# Talking Shop

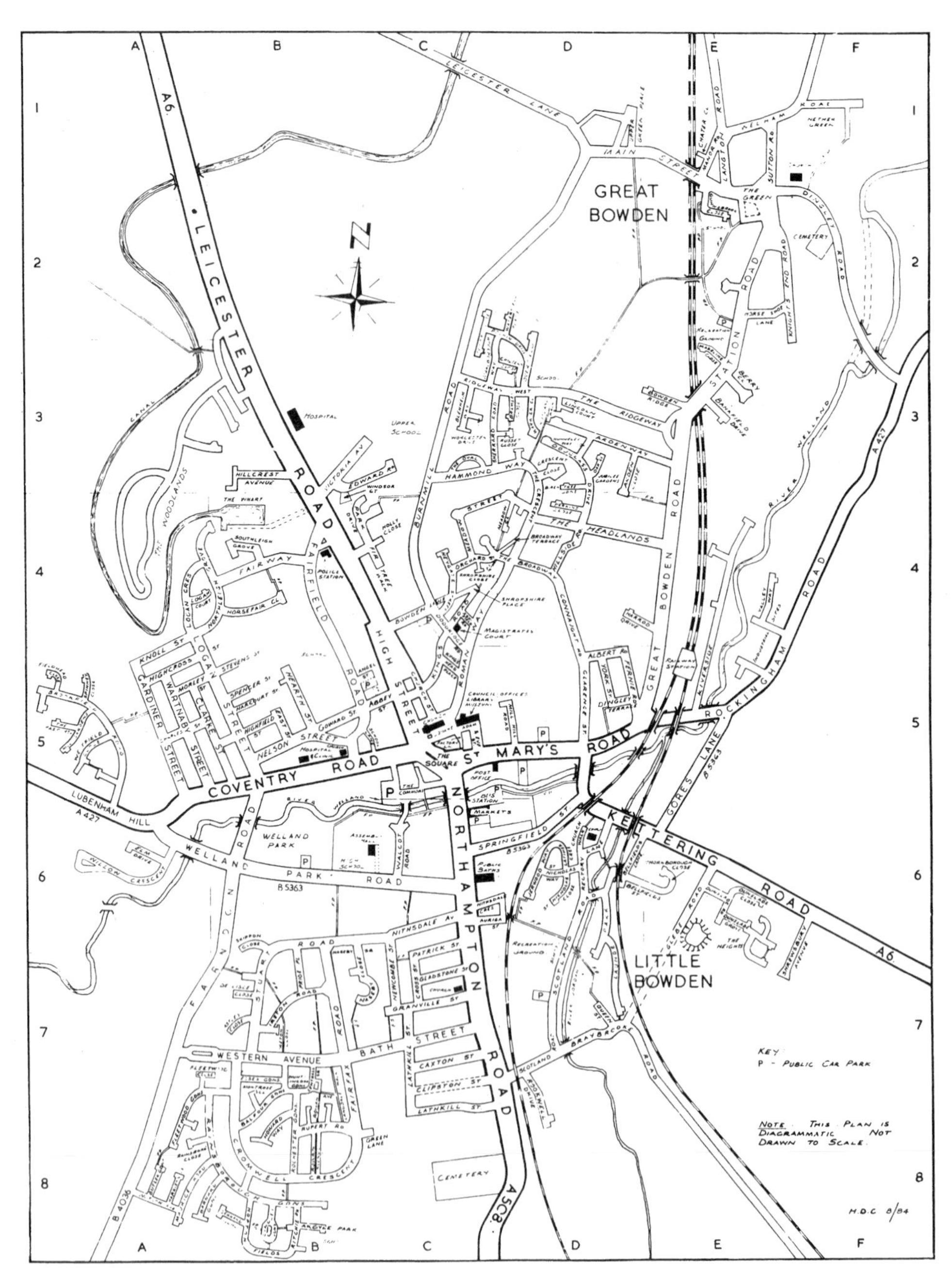


Street plan of Market Harborough in 1984

# TALKING SHOP

## AN ORAL HISTORY OF RETAILING IN THE HARBOROUGH AREA DURING THE 20TH CENTURY

*Sam Mullins & David Stockdale*

ALAN SUTTON PUBLISHING LIMITED

LEICESTERSHIRE MUSEUMS, ARTS AND RECORDS SERVICE

First published in the United Kingdom in 1994 by
Alan Sutton Publishing Limited
Phoenix Mill · Far Thrupp · Stroud · Gloucestershire

---

First published in the United States of America in 1994 by
Alan Sutton Publishing Inc · 83 Washington Street · Dover NH 03820
in association with Leicestershire Museums, Arts and Records Service

Copyright © Samuel Mullins, David Stockdale and Leicestershire Museums, Arts and Records Service

All rights reserved. No part of this publication may be reproduced, stored in a retrieval system, or transmitted, in any form or by and means, electronic, mechanical, photocopying, recording or otherwise, without the prior permission of the publishers and copyright holders.

British Library Cataloguing-in-Publication Data

Mullins, Samuel
Talking Shop: An Oral History of Retailing in the Harborough
Area during the 20th Century
I. Title II. Stockdale, David
381.10942544

ISBN 0-7509-0724-X

Library of Congress Cataloging-in-Publication Data applied for

DEDICATION

To the shopkeepers, shopworkers and shoppers of Market Harborough who contributed so readily and enthusiastically to the research for this book.

Typeset in 11/13pt Garamond.
Typesetting and origination by
Alan Sutton Publishing Limited.
Printed in Great Britain by
Ebenezer Baylis, Worcester.

# Contents

# The Leicestershire Remembered Series

This series by Leicestershire Museums, Arts and Records Service aims to publish substantial accounts by the people of Leicestershire and Rutland of everyday life in the past which have a distinct bearing on the present.

The third volume in the series differs from the previous two by using a synthesis of transcribed oral testimonies from over sixty people, rather than the written reminiscences of one man or woman. This consort of voices has then been amplified and interpreted by more traditional documentary historical research. Both authors are former members of staff of Leicestershire Museums. Sam Mullins (now Director of St Albans' Museums) was founding Keeper of the Harborough Museum from 1982 to 1987, and David Stockdale (now Assistant Keeper of Human History, Dundee Art Galleries and Museums) was Temporary Research Assistant for the 'Shops and Shopkeeping' project during 1986.

Other titles in the 'Leicestershire Remembered' series are: O.D. Lucas, *One Man's Wigston: Sixty Years' Recollections of Everyday Life in Wigston Magna* (1993). Maurice Woodward, *A Coalville Miner's Story: Sixty Years' Recollections in the Leicestershire Coalfield* (1993).

Steph Mastoris
General Editor

# Preface

In the last decade of the twentieth century the British have become a nation of shoppers. Consumerism is the ruling dogma and shopping is viewed as a prime economic activity. Commentators frequently judge the health of the nation's economy by how much we spend in shops, rather than by how much we produce in factories. Shopping is a universal activity for every man, woman and child in Britain today. The incessant pace of change in the retail industry in recent years is now almost taken for granted. Developments over the last twenty years have led to the cloning of high streets with the same retail outlets, globally sourced goods being available in every locality, the move out-of-town by large sectors of the industry, and the replacement of cash by a range of electronic point-of-sale innovations.

These developments have brought profound changes for traditional town centres, for shopworkers and for shopping itself. Yet the roots of modern retailing can be traced back a suprisingly long way, through post-war prosperity and rising living standards, past the ambitious corporatism of large retail businesses in the years between the wars, to the pioneering innovations in trading of the late Victorian period.

But despite its importance, there is a great dearth of published work on this retail revolution, especially for the period since the 1930s. There have been several national studies, useful biographies and company histories, but very little of a general nature. It was with this in mind that in 1986 the staff of the Harborough Museum (a branch of the Leicestershire Museums, Arts and Records Service) embarked on a research and exhibition project to record the retail history of Market Harborough and its hinterland. By interviewing many people who had owned, worked in and patronized the shops in this area of south Leicestershire down the decades, we soon realized that the project offered considerable insight into many of the revolutionary changes in British retailing during the twentieth century.

By examining the grassroots of provincial retailing, our research does not illustrate the cutting edge of change, but rather the process of change as it filtered down to the high street of a small market town; for instance, self-service was first introduced in Britain in the late 1940s, but it only reached Market Harborough a decade or so later. In this, we believe we are making an original contribution to the history of retailing. In telling the story of one urban shopping centre, and its place in the national picture over the last hundred years, we have focused on changes in daily life on both sides of the counter – for customer and trader alike. Nor have we lost sight of Market Harborough's distinct identity as a community. We hope that those who know the town, as well as those who do not, will appreciate how the shopping habits of Harborians between the 1890s and the 1980s throw a raking light across the social history of both this Midland manufacturing and market town and the legion of similar towns up and down the country – the Market Harboroughs of England.

From the earliest days of our research, we realized just how large a subject we had embarked upon. Inevitably we have concentrated on areas for which the sources were strongest, to the neglect of such important retail trades as soft furnishings, electrical goods, pharmacies, newsagents and sweet and tobacco retailing. As a result, this book considers shops and shopping from three different angles. The first three chapters introduce the general pattern of shopping in the twentieth century from a Market Harborough perspective. The next two chapters consider how the organization of retail trade shaped the lives of those who worked and served in them. The final chapters look in depth at five individual retail trades.

We were very fortunate in the number and quality of responses to our pleas for information and it is the richness of the personal views offered by the people of the Harborough area that underpins *Talking Shop*. Some of our respondents may be disappointed not to find themselves quoted directly, but all those listed in the Sources have contributed materially to this book and their full reminiscences are preserved for posterity on tape and in writing in the Harborough Museum's sound collection.

Reminiscences of customers and shop staff do tend to emphasize an optimistic view of the past, recalling high standards of service, the personal touch and the social nature of shopping. Very little was forthcoming about sharp practice, low wages, poor standards of hygiene or inferior quality goods. This roseate perspective is inevitable in the gathering of oral material, but we have earnestly strived to keep this in proportion in our account. In the same way, our determination to bring the story up to the very recent past of the late 1980s has provided some of the most challenging aspects of our investigation. Our recordings of current shopkeepers and store managers led to problems of perspective, for in dealing with the last ten or so years it was not easy to judge what the long-term trends might be and distinguish them from short-term hiccups.

The final twist to this century's retail revolutions has been the drastic downturn in retail fortunes during the time that this book has been written. From the euphoric boom of shop openings and supermarket building in the early and mid-1980s, the whole retail sector has found itself pitched into a severe and prolonged recession in the late 1980s and early 1990s. As a consequence, retailing has lost some of the gloss it acquired earlier and the interviews recorded in those years can be viewed in sharp perspective today. Also longer-term trends have been at work since this book was researched, most important being the increase in Sunday trading and ever-more flexible working patterns. In addition there have been a number of important changes to the local structure of retailing in Market Harborough, and we have asked Steph Mastoris to sketch these in his short Postscript.

We hope this book will be widely read and enjoyed, not least in Market Harborough itself, as it has much to say about the culture of the small country town. It is also to be hoped that we might encourage colleagues in other history museums and in the field of local and social history to look at their own localities and provide a contrast to the local picture from the East Midlands. There is considerable scope to take the account of our most successful industry of modern times a great deal further than has been possible here.

We both owe a great debt of gratitude to the large number of past and present shopkeepers, shopworkers and shoppers who replied so readily to our appeals for information; all are mentioned in the Sources. They allowed us to copy family photographs, see business records and above all explore their memories. We trust we have done them justice.

More particularly, thanks are due to Nora Kavanagh's indefatigable searching through the local newspapers which opened up a rich vein of advertisements, bankruptcy cases, shop openings, public announcements, sales lists and criminal cases. John Carter's local knowledge both opened doors and prevented us falling through them. Deborah Boden worked on the later stages of the project and offered invaluable assistance when both authors had moved away from the town, while Jan Gough and Yvonne Hayhurst assisted with the transcription of the tape recordings. The late J.C. Davies, the Harborough historian, was, as always, a most obliging source for everything to do with Market Harborough, ever willing to share his encyclopaedic knowledge of the town's history and always willing to encourage the research work enabled by the new Harborough Museum. Finally our thanks go to Steph Mastoris, the present Keeper of the Harborough Museum, and his tireless staff without whom this book would most certainly not have been published. As we moved away to pastures new, he refused to lose sight of the conviction that publication is the only justification for research, and dragged us back to the word processor and brokered this book with Leicestershire Museums and Alan Sutton Publishing Ltd.

Sam Mullins and David Stockdale
St Albans and Dundee
June 1994

# Introduction

Market Harborough is situated in the middle of the southern border of Leicestershire, about half-way between the cities of Northampton and Leicester. Since its foundation as a 'new town' in the mid-twelfth century, Harborough has served a hinterland of about an eight to ten-mile radius. Within that area in the mid-nineteenth century, over fifty villages were served by country carriers who ran regular conveyance for people and parcels to and from the town on market and other days. Market Harborough's circle of influence was interrupted in its south-eastern corner by Desborough, Rothwell and Kettering, each market centres in their own right, and Kettering, a manufacturing centre of growing importance, but of severely localized influence. Country carriers from this area also extended to Uppingham, Lutterworth, Kettering, Northampton and Leicester, but Harborough was the regular centre to which the district on either side of the Welland Valley looked for goods and services, for the sale of livestock and country produce, and for gossip and news of the wider world. For several hundred years the roads were especially busy on Tuesdays with carts, vans, livestock on the hoof, farmers and labourers, all making their way to the weekly market in Harborough.

> Surrounded on all sides by rich grazing lands which carry a large head of stock during the summer months, Market Harborough is a natural distributing centre for a large number of fat cattle and sheep . . . a considerable amount of business is concluded each Tuesday. (*Market Harborough, the official guide* (1940))

As well as this agricultural setting, Market Harborough has had an almost equally long history of urban trade and industry. The modern town has therefore been home to a socially diverse population, as befitted a manufacturing market town. Just how diverse can be seen in this second extract from the 1940 official town guide. Apart from a few variants, this could have been written at any time in the first fifty years of this century:

> For Hunting, Market Harborough has long been a favourite centre. . . . There is little difficulty in finding congenial society for the sportsmen in this neighbourhood. Hunting boxes are numerous. . . . That industries already established in, or just outside the town, do well is evident from the prosperity of numerous firms. Among them are firms engaged in light engineering work, the manufacture of corsets, patent foods, and accumulators, in the preparation of bent timber, wood turning, type founding, leather tanning, silk weaving,

aircraft component manufacture and the making of shoes and rubber goods. A considerable proportion of female labour is employed in most of these activities. . . . Perhaps in no town of a similar size are there so many 'owner-residents'. . . . The home conditions being comfortable . . . it follows that the workers at Market Harborough are, on the whole, a contented class.

This was the sizeable, mixed community which was served by a thriving commercial centre of retail outlets. All of Harborough's shops, whether independent or branches of chain stores, had their own niche and were sufficiently specialized to meet the needs of a particular cross-section of local customers.

An aerial view of Market Harborough, looking north, in early June 1935

## SECTION ONE

# SERVING THE TOWN

# *Chapter One*
# The Customer Comes First

*You used to thank them for their custom.*
(Sales assistant at Wood's the draper's, 1930s[1])

*I loved selling . . . to have two or three customers on the boil at once, to serve them well and see them go off well was a great satisfaction.*
(Assistant, Co-op menswear department, 1930s[2])

A revolution in retailing since the last war has completely changed the way in which shops treat their customers. Self-service and supermarketing have all but eliminated any contact between shopkeeper and shopper. The customer is wooed with full-page advertisements, television commercials and 'unrepeatable' offers but modern supermarkets are an impersonal environment in which to shop. Indeed, in the late 1980s Tesco felt it necessary to introduce a staff training scheme in customer relations: 'Customer 87'. Chairman Ian MacLaurin was quoted as being dismayed by his company's fifth position in a customer survey: 'I'm afraid we concentrated so hard on getting the trading right that we overlooked the importance of staff–customer relations'.[3]

Tesco's solution was to give customer service training to all staff at every store. At service counters, staff were encouraged to greet every customer with eye contact, a ready smile and 'Good morning, what can I get you?' The transaction had to end with a 'Thank you' and a 'Goodbye'. A similar drill was laid down for checkout staff. This concern for customers was both laudable and profitable. It is of course still characteristic of many smaller shops. In the not-so-distant past, it was the norm in every shop in the high street: 'Every customer, you tried to make them feel they were the most important customer'.[4] In the first half of the century, Market Harborough's shops catered for a large working class, which included a significant number of women workers in the local factories, a middle class of clerical workers with a sprinkling of professional people, an influx of farmers and farm workers on market day from the surrounding area and the well-heeled permanent residents of (and seasonal visitors to) country houses and hunting boxes near the 'best headquarters in the world for fox-hunting'.[5] Each and every one could expect a high standard of service in the town's shops:

I can remember when I first started there [Symington & Thwaites, a quality grocer's, about 1923] selling a lady's mantle [dress]. We didn't have it, we didn't stock it, we had nothing to do with it, but an old lady in the country wanted one and she couldn't get into town, would you get it? So, of course, we got it for her, from Wood's. And anything like that, if anybody wanted anything, we'd always get it if we could.[6]

My father [Mr John Wood] was the owner, and . . . Lady Zia Wernher, she used to buy a lot of linen from him and all that linen was marked with her name. And my father used to do that, he used to print it with Indian ink on her linen.[7]

People from outside the town, the country, used to come in a horse and trap. I remember one, a man from Ashley. . . . He came in, he'd got a high trap and quite a high horse, it was a high stepper, and he called out for somebody to come and hold the horse, so the boss sent me out. Well, I'd never held a horse. . . . It kept lifting its feet up and stamping the ground and tossing its head. . . . He gave me the reins and left me! I was scared stiff . . . I got *6d* for it anyway; it was a lot of money then, when your wages were four bob a week.[8] (Apprentice at Smith's grocer's, St Mary's Road, about 1912)

Jack Stokes' small general store opposite the Harboro' Rubber Co.'s factory on St Mary's Road, Market Harborough, 1920s. Mr Stokes is in the centre, flanked by the delivery boy (with his handcart) and the shopman

Treating your customers well was neither servility nor just politeness. It made sound economic sense. A satisfied customer was more likely to remain loyal to the shop. The extended personal contact of counter sales also gave a good shop assistant the chance to suggest additional purchases. It was normal in every shop for the customer to be greeted as soon as they came through the door. At Wood's on the Square, the proprietor Mr John Wood generally did this himself: 'He would open the door for them and say, "Good morning Mrs So-and-so". . . . As I say, he was very polite and then . . . he'd say something like "Can I help you?", and they'd say they'd like stockings, and then he'd say, "Mrs Houghton, could you please show this person . . . ", and it was all very gracious'.[9]

Mr Wimlett started as an apprentice at Webb Bros, a gents' outfitters in Church Street, in 1923. It was one of his tasks to greet customers at the door:

> If I met you at the door and I didn't know who you were, I should pass the time of day to you, 'and what can I do to help you?'. If you said you wanted a suit, I should immediately call Mr Ward the manager and he would come along with his tape round his shoulders. . . . If he were not there, the assistant, what we called the First Sales . . . he would do that.[10]

> It was 'Yes Madam, Yes Sir, No Sir'; when a customer came in, you went round and put a chair there for them. They sat down, they gave an order, you took it down.[11]

Having taken the order, this was the assistant's opportunity to suggest or show a range of products, to jog the customer's memory, to allay any doubts or to give advice if asked for it:

> First of all to greet your customer with a smile, that's a most important thing. Never scowl, no matter how much they make you cross, don't show it, be pleasant. That was the first thing I had to learn, how to be pleasant, whether I liked it, whether I'd got toothache, whether I hated the sight of the bloke who'd just come in. . . . You'd got to sink your personality for that but at the same time present your products, whatever they are, honestly. Don't lie about them. If it isn't very good, avoid saying that it's very good.[12]

> When it came to a customer, she came to the counter; two pounds of sugar, half-a-pound of tea, bar of soap, packet of powder, that sort of thing. You put them on the counter and you started, 'Anything more Mrs Smith? Soap, soda, starch, blue, matches, candles, boot polish, black-lead, salt, mustard, pepper, rice, tapioca, cake flour, sponge mix?' That's how we used to go on you know and, 'Yes, yes, I'll have one of those' and that's how you made your order up.[13]

> You'd got to make a sale and if you hadn't got – you knew you hadn't got what they

wanted – but you had to try and make a sale, pull all the drawers out.[14] (Draper's assistant, 1930s)

If you'd served a customer and sold her one or two extra items . . . you thought you'd done a good job.[15]

The service provided to customers did not end when a sale had been concluded:

If they were lucky enough to have a motor car, you would put [their groceries] in a box and take it out to the car for them. If they didn't, no one would dream, as my wife does now, of walking round the town with a trolley and coming back and lifting it into a car. That would be delivered; no charge for the delivery, it was just part of the service a high-class grocer or any other trade would give.[16]

Price competition was limited by the system of resale price maintenance. Until the system was finally dismantled in 1964, some resale prices were fixed by groups of manufacturers and distributors, with an estimated 30 per cent of goods sold being subject to RPM by 1938. The extent of price maintenance, however, varied widely between different trades and even between types of shop within a particular trade. This allowed for a certain amount of competition on price, notably in the grocery trade.[17]

Nevertheless, with labour relatively cheap, shops between the wars competed as much on the quality of service they offered, as on price. This was true of both independent and *multiple* stores (the contemporary name for the large retail chains). The Co-operative Societies also offered the discount of the dividend. The level of service offered by Hodby's of Nelson Street to keep their customers was by no means untypical:

We did a lot of sending out to customers for orders. Many customers had three visits a week. . . . We would have sent errand boys or young assistants on Tuesday round to certain people. . . . Quite often they'd come back and say Mrs Smith would like her order so that she can cook so-and-so for dinner. Thursday was a day when my father went out and called on a lot of those people who'd already been called on on the Tuesday. He fetched the main weekly order and again after he'd perhaps been away from the shop for about an hour, someone would go and waylay him as he came out of a person's house and come back to the shop with two or three orders and start getting them up so they could be delivered by lunchtime. Thinking back, it's absolutely crazy![18]

In the competition for custom, some traders offered extra services. Clothing shops such as Hepworth's and Wood's sent out suits and other clothes on approval, using the services of country carriers. Most of the town's shops made up orders brought in by carriers on market-day mornings from the country villages around, for collection before their return journey in the afternoon. The carrier commonly negotiated a brokerage or cut, usually a penny in the shilling, for bringing such trade to a shop.[19] The Market Harborough branches of W.H. Smith and Boots the Chemists for many years maintained subscription libraries for customers to borrow books, while earlier in the century independent shops such as Wilkinson's the printers had offered a similar service. Between the wars many poorer households had their Sunday lunches cooked for a penny by the town's bakers, such as Joe Jinks or Mr Murkitt in Church Street:

> That was a regular thing on a Sunday morning because . . . all these little cottages [the yards off Church Street and King's Road], none of them had got very good cooking facilities. . . . In fact our oven would be full. . . . They'd bring their beef or whatever for roasting and their Yorkshire pudding in a jug and they'd leave it to him to pour round the meat at the right time to do it. . . . Except for the afternoon, Sundays were as busy as a day in the week.[20]

Customers expected to be given credit by many shops, monthly or longer billed accounts for the wealthy and weekly tick for the poor (see Chapter Two for such

W.H. Smith's shop in St Mary's Road, 1930s. Like most of the chain, this store was well-situated for the trade which passed to and from the railway station

arrangements). Shops stayed open for as long as they could to attract customers, within the limits laid down by shop hours legislation brought in during the First World War and made permanent by the Act of 1928.[21] While these laws laid down maximum shop opening hours, they did not place a limit on the number of hours worked by shop staff who could of course be working while the shop was shut. On Friday and Saturday, shops might open to ten o'clock or later to catch wage earners who had been paid that day. This applied particularly to small independent shopkeepers and the national and regional chains of shops who were dependent on the working classes' trade. Mrs Springer remembers the long hours of opening at her parents' small bakery and grocery shop, Murkitt's, in Church Street:

> Friday night was always very busy, from say five o'clock until nine o'clock. Saturdays, all day Saturday, right up until nine o'clock Saturday night there was always customers coming in. In fact you'd still get somebody at the back door on Sunday morning, even though you'd been open till nine and ten o'clock on a Saturday night.[22]

Competition was keenly felt over opening hours. Mr Ingram worked at the Maypole Dairy in Kettering from 1925 to 1939:

> Half-past eight in the morning, until the shop closed at seven . . . Opened till eight on a Friday and it was eight on a Saturday; except say Christmastide or bank holidays and competition was so keen that they all used to watch one another for closing, like Lipton's, Home & Colonial, all the whole lot. Don't you dare close half a minute before a competitor![23]

While all customers were treated with what might today be regarded as exaggerated politeness, some were courted more assiduously than others. Head servants from local country houses, for instance, were important customers because of the size and status of orders for which they were responsible:

> Lubenham Hall, Langton Hall, Sulby Hall, Rockingham Castle, all those places. You always dealt with the butler, the cook and the housekeeper, they ruled it. . . . The butler, he'd give his order for the things he wanted [wines and spirits], the cook would order the food and things, the housekeeper would order the cleaning things.[24]

Mrs Elizabeth Bristow was cook-housekeeper at Thorpe Satchville near Melton Mowbray (Leicestershire) in the late 1930s. She was responsible for ordering all food, drink and cleaning materials, mostly from local shopkeepers in Melton Mowbray:

> We had people say, 'Here's my card, I'm from so-and-so at Melton Mowbray, we've started a new business and I wonder if you'd be interested in giving us an order. . . . I did quite well with that because Warner Bros, Mr Cobley was the manager, he would come

> and say, 'I'm setting up a new department, we're going to have so-and-so and so-and-so. . . . He would deliver then, it always came by van you see. They'd bring you a little note with it all and I would check it off and put that on the file and at the end of the month you got your bill. Well, I would take that to the Captain, all my bills, all initialled you see, to say we'd had the stuff and sometimes straightaway he would write a cheque for it or maybe the butler would come out in the evening with a silver salver and all the cheques would be on top of the salver for me to pay. If you paid them within the week sometimes I've had as much as 30*s* back from the fishmonger and the greengrocer. It was worthwhile putting yourself out to try and get everything done up to date.[25]

> Often they would have the housekeeper or the butler come to the shop [Symington & Thwaites] and they'd be taken down the cellar with a cheese-iron – they'd bring their own cheese-iron – these butlers and housekeepers used to come round to taste the Stiltons.[26]

Only the high-class stores and some of the larger shops were able to serve the country house trade. Each shop attracted its own range of customers, and the style and range of services on offer made a large contribution to customers' loyalty. The bond between shop and shopper was a complicated one, to which church or chapel connections, friendships and family ties, long-established habit, and services such as credit, savings clubs and dividends all might contribute. Loyal customers were not necessarily the big spenders. At the butcher's shop every cut, even the bits and bones, had its customer as did stale cakes at the bakers:

> I don't know how my mother used to cope honestly I don't. I've been down to Frost's [Church Street] for a penn'orth of pot herbs – a carrot, an onion and a parsnip and sometimes they'd put in a swede – a penn'orth of pot herbs. Across then to what was Star Supply for three penn'orth of bits of bacon. . . . Round to Garner's [Adam & Eve Street] for pork bones. We'd have a rabbit and in this big old pot she'd make steam puddings.[27]

Shopping in the 1940s and early '50s was drastically affected by the wartime introduction of rationing, which placed severe restrictions on customer and retailer alike: 'During the war there was no freedom at all because everybody was on coupons and you could only have so much and that was that. People would try to curry favour to get another two ounces of corned beef. . . . While I was [a sales rep.] on Brooke Bond's, they'd do anything for a quarter of tea'.[28]

Foodstuffs were the first to be rationed. The sale of bacon, ham, butter, margarine and cooking fats, sugar, meat (with the exception of poultry, offal and rabbit) and tea was limited to set amounts in 1940. Cheese, preserves, chocolate and sweets were added to the list during the next two years. Many other grocery lines could only be bought with 'points', or rationing allowances, and the distribution of milk and eggs was tightly controlled. Clothes and footwear rationing was introduced on a points basis in 1941. Right across the retail economy, the government laid down levels of production for civilian consumption and attempted to fix product ranges, prices and profits.[29]

None of our respondents who had worked in shops during this period made explicit reference to the favouritism, fraud and black marketeering that is known to have accompanied shortages and rationing. Probably the most common practice was the keeping of goods 'under the counter' for favoured customers. Some hinted broadly that rationing 'used to be the biggest fiddle out' but most were coy on the subject of its evasion. Rationing made extra paperwork for the retailer and could easily lead to strained relations with established customers:

> You could only let anybody have just what they were entitled to. It made a big difference. There was all the coupons to count – sweet coupons, clothing coupons, you used to bank them – . . . . The bacon and so forth, they used to assess you on the number of customers you'd got [who were registered], plus the number of emergency coupons you'd collected during the month. If anybody had come to stay for a week, they'd have a set of emergency coupons, they'd got to spend them somewhere. You'd keep them, send them into the Food Office and they'd increase your quota.
>
> There was a certain class of customer who thought you could let them have a lot of extra bits and bobs, and you hadn't got them. . . . Some did [get offended], but the majority accepted it.[30]

It is possible to trace radical changes in the relationship between shopkeepers and customers to this period. The rationing system virtually tied a customer to a particular shop. There was hardly any point in taking your custom to another shop, similarly encumbered by shortages and rationing restrictions. Service had been the principal area of competition but all shops, both large and small, were hampered by the loss of staff to the war effort and their replacement by often untrained assistants. Familiar routines of customer service were severely disrupted by the war. By the time rationing ceased and normal service might have been resumed, far-reaching changes associated with self-service and price competition hustled the retailer off in other directions. Wartime restrictions threatened many shopkeepers' livelihoods as staple items became restricted or unavailable. Michael Kelly remembers the problems in his uncle's greengrocery and florist's shop in St Mary's Road: 'It was a tremendous job to carry on the business at all, because the fruit allowance [to the retailer] was so small, if you got it at all. You just couldn't run a business on that sort of quantity'.

One of the Kelly brothers, Richard, found an enterprising solution by turning his hand to making jams, pickles, sauces and meat spreads at the back of the shop:

> [He] could buy American 'Spam' and [with] a bit of flavouring and gelatine he could make a very, very passable – I think they would call it – pâté today. And he was able to get hold of these little wax tubs that they used to put ice-cream in. He could sell them as quick as he put them together. You see, people were rationed and they hadn't got much meat. . . . So they sort of got by with that and the flower trade and the home-produced veg.[31]

The climate of austerity and economic controls continued after the war. Rationing was maintained on clothes until 1949 and on foodstuffs until 1954 because of shortages. Though no boom period for retailers, fixed prices and rationing guaranteed returns and also restricted price competition. Geoff Johnson set up in business as a gents outfitter on his own account in Market Harborough after leaving the RAF. He maintains that rationing gave him the breathing space he needed to get established:

> It was also a godsend, because you couldn't ruin yourself by overbuying, even if you could have got it. You recouped your coupons from your customer and you paid them into the bank. The bank credited you a percentage. It made it so you had a little increase all the time. You couldn't overspend because you got your money and your coupons the same time you sold your goods [and] you'd always got a little increase in your money. I wouldn't have been able to do it if it had been a free-for-all.[32]

With the eventual removal of rationing, previously scarce goods came back onto the shelves in abundance. There was a certain similarity between conditions in the 1930s and '50s, with more goods than ever coming under the system of resale price maintenance which reached its peak in 1955.[33] Price competition, however, was already gaining ground in the grocery trade. Significant changes also resulted from the steadily higher cost of labour. The increase of such costs was a powerful incentive for retailers to try new ways of serving their customers.

The most potent new idea was self-service, an innovation from America. Self-service only became possible as more goods came pre-packed from the manufacturer. On a national scale, the British pioneers of self-service in the late 1940s were a number of Co-operative retail societies, to be joined in the early 1950s by the Tesco chain.[34]

Variety chain stores or bazaars such as Woolworths, however, had long had open layouts in their stores which encouraged customers to walk around and examine merchandise freely. Open layouts and the lack of pressure to buy had been originally introduced by Gordon Selfridge in his London department store before the First World War.[35] The principal advantage from the shop's point of view was that the shop assistants spent less time serving customers as the open display of goods relieved them of the need to show goods individually to each one. The options for purchase were presented in the passive display of merchandise rather than by the active suggestion of the assistant.

Vivien Window from Desborough worked as a 'Saturday girl' at Woolworths in Market Harborough in 1956:

> Woolworths was almost the start of self-service in that you could see and handle things before you bought them. But of course you still had to catch the assistant's eye. . . . And this is why we were always in trouble for chatting; our supervisor sort of walked around the rows, looking, and if we were chatting and there was a customer waiting, heaven help us! . . . It was a great temptation to stand and talk if you had a few minutes spare and particularly for young girls.
>
> We would be in the middle and the counter would be all around us. They were wooden counters, they were about waist high . . . and they sloped gently towards the customer so that obviously they could see everything and we stood behind them. . . . Sometimes they

The middle portion of the west side of the High Street, Market Harborough, *c.* 1936. The shops on the left are: Eaton's the ironmongers, Boots the Chemists, Goward's the grocers and Woolworths

> were velvet lined, particularly for jewellery, and they had thick glass slotted in so that they made boxes.
>
> The counters were open at the back, so we kept our stuff [i.e. the stock] underneath and people would often pick it up from the front and you'd say, 'Would you put that back please and I'll get you one from underneath' or else the wretches would hand them to you, and if you were in a good mood you'd let them pay and just get another one out. One of the jobs of the supervisor was to make sure that the boxes were always filled . . . and if people took from the front and you were run off your feet and didn't put them out again, there again, there'd be trouble, you might be losing custom . . . and if you were very busy, it was quite hard work keeping the fronts filled up.[36]

Self-service proper arrived in Market Harborough at the end of the 1950s, when it was introduced by Burton's, a Nottingham food firm, then the owners of Symington & Thwaites on the corner of Adam & Eve Street and St Mary's Road. Shortly afterwards, Fine Fare bought out the retail division of Burton's as the former assistant manager remembers: 'They immediately changed the character within a year . . . downgraded in my opinion . . . they went pure supermarket then . . . they cut the staff right back – I think I had about ten or a dozen staff, that's all'.[37]

By this time (the early 1960s) up-and-coming grocery chains such as Fine Fare were competing hard on prices. The then assistant manager at Fine Fare, Mr Lee, was responsible for carrying out the new owners' marketing policies:

> And I'll guarantee a customer would come into that shop . . . they'd come in with the intention of buying one thing or two, they'd go out buying half-a-dozen. The way you laid the shop out . . . It pays to lose money on certain articles to get people in the shop; we've sold sugar, at Fine Fare, at less than cost price, to get people in. . . . Once you've got them in, you've got them. . . . They'll walk round the shop and pick something else up at a higher price. That's where you make your money.[38]

Special offers were always placed at the back of the store to make shoppers walk right through the merchandise. Ploys such as this were necessary because there was no longer an assistant available to deliver a sales pitch. Staff trained in the traditional style of trade might find it difficult to adapt to this new anonymous style of selling. The International store at 12 High Street changed to a self-service system with checkouts in 1965–6. The manager at that time was Mr Neville, 'a true grocery man':[39]

> He used to wear his white jacket and always his apron, a clean white apron, over the top. . . . He was always out in his shop, because I think he was so used to being behind the counter, you see, and greeting people. So when it came to the supermarket, he was

> still out in his shop walking around, greeting all the people that he knew because they were all his customers, chatting to them, asking how their families were, making sure they had the things they wanted.[40]

For economic reasons – faster turnover and lower staff costs – self-service and checkouts had come to stay. Delivery services were maintained for a few years, often at a charge, but were then also largely phased out in the quest for lower prices. The new way of shopping was also a response to the increasingly high proportion of the population who owned cars: 'The method of shopping was changing, it was moving from walking to the shops to taking the car, leaving it in the car-park and going to the nearest shop'.[41]

The heyday of price competition came in the 1960s and '70s. In 1964 resale price maintenance was finally removed, permitting an acceleration of the price war between supermarkets, especially in the fiercely competitive grocery sector (see Chapter Seven). While prices have remained important to the shopper to this day, other factors such as convenience and brand quality or loyalty have also become major considerations.

In the 1980s 'customer service' came to mean more than simply serving

Mr Arthur Swingler selling fruit and veg in the covered market, Northampton Road, Market Harborough, September 1988 (Photograph by Doug Millhouse)

customers. The phrase was used by managers of large stores to include lower prices, staff training, bright colour co-ordinated interiors, signposting, labelling, stocking wider ranges of goods and keeping the trolleys in working order. As a Tesco store manager, Mr Ken Wylie saw this development at first hand:

> Certainly in the last five years [1981–6], the company has changed dramatically. The needs of the public have been totally different. I think the public won't accept going into a store that's dirty, that's got bad customer service, that hasn't got a good pricing policy, where staff are rude, where people aren't skilled at the business . . . obviously we're going to be as good as the people we employ and the people we employ have got to be trained to do the job properly. That's what the company now concentrates a lot on. . . . There's a full training programme from the minute they start with the company.
>
> It was costing the company around £4 million a year to give these carrier bags away, as they cost 2p each [to Tesco]. The company had a new carrier bag made which is a lot larger and stronger and can be used eight, nine or ten times. . . . I think the company spent £1· million on carrier bags last year. It was a cost-effective exercise. The customers get a better product, they don't walk into the car-park and all the groceries fall out of the bottom.[42]

Mr Frederick Lee worked in several grocers' shops in Market Harborough from the late 1930s to the early 1960s. He believed customers tended loyally to use one shop for certain goods until late in the 1950s, a loyalty reinforced by the high level of personal service offered by the independent stores: 'Loyal until the end of the Fifties, then it changed completely. They went where the price was [cheap] then, particularly the younger housewives, not the old people'.[43]

Self-service was only able to spread as the proportion of pre-packed goods increased and as counter service became less of a necessity. The loss of personal contact was regretted but the new system did make shopping quicker. At the Maypole store in the mid-1960s 'it was all wrapped [by hand] . . . you see you had to stand and wait, whereas now people haven't got time to stand and wait, have they? . . . Supermarkets I think are very indifferent places and I think people shop in them now for pure convenience'.[44]

Self-service is by no means universal. Counter service has remained a necessity in more specialized shops – bakers, delicatessans, florists, jewellers, electrical goods. Indeed within larger supermarkets counter service has been reintroduced for specialist sections such as bakery, cheese and provisions. More specialized products still require the advice of counter staff, while high margin goods such as cosmetics justify counter staff for their sales abilities:

> Well lots of people still need advice [with cosmetics]. You get it if you go in the bigger

> Boots . . . they let out to so many agencies, for different companies to have a stand to sell their goods and they're on commission. So you see you do get advice from them, but you also pay much more for whatever you're buying, because you're paying for the name aren't you?[45]

Whenever customers and shop staff come into contact, the old rules still apply – 'we were always told that the customer's always right, we always had to be polite':[46]

> One lady came in one Saturday morning. It was very, very busy and she brought this great big teddy-bear in, sat it on the chair next to the child and said, 'My little girl would like some wellington boots to fit this teddy bear'. It was just when Rupert Bear was about you see and of course we sold little blue wellingtons and little red wellingtons. Well how the heck can you possibly get a pair of wellingtons on a bear? But this is what I was expected to do.[47]

# *Chapter Two*

# Cash, Clubs and Credit

*'Gain We Must': G = 1, A = 2, I = 3, and so on.*
(The key to a letter-code used to mark stock prices on goods at Symington & Thwaites in the 1920s and '30s)

In the early part of this century, customers paid for what they bought in mainly three ways. The Edwardian shopper could hand over cash, have goods 'booked' or 'on account' or pay regular instalments into a purchasing club. A fourth method, hire purchase, was restricted before the First World War to a few large items such as pianos and sewing machines, although it became widely used between the wars for all sorts of household goods, particularly furniture.[1]

Despite the strictures of poverty, for many families the payment for all goods by cash-on-the-nail was a matter of some pride:

> My mother had been out in the afternoon and the baker had called and left two loaves of bread and left it without the money. Before I had my tea, I had to run from Kibworth Harcourt to Kibworth Beauchamp where the shop was and pay for these two loaves of bread. It was a crime to owe any money.[2]

> My mother would never have credit, no. Money had got to be on-the-nail. If she couldn't afford it, she wouldn't have it. No, she'd never get into debt . . . she wouldn't have the packman at the door. 'You'd wear your things out before they were paid [for]' she used to say. So she wouldn't have anything [on credit].[3]

The taking and handling of money was a major part of shop work and reckoning up the prices of goods 'on the counter' was an essential skill for shop assistants: 'My God . . . if we'd put it down on a piece of paper to reckon it up, we should have been told off for it'.[4]

> You got all your things on the counter and you added the price on and on, done it all in your head. No such thing as writing it down. Parcelled it all up and then took the money and give the change. We used to have a change board at one corner of the shop and it'd have like a couple of mousetraps on it and you'd have one for ten-shilling notes, one for pound notes, and then there was a ledger, and you'd have all 10*s* in silver, two half-crowns, two [florins] and a shilling so that you could give change according to whatever the customer gave you. . . .[5]

In larger shops there was often a division of labour between the counter assistant who served the customer and a cashier who made out receipts and gave the change. This was also the practice in shops such as butchers, provisions merchants and fishmongers, where it was important to separate the handling of money from the handling of fresh food. The cashier generally had her own cubicle or desk where money and the shop's account books were kept. The central Co-op store in the 1920s followed the common practice where the counter assistant made out a bill and the customer took this to the cash desk to be paid before leaving the shop. Some large shops had mechanized cash transport systems, which allowed the assistant to take cash but centralized change-giving and book-keeping with the cashier:

> We had the old overhead railways to put the money in: you pulled the lever on a spring, put the money in the cup and it went up to the desk, and money came back, the change. . . .
>
> Often it was quicker to run to the cashier and hand your thing over and get your change than it was to put it on the railway and wait for it. But at the other end of the shop, they probably saved legs by using these.[6]

Winnifred Hardwick was a cashier at Wood's the drapers on The Square at Market Harborough in the late 1920s:

> Miss Miller was the head-cashier and book-keeper, and I used to do the change and help her keep the books [both for cash takings and credit accounts]. I had to do the dissecting – hated it – everything had to be dissected; we had a special dissecting book and all the dockets from the cash that day were all put in their proper places. Everything that was sold had to be written down in the day-book. It wasn't a very easy job.[7]

Cashiers in the town's shops were gradually replaced by the use of mechanical cash registers. One of the first shops to introduce this innovation was the Co-op's central branch. From around 1930 each counter assistant handled money for the first time and was made personally responsible for it:

> When you went out anywhere, or when you went for meal time or anything, you locked up your till so conscientiously and turned your check-book over and nobody was allowed to touch it. . . . If during the time you was using it you ran short of change, you locked your till and then went up to the counter – 'Can you give me any silver?'. . . At the end of each day before you started cleaning up or anything like that, you had to cash your till up. Then that went in turn to the manager. He had to check each one off and then he'd summarise it into a main statement. Then you had to report back to say how your cash tallied with your check-book the following morning. Anything wrong, you soon knew about it.

> I don't know whether that was a good system or not, each having a till. If you was busy at the counter and you had to go to somebody else and ask them if they could change a note for you – it was all delay and it was all extra work. I think the cash desk system was the best myself, although it was a heavy job on busy days.[8]

There were also occasions when cash never changed hands. The traditional practice of barter was still used by local farmers well into this century. Grocers bought some of their supplies from local farmers, especially butter and eggs and it was common for farmers to offset their grocery bills against produce supplied to the grocer. In the 1930s, when the Depression had a severe effect on agriculture, farmers were sometimes obliged to settle their bills in kind with all types of retailer: 'If they hadn't been able to pay their bill, they'd probably bring in a pound of butter or something'.[9]

The usual way to pay for items you could not immediately afford was to ask for credit. For many working-class families the notion of paying cash as a sign of respectability had to be sacrificed through economic hardship. For such customers, the shopkeeper's usual practice was to book goods through the week for settlement at the weekend when wages were paid and debts discharged 'and then start again for the next week'. Shops stayed open later on Fridays and Saturdays to serve the customers who had just received their week's wages and their housekeeping: 'People would probably have credit all week and hopefully they paid you on a Friday night. Well by the time they'd paid what they owed they had started having the rest of the week on credit almost immediately'.[10]

Norman Marlow worked at the Husbands Bosworth branch of the Co-op in the late 1920s. Their customers were predominantly agricultural workers and factory workers who cycled daily into work in Harborough, Lutterworth or Rugby: 'Co-op business was all cash, supposed to be, but . . . in these outlying villages you had to do what other people did and run a book'. In these circumstances, the Co-operative Society's long-standing rule against giving credit was waived at the grass-roots level. But such unofficial credit caused problems for the shop manager at the annual stock-taking when all money and goods had to be accounted for: 'So if the book [was] owed £20, Mr Kilsby [the Husbands Bosworth branch manager] had to make that right through his own pocket. He'd get it back of course when the people paid, but to cover that one weekend period, he'd have to find the money'.[11]

Giving credit also created extra book-keeping. Mr Wimlett's father was manager of Eastmans, a multiple butcher's shop, just before the First World War: 'Father, while he was with Eastmans, his Sunday morning was spent in making up his returns, and he had to show every debt of everybody living in the district, whatever it was . . . . He'd have all the names down and how much they owed, and that had to go into the office ready for Monday mornings'.[12]

A grocer who went into the family business at the end of the First World War recalled that at that time the shop wrote out credit sales three times – in a day-book, in an alphabetical ledger and then on a weekly bill. Most of this work was done in the evenings, 'It was a very involved and time-consuming way of having goods'. In this shop, the books were superseded by the McCluskey system, a spring ledger for filing duplicated bills.[13]

The other form of credit was the regular account. This tended to be the expectation of the respectable middle-class customer. No stigma was attached to this. Indeed it was regarded as a mark of social status. To attract and retain the trade of wealthy middle-class and upper-class customers, shops offered long-term credit, usually for a minimum of a month. Unlike other credit terms, long-term credit usually involved an extra charge.[14]

The practice at Miss Stiles, an independent chemist on the corner of Adam & Eve Street, was typical: 'We had an accounts book and everybody with an account would come in and Miss Stiles would send the bills out every three months. . . . Every time somebody came in with an account, we had to write everything down in this book. It was mostly farmers, veterinary surgeons and Bowden House, Fernie Hunt, mostly titled people'.[15]

Giving credit was an essential service provided by most shops but it always contained an element of risk for the shopkeeper or manager. Credit also meant money tied up. The shopkeeper's own creditors, the manufacturers and wholesalers, had to be paid and other costs such as wages, rent and rates had to be met regularly.

The balance between cash trade and credit varied from shop to shop. At Webb's, a gentleman's outfitters, between the wars it was 'all cash transactions': 'There was a credit trade if you were of good standing. You'd got to be someone – well, like my father, he would have been, another manager in the town, you see, or you'd got to know they were affluent people. Otherwise credit was frowned on. It was such a job to get the money'.

Other shops, especially those in the food trades, simply could not afford to be so choosy. Mr Ron Hodby estimated that in his family grocer's shop in Nelson Street, New Harborough, 60 per cent of their business in the 1920s and '30s was done on credit.[16]

Shopkeepers and managers had to use their judgement and knowledge of their fellow townspeople when deciding whether to extend credit. A former cashier at Wood's the drapers thought that Mr John Wood, the owner-manager, was too ready to offer credit:

> We'd give credit for anything! We on the desk used to say sometimes, 'Well I don't think

Staff of Jeyes, the chemist, Church Square, Market Harborough, 1960s. From left to right are, Miss Wood, Miss Holton, Miss Morris, Mrs Kemp (not staff), Mr Heywood and Mrs Mingle. (Photograph by another member of staff, Mr Kemp)

you ought to send any more to her, she owes so much already'. Boss would say, 'Oh, well, let it go', so we used to let it go. . . . But some of these very well-off posh people used to run up big accounts and then they'd come in and say, 'Would you take off this?', but they'd leave the balance because they couldn't afford to pay for them. And then we'd let some more go, same house, as she'd paid. . . . They were all as bad, often, as ordinary people, although I think some of the parsons were worse![17]

There was always the fear that if a shop refused credit, it would lose the customer to a rival concern 'and you wouldn't get what they owed anyway'. Once one shop offered credit, all the others were obliged to in turn. It was a merry-go-round that was almost impossible to get off. As one village shopkeeper said, 'Some would swap about; you'd know if someone got into debt at one shop, they'd start with you!'[18] Since credit sales were so important to most businesses, every shopkeeper had their share of bad debts. This was true in the villages as well as the towns, in the depressed 1930s and the more prosperous '50s and '60s. Charles Kirby's mother ran a small shop in Slawston in the 1920s:

> The biggest thing in a country village was your debts. Well, take farm labourers, at that time of day they was only getting about thirty bob a week. Well, I mean, if they got behind one week it was a job to pull up. . . . You couldn't blame them because they

Coats and hats in the Ladies' Department of Smith's, The Square, Market Harborough, 1921

didn't earn it so they couldn't pay out. Farm labourer, if he got a wife and a family and got to pay house rent and got thirty bob a week, there wasn't much left for food was there?

We heard the same story about other shops and the credit they offered:

Obviously you often got bad debts. You chased them where you could but because you knew everyone personally you did tend to let credit run on. . . . The fact that you were so personally involved with these people, you knew their problems and that, it made it difficult I think at times to be a bit hard-hearted, which she [my mother] wasn't anyway, I suppose not a good businesswoman.[19]

Debts were by no means always a matter of poverty:

We had lots of monthly accounts . . . one or two let us down, but they weren't the ordinary working people, they were people who you would have thought knew better and had more money. One or two hotel keepers skipped off and left us holding the baby, but nothing you could do about it. If they hadn't got the money, you couldn't get it. . . . Even for such things as funerals, I never got paid.

I suppose really we had quite a lot of bad debts . . . well, in the grocery trade today you have to pay for the stuff immediately you have it don't you.

Although they didn't always pay, you had to write them off in the end.[20]

Another common way of buying goods was through a club into which the customer paid regular sums of money. Clubs were more akin to thrift than credit, although obviously they were provided by shopkeepers to encourage trade. Christmas clubs, for example, which started in the nineteenth century, enabled their members to buy the full festive fare, but spread payment over a lengthy period prior to Christmas.[21]

Purchasing clubs were primarily for 'ordinary working people' and were consequently run for the most part by shops with a significant working-class trade for relatively expensive items. The Market Harborough Co-operative Society, for example, ran drapery, furniture and coal clubs in the 1930s. Perhaps the most popular clubs in the early part of the century were the clothing and footwear clubs run by many drapers and outfitters in the town. As in the other clubs, the clothing club spread the major expense of buying clothes or material over a period of regular instalments:

And of course we used to run a club, a clothing club . . . and people used to pay so much a week or month – whatever they wanted – a shilling a month if they wanted it. And

> then once a year they'd come for all their goods and, of course, it was already paid for. And they had a good discount. Some of them used to buy quite a lot of stuff on the club. The town people, as well, they used to come in and put [down] 2*s*; 'Will you put 2*s* on the club?'

Club money represented an important source of cash-flow for the drapers and clothiers who had to buy expensive stock months in advance of it being sold. Its importance is suggested by their willingness to offer discounts on clothing club sales.[22]

Paying by hire purchase was a more rigid system than either clubs or informal, week-to-week credit. It was a contractual agreement where a deposit secured the possession of the goods and the balance plus interest was paid off by instalments. Hire purchase covered a widening variety of goods between the wars and became extensively used by the 1950s, partly replacing some of the earlier club arrangements. For the retailers it encouraged custom while providing steady payments and interest to cover the length of payment. For the customer, the purchase could be taken away immediately for a relatively small deposit and unlike arbitrary credit, buying on the 'never-never' did not limit the likelihood of further credit being given.[23]

The introduction of self-service, which came to Market Harborough in the late 1950s, brought a new division of labour and a change in the method of handling cash in the larger stores. At the International supermarket in the mid-1960s, some assistants staffed the checkouts while others made up orders and filled shelves, as Josie Walker recalls:

> I worked checkout in those days. . . . It was a very quiet period and we were just sat there and sat there, doing nothing. . . . And I said to [the manager], 'Mr Neville, would you mind if I had a bucket of water and I could wipe those fixtures down just by the checkout, then they'll be nice and clean for when the order comes in'. 'Mrs Walker, you do no such thing!', he said, 'You are employed as a checkout assistant and that is where you remain, you do not leave it.'
>
> You had to do all your own cashing-up; each checkout did their own in those days. And it had to be right, and you had to stay there until it was right, or else put whatever money you were short in yourself.[24]

Large amounts of cash are handled at shop counters and checkouts today, alongside payment by credit and debit cards, and cheques.

> It is quite hard work. I mean even working on a checkout and sitting there is very tedious, and I wouldn't work in a supermarket now for all the tea in China, with those complicated tills. . . . You've got to put different goods through at a certain code.

> We went, just out of curiosity to Asda [in Corby] one Tuesday. Well, if you want to see checkouts you want to go there. If they've got one checkout, they must have twenty-four. And they're all full, and the baskets and trolleys are piled high. . . . Oh, I'd go spare. It must be awful, mentally, you know, all the time on that till just sitting there.[25]

With the advent of bar-coding in the 1980s, the large chain stores were able to centralize all stock-taking and ordering procedures on computer, an operation which assisted the tight control of sales policies from head office. At Tesco in Market Harborough, for instance, the stock levels were entered onto a small hand-held unit overnight and passed through a modem down the telephone lines to the head office computer, enabling automatic replenishment of stock within forty-eight hours. Chain stores now use a laser reader to read bar-coded price labels at the checkout directly into the till. Initially customer suspicion of bar-coding meant that the stores did not dispense with individual price stickers straightaway, despite the unnecessary labour involved, but as bar-coding became familiar this part of shopwork disappeared.[26]

Credit, whether free, at low interest rates or through a credit card remains an important selling device and many stores now issue their own credit cards. Research in the late 1980s suggested that card holders spend up to six times as much as they would if armed only with a cheque book or cash.[27] If used to gain credit, high interest rates are incurred, although an increasing number of people use credit cards to spread payments for purchases. Others simply use the cards as a convenient method of payment, writing a single cheque for all the purchases at the end of the month. Credit cards overcome the last inhibition to buy: 'can I afford it?'

Credit cards issued by finance companies and banks removed the risk of trading on credit from the shopkeeper and manager in return for a percentage charge on each card-based transaction. From the mid-1980s, however, most of the large variety, clothing, furnishing and departmental chains sought to recover the increasingly important credit business from credit card companies by introducing their own in-house credit cards. The large chains are now prepared to shoulder the risk of defaulted payments. A credit card which can only be used within one chain of outlets or a group such as Storehouse encourages both impulse buying and the brand identification and store loyalty which lies at the heart of current retail marketing strategy. The in-house card also retains the commission for the store which would otherwise be lost to the credit card company.

Purchase by instalments has also been extended beyond the high street shop to include by mail order. The potency of the catalogue which can be browsed through at leisure in the home has long been recognized. The catalogue, both prior to Christmas and through the year is now widely used both as a selling device and a reinforcement of store loyalty. Increasingly in the late 1980s, the catalogue sought to sell not just a range of products but a style of life for the consumer in which to participate through purchase.

## *Chapter Three*

# Doing the Rounds

Shoppers in the 1990s collect their purchases themselves. Planners, retailers and developers seek to make this process as smooth as possible by ensuring adequate car parking is available close to both high street shops and out-of-town hypermarkets. This has become the norm, however, only in the last twenty years. For much of the century most retailers won and retained their customers by competing on service rather than by price. A rapid delivery to the doorstep, often on the same day, was an indispensable part of that high standard of service. While we now contemplate the possibility of shopping at home by computer keyboard and teletext display, the delivery of goods to the home was a universal feature of the retail trade up to the late 1950s, even among some multiple stores. Most shops also furthered their trade by a weekly order round, calling at homes to collect orders from the housewife on a regular basis. As a former Co-op manager remembers of the inter-war period: 'I should think 75 per cent of the people shopping with grocery orders, they didn't carry a bag with them at all. You wrapped the groceries in a brown paper parcel, tied it up and handed it to the person. Or if she wanted it delivered the following day you put it in the warehouse at the back'.[1]

The vigorous competition to be found in the grocery and provisions trade led most shops to offer an order and delivery service. The Market Harborough Co-operative Society was no exception. In the 1920s and '30s each of the out-of-town branches had their own roundsman who made deliveries in a Morris van. Orders for Foxton and the Langtons were taken by Mr Copson when shop-boy at the central Co-op store:

> They had a round, on Tuesdays it used to be the Langtons way and Wednesday it used to be Foxton way. I used to go myself, push-bike of course. You started at half-past eight into West Langton, then gradually worked your way round and finished up at Tur Langton, perhaps at one o'clock. I used to do the area, Braybrooke, Arthingworth, Kelmarsh, Clipston, Oxendon one day; Lubenham, Farndon and Marston another day, collecting orders. Some people used to have the orders written down. You scanned through it and 'Anything else Mrs Smith?' Otherwise you always carried an order book and you went in the house, sat at the table and you started off. As she named the items you wrote them on your order form.
>
> The delivery in Market Harborough of groceries used to be by horse and cart. . . . The chap used to do it regular from the Central [branch]. He'd finish his job

The baker Bill Pateman taking orders from Mrs Norton of Lubenham, *c.* 1906. Doorstep delivery was all part of the service offered to customers by most retailers

> perhaps half-past eleven and he used to give his horse a feed while he came down and sorted his parcels out. He used to put them all out in the yard, in rotation [by] the streets and then he used to put them on his van, and Thursday, Friday, Saturday, he used to have two cart-loads for delivery and he used to stack them perhaps five or six high nearly up to the top. He used to work hard, it was really hard work.[2]

The five Co-op branches in Harborough itself and Great Bowden relied on a boy on a bike, or used a milk roundsman from the Central Premises to deliver in a dray. Deliveries in the town were by horse and cart right through the 1930s, during the war and into the late 1940s. Hand-trucks were also used before the last war.

Symington & Thwaites, the largest of the town's independent grocery and provisions merchants also maintained a large order trade, particularly with the district's country houses. At the turn of the century this was carried in liveried horse-drawn vans with the firm's name proclaimed on the side. By the early 1930s, they had been replaced by a fleet of three motor vans. Mr Hubert Reeve first 'travelled' for them in the late 1930s:

I used to go out travelling in the town for a start. I used to go out two or three days a week getting the orders. Then I had to come back and get them up. Then a bit later on still, I started on the country round. . . . I used to go up to Dingley Hall when Earl Beatty lived at Dingley, and of course I had an order from there that filled the big van; I had to take it up specially. . . . We reckoned to go there once a fortnight and deliver a van load but often they'd ring up and expect it delivered the same day or at the latest the next morning. Of course we had to deliver it, but usually it was a big enough order to make it worthwhile. . . . We used to go to Rockingham. They used to let the castle for the hunting season and there was an American came to live there, and we thought old Beatty had a lot of stuff! . . . We had a biggish van and he had to go twice for one order; sides of bacon, sacks of flour, hundredweight box of lump sugar, everything on a big

Symington & Thwaites' modernized shop-front, *c.* 1930. By this time the business had extended along St Mary's Road and the horse-drawn delivery vans had been replaced with motor vehicles

scale. 'Course, they'd got a lot of servants and they did a lot of entertaining. It was quite an order when we got it.

It was always 'Good morning' or 'afternoon', whatever it was. They were regular customers. There was no 'patter' at all but [I] just went in and sat down and they paid the bill for the last fortnight's groceries and then they told me what they wanted and I kept suggesting other things; anything I thought they might want. No sales patter, not anything like that, we didn't need it. You'd got to know the people. Ordinary suit of clothes, collar and tie and when I finished I said I'd never wear a collar and tie again because you used to wear it in the summer as well and it used to get hot, and it used to get damn cold in the winter. There was no heat in the car then. I had a regular wage and a small commission, only about half of 1 per cent. . . . 'Course, if anybody fresh came into the village, we'd go and look them up. . . . When Fine Fare took over [in the 1960s] I had half-a-crown for every fresh order that we kept for a month.[3]

Officially the Co-op did not give credit in any form, even on goods delivered by the roundsman. To avoid the handling of cash, the Harborough Co-op used a system of checks for bread and milk rounds (as other Co-op Societies did):

They was a printed disc. The milk disc used to be round and the bread disc was octagonal. And of course they had 'Market Harborough Co-op Society, 1 pint' or '2lb loaf' and people purchased them in the Grocery . . . had them with their orders. . . . Her milk checks she purchased once a week and the same with bread. And all you did, when the milkman came, you just gave one check for one pint, and the cash was all handled through the Grocery department.[4]

Between the wars there was resentment among Co-op deliverymen at the increasing workload caused by the growing size of the town. The same number of bread and milk roundsmen were delivering to more and more customers, so they were working longer hours without any extra pay. This grievance fuelled support for unionization among the delivery men. Another drawback to working on deliveries came when the firm had its annual outing to the seaside, 'Morecambe, Blackpool or somewhere like that'. All the employees went except for 'a man from the Dairy. He had to stay behind to take the milk in from the farms. And they used to draw lots for that'. There were occasional 'advantages' too: delivering milk on Christmas morning meant plenty of offers of drink till 'In the end I couldn't see me truck!', and taking dividends out to members in the country earned deliverymen the odd tip.[5]

The delivery men and other service staff were the bottom layer of the Co-op's labour force, working long hours and expected to help wherever needed. 'I've had to come off delivering milk in the morning, very often, go back home and change me clothes and deliver coal in the afternoon.' Most of the roundsmen from the Central Premises working in the Dairy department went onto general deliveries (bread and groceries) after they'd finished their morning's work for the Dairy. 'I'd start at seven [a.m.] and I'd be lucky to come home at six [p.m.]. . . . If you hadn't got your round done you had to stop and do it you see.'[6]

Mr Geoff Johnson started at the central branch of the Market Harborough Co-op in 1926: 'I went straight in. Keep the place clean for a start and run the errands, and then unpacking and then you gradually began to serve the customers. You were a general dogsbody really. You wouldn't dream of letting anybody carry a parcel if he [the manager] could send me out on a bike. It was enjoyable in the sense that you escaped when you got on your bike, you were away from the eye of the "Almighty" weren't you'. Although pedalling the Co-op's heavy shop bike with its cumbersome basket across the broad reaches of the Welland Valley in all weathers was undoubtedly hard work, for Geoff Johnson there were definite compensations to be found on the country round:

> Great! Half the week in the fresh air . . . . On Mondays I spent all day in Kibworth, a straight run along the A6. . . . After a few calls selling bits and pieces, but mostly Co-op stamps [savings club stamps], I arrived at old Polly Ward's. Ten minutes sit-down and gossip brought me up to date with all the goings-on in Harcourt. . . . The afternoon calls were close-packed, and I sold a lot of savings stamps; very often the money was left ready and I was able to get round quickly. . . . With luck I could finish my calls by five o'clock, bike back to Harborough and be cashed up by six. Sometimes in bad weather I went by train, taking the bike. On Wednesday mornings I did Oxendon and Clipston, with occasional calls at Arthingworth and Kelmarsh. . . . One of my favourite calls in Clipston, was on old Miss Mutton. . . . Without fail there was a cup of cocoa and a piece of cake on the table, and we had many a good talk over these elevenses. . . . After this call I got my skates on and raced round to finish by 12.30 at the latest, so as not to miss any of my precious half-day. At Husbands Bosworth [Thursdays] I started my calls in Honeypot Lane. . . . I always had my midday sandwiches in the bakehouse [attached to the Co-op branch shop] with Jack Stanyon and heard all the latest goings-on in Bosworth.[7]

The shop bicycle was synonymous with deliveries for most of this century. Cycles with a carrying capacity had been available since the days of the 'penny-farthing'. The diamond-framed tradesmen's carrier cycle with small front wheel and tubular support for a large basket on the front was available from most cycle manufacturers between the wars for £6 to £8. Invariably finished in black, with its only decoration the shop's name on a plate inside the frame, the shop bike was heavy, being built to last, hard work uphill and unstable if overloaded.[8]

Mr Raymond Tack worked for the Co-op at this time as a milk roundsman:

> I used to have a two-wheeled truck and it had a 17-gallon churn hung in the centre. And then it had a tap and you used to fill your bucket from the churn. You used to have two 2-gallon buckets, one hanging on each handle as well. My first stop was R. & W.H. Symington's here, their canteen, two gallon of milk to them. But it was pretty hard work to push the old churn and that. And going up where the Stall Market is now [Northampton Road] that slope up there, if it was wet or had been snowy, I couldn't get a grip. There used to be quite a lot of chaps coming down to their work in the factory, one or two of them would give me a push up till I got to the top. I used to start off at Springfield Street, Auriga Terrace, Nithsdale Avenue, Newcombe Street and I used to do all them. I used to have on average about 300 calls . . . perhaps just over 20 gallon of milk. I was allowed one-and-a-half pints for spillage. If I was over that one-and-a-half, I used to have to pay for it. Some used to pay for the milk, but some of them had a Co-op disc. Very often the weights-and-measures man would be waiting for you. You'd perhaps just come from a customer and you'd put a pint of milk in the jug for them and all of a sudden he'd appear around the corner. 'Right' he'd say, 'Come on, we'll measure it out'. And you're in for it if you'd given under and he also didn't like it if you'd given too much! . . . I'd start at seven and I'd be lucky to come home at six. If you hadn't got your round done, you had to stop and do it you see. There was no set time for you, no booking-in or anything like that.[9]

While the country round is a nostalgic symbol of the complete service once offered by shops, come rain or shine, the roundsman had to be out with his bike. The round was important to the survival of the shop, particularly a private shop, in the face of vigorous competition from the aggressive multiples. Developing a round created a regular and loyal circuit of custom for the shop. In an age before near universal access to a car, a large number of potential customers were unable to get into town regularly, especially in the country villages. If the customer couldn't get to the shop, the shop had to come to them.

The crucial importance of the roundsman is demonstrated by Mr Ingram's account of the Maypole Dairy branch in Kettering. In the early 1930s trade was poor in the shop and, most unusually for a multiple store, country rounds were embarked upon to improve the Maypole's turnover. Rounds were set up to Desborough, Rothwell, Burton Latimer, Thrapston and Islip. In 1932, as the new town around Corby's redeveloped steelworks began to be established, Mr Ingram was set on developing a round there:

> Corby made Kettering. . . . Once they started altering that steelworks, our firm was straight onto it. We'd got to get in there, so for about a year we went to the old Corby village and start and get a few customers together. Then I watched for when the houses

A milk delivery roundsman on Northampton Road, 1920s

started to go up. I remember when the first went up in Bessemer Grove. Every time you went you watched to see curtains going up. Try and get all the customers you could. It worked – I used to go on Mondays, deliver Saturdays, and then it got to Tuesdays and then Wednesdays, as all the houses keep going up, more people kept coming down, Scotch people and all the rest of it. I got on ever so well. I was spending three days a week on my bike going all round collecting the orders. I didn't go back to the shop for two days because it wasn't worth it. I'd go in Monday, collect me book and things like that. Thursday morning I'd be sat upstairs writing all the orders out and then on Friday we'd be all day long, probably up to midnight packing them all into parcels. . . . And then they hired a man from Corby with a lorry and he used to come in Saturday morning and we'd be all day Saturday delivering. I worked it up at nearly £100 per week. Now a £100 a week then was a lot of money.

No order was too small. Even at the country rounds, you had to go across a field to a house for a quarter of tea. You'd do it; you were out to sell everything you possibly could.

You daren't refuse an order. . . . Imagine all those big housing estates up round Stephenson's Way and all the way round Occupation Road. There weren't any roads you know and we used to have to wear wellingtons. You'd never seen anything like it! . . . When you were on the country rounds, booking the orders, we'd got these pads with the carbon through and you'd book down what the customer wanted next delivery. You used to knock at the door and if they didn't answer, you used to open the door and shout 'Maypole!'. I know there's been many a time when I'd been wet through back in them early days. I often used to wear a bowler [hat] on a wet day because they were the best hats: with a trilby you'd get wet through, but with a bowler, every now and again you just let it run off.

During the Kettering Maypole's problems in the early 1930s, promotional rounds were resorted to:

Head office or inspectors, they'd pass it onto the managers what they wanted them to do to try and increase sales of this, or if sales were lagging. . . . Trade was so bad at Kettering that even my first year [1925], I had to go out round the streets all round the houses. . . . We had a little one ounce pack of tea and we used to do up either two ounce or four ounce scrolls of margarine; you'd weigh it up and others would roll it. You used to pack all of them, you remember the baskets like bakers' baskets, and I used to have to carry that while the other two knocked at the doors. And many's the time my arm's been red with carrying that basket nearly all day. That's to get trade, every penny you could get, things were so bad.[10]

Shops without their own roundsman could make use of the carriers who ran regular services to and from the country district into Market Harborough. Until the advent of the motor bus between the wars, the horse-drawn carrier's van formed an important link between the town's shops and their rural customers. Not only did the country carrier provide transport into the town on market days, he also delivered and collected goods and parcels, and acted as a shopping agent for goods not obtainable in village general stores for the rural customer. Arthur Wilford's father was the Naseby carrier until the Second World War, running into Northampton on Wednesdays and Saturdays, and Market Harborough on Tuesdays:

Going to Harborough on Tuesdays . . . . The first thing of course was to get the horse ready, making sure he'd had a good feed and making sure he'd got a feed with them, a bag of corn and all the rest of it, for when you got down to your destination. Quite a few folks would bring things along the night before which were stored in the house and they would be put on the vehicle, usually, if possible in the order they came off. There was an art in loading, to make sure you didn't have to shift everything to find something else

George Barwell and his carrier's van on the road to Uppingham, *c.* 1910

because ten-to-one you'd be gone by somewhere and you'd find something you'd got to go back for, so you'd got to do it right. Anything important, it used to go down in a pocket-book: Dad always carried a pocket-book and he noted everything very carefully in that book and then you set off round the village, followed by the old dog, who wouldn't miss his Tuesday run. I think the old dog was interested in the local bitches and all that you know!

Anyway, you'd go around the village and make certain calls. Always used to call at the pubs for a start, because if anybody'd got anything, they used to leave it in the pub if they were there perhaps the night before and say, 'Will you give this to George Wilford tomorrow morning for me to do at Harborough?' Then, of course, finally they'd get out of the village, although there were a lot of folks used to stop him [while] going round the village ordering little bits and pieces. Folks would want little bits of grocery and all that sort of stuff you know, another thing shoes, and not so much ladies dresses but perhaps underwear and things like that and kid's shoes, school shoes, men's shoes, anything like that, and there used to be certain shops in Harborough where you used to take the orders and there used to be a bit of a fiddle in that because you used to get a penny in the shilling discount for the paying. Whatever it cost, Dad used to get a penny in the shilling, that was the recognized thing.

Then of course, through Clipston, call at the two pubs in Clipston, down at Farndon, call at the pub there . . . one or two of the biggish houses in Farndon, they always wanted you to call, because they'd always got something, you might bring pig-food or whatever. It would probably be on account, you wouldn't have to pay for that, but you brought it. The first thing, when you got down to Harborough, was to go around the town delivering anything that had to be delivered and then if there was any empties for anywhere . . . they were taken back to the various shops like the big grocers shops and places like that and then there was a lot of things 'on appro', if you know what I mean, on approval. Say they'd want a suit for a boy of so many years you see, so these appro firms like Hepworth's and one or two more down in Harborough, they would pack up three or four suits in a pack you see and then they'd chose one of these suits, if it fitted and so on, keep them for the week and then they'd go back. The same thing would happen over shoes.

When we got down to Harborough, as I say, it was delivering all the bits and pieces round together with orders. If you'd got any orders for some of the big places, you dropped them in as you went by otherwise you had to walk round. And then on to the old Cherry Tree . . . where the ostler took over then. You went in and the ostler took charge of the horse and the dog went with him and laid with the horse all day. The ostler went off with the horse's feed, gave him a bucket of water and generally looked after things like that and he would look after goods as they were brought, you know, when firms brought things and left them there, he would keep his eye on them all the time. The ostler would keep his eye on folks who come in because obviously there was nothing to stop somebody pinching things which were left [for the carrier]. That often came off; somebody would be around pinching.

The van, that was the apple of my grandfather's eye, it was absolutely the latest, there was nothing like it in the vicinity at all when that was brought out. It was a two-horse vehicle, but you could have a choice of one or two horses because it had got a single or a double pair of shafts which were a little bit narrower and they went out wider and the two horses were connected together with a pole. . . . It had what we called a box seat in the front where the driver sat and any privileged party sat on there. There was always a fight to see who was going to sit on the box in front if there was a crowd in the van. Along the sides of the van were some seats which were portable in the fact that they could be hooked in or folded up and parked out of the way, so if you hadn't got many passengers and a lot of heavy stuff or bulky, you could shift these seats and the same across the back. The van it would hold four down each side, easy, hold four, and one at the back if normal adult, two kids could sit there and two at the front, one each side of the driver you see. These seats were beautifully upholstered, right thick upholstered you know and at the back there was a door which opened outwards and there were fold-down steps which used to come down and that was used when the vehicle was used as transport for a crowd going to a dance or something like that where all the ladies were made up and all that, instead of getting up in the front end they got up the back end with the door open. And in my very young days, it used to be used going round the countryside taking folks to these dances and whatever. It was the only means of transport then.

When it was due for repainting it used to go in there for a week and it would be a chocolatey-coloured brown with . . . red and yellow on the sides; they were adverts, used to have a great big long 'Lancaster and Wells, Wines & Spirits, Northampton' advert all along each side. They used to pay about a pound a year for this advertising. And then there was a clock inside, 'This conveyance leaves at . . . ' and you could set the clock at whatever time so they knew what time you were going to take off see. . . . It always had the name on the side, it was 'George Wilford, Naseby, carrier to Northampton, Wednesdays and Saturdays, Market Harborough Tuesdays' on both sides.

The carrier's business, consisting predominantly of many small transactions, was done on credit:

If it was £2 or £3, well Dad said 'I want the money then' you see. There used to be a few jibbers you know, . . . shocking bad payers, and Dad would pay for their boot repairs and whatever, 'Oh, can't do it today, I'll come down, bring the money down'. They wouldn't come down. Next week, he'd say, 'What about last week's?' 'Oh no, can't pay, we'll come down' and it went on. Eventually it would get to the point where Dad would say 'Well I'm doing nothing else for you until you pay up'. One common thing out in the country in those days, I suppose folks had got very little money, was to go to the Home & Colonial in particular in both Harborough and Northampton for margarine. If you bought a pound of margarine, it used to be 4*d* or 5*d* a pound, you'd get 2lb of margarine, they'd always give you one extra. For every one you bought you got an extra one chucked in. That used to be a regular thing, 'Bring me so many pounds of marge', and you'd get somebody who had a particular fancy for somebody's sausages, something like that, so you'd go to that particular butcher for a pound of sausages.

Holidays like Bank Holidays in particular, it would mean another vehicle going as well. They used to use a big spring cart, but what they used to do, if possible they used to book. You wouldn't go and jump on the carrier's van, you had to book in advance or else you didn't know you were going to get a ride. There used to be big bookings, so you knew what you had to take in the way of transport. If we were pretty well packed up and there was no ice, there could be three more sitting on the back of the vehicle which had

George Moore, of Moore's Dairies, delivering milk from the churn on a handcart in St Mary's Road, Market Harborough, 1950s

> what we called the 'cratch' which dropped down or hooked up out the way. Of course, you always used to keep it hooked up because kids were a blasted nuisance, running behind and jumping on that for a ride. Oh they were a bloody nuisance and you'd hear somebody say, 'Whip behind mister!'[11]

The first multiple grocery and provisions shops had traded on a strictly cash and no frills basis, with a very limited range of items sold at well-advertised and highly competitive prices. By the 1950s the established multiples had broadened their stock considerably and where before they had undercut the independent grocer on a few items – butter, margarine, bacon, jam – they were now competing across a broader spectrum. As these basic shops moved upmarket, they were inevitably drawn into competing on service and this included an order and delivery service. Mrs Prince worked at Lipton's in their small store at 8 High Street from 1959 to 1961 where an order round was still part of the trade:

> There were quite a few orders. Mostly they were for delivery on Fridays, some on Thursdays. You always did them up in advance and then you had a list of things like bacon and ham, and that was all put in next day so that it was fresh. A boy from the grammar school used to come after school and he had the old bike with the tray on the

> front. We used to load it up . . . he used to lift the flaps on some of the boxes and tie string round the whole lot to keep it on. I can only remember him coming back once and said he'd fell off. We used sometimes to have to swap the eggs.[12]

The change to self-service in Market Harborough around 1960 saw the end of the shop bike and the delivery round in the grocery trades. The creation of car-parks on the Commons and behind both sides of the High Street subsequently provided for the increasingly car-based shopper. Proximity to a car-park is now crucial for the supermarket as witnessed by the Co-op's move out of its prime High Street position to Coventry Road and the extended Commons car-park.

Few shopkeepers find a delivery round a paying proposition today, although some supermarkets are once more experimenting with home delivery. Most of the liveried vans seen around the town are delivering stock to the shop rather than orders to the home. Alan Bott of Gregory's the butcher's is an exception, delivering mostly to house-bound pensioners and bulk customers such as restaurants (see Chapter Eight). Several village shopkeepers do deliveries, regarding it more as part of their wider social duty in the community then as a strictly economic function.

The post office and garage, Naseby, 1920s. On the extreme right can be seen a motor bus used by the enterprising postmaster, Endor Halford, for his passenger and goods transport service into Harborough and Northampton

Again this tends to be for the benefit of elderly customers. As the numbers of car owners and especially second car owners rises, the delivery service is unnecessary. With the numbers of working women also rising, the reception of a delivery has also become problematic. The delivery round used to be an essential part of the service provided by most shopkeepers for their customers. Today the more mobile consumer looks towards different areas in the retailer's service: quality, value for money and accessibility by car.

## *SECTION TWO*

# *BEHIND THE COUNTER*

# *Chapter Four*
# Workers, Managers and Owners

The service that a shop provides depends ultimately on its staff. In the twentieth century the experiences of shopworkers in large private shops and branches of multiples have revolved around changes in training, the increased employment of women workers, and the low level of unionization in the retail trades. The job of the manager has evolved from that of the skilled retailer in charge to a more administrative role. At the same time there has been a wholesale decline in the numbers and importance of private owners.

## THE SHOP-FLOOR

> [As for] my youngest sister – my father said he was tired of us going into shops, he said 'Why don't you try the factory?' – 'course she went into the factory and she got loads more money than we did. And I don't suppose she worked half as hard as we did, on our feet all day. (Female shopworker, 1920s[1])

Work in a shop between the wars was an attractive prospect to school-leavers of both sexes in Market Harborough. A job as a sales assistant had a higher social status than the main alternatives – factory work, farm labour, or earlier in the century, domestic service: 'I wanted to do shopwork, you know. I don't know why. I didn't fancy myself sitting in a factory machining all day. . . . And I was lucky really, at the time, they had a vacancy for an apprentice. But it was long hours, and you're standing on your feet all day'.[2]

Formal apprenticeships protected entry to a trade, particularly among shops that served the wealthier end of the market and were supposed to offer a good training. Joyce Gardiner was an apprentice at G. Nephews, a large drapery store right in the centre of Leicester, in the late 1920s. Her early working life gives a glimpse of the practice that had been the norm in the draper's trade in the midlands and south of England thirty years previously. 'I wasn't allowed to serve customers for twelve months. . . . I lived in. We lived over the place – There was a matron, and meals were all cooked and everything. It was very good. . . . Not paid anything, no. My father had to pay something to start with!' Charles Kirby served his apprenticeship at a high-class butcher's in Leicester, just before the First World War, staying with his aunt in town. He was there two years and was unpaid: 'I only used to take the meat out on a bicycle with a carrier on the front'.[3]

Trainees were more likely to be called apprentices in private shops, but often there would be little or no difference in the training received by an apprentice in one shop and by a 'junior' in another. Joan Freestone was 'apprenticed' at Wood's the drapers for three years from 1931:

> Nine o'clock we used to start. Well you'd have to dust and tidy up, and get the counters straight. [And] do stock-taking, help with that, see what we were short of . . . and then I think we used to go and make tea for the bosses. That was how we first started, when we did the dusting, the donkey-work.
>
> You learnt, went through all the departments – You just went under the 'First Sales' and the 'Second Sales' [assistants], and they showed you how to serve a customer, and what to do, and making receipts and bills out . . . and then when you served your apprenticeship, you went as Second Sales and then First Sales.[4]

Only in those trades which still combined craft and retailing (baker or bespoke tailor for instance) and those with a professional status (such as a pharmacist) was training more rigorous. Under these circumstances it involved learning far more than how to serve a customer and having a knowledge of the goods for sale.[5]

An apprenticeship or junior position was not always the bottom of the ladder. In some trades it was possible for a young boy to start as an errand-boy, often while still at school, before being promoted to shop junior. There is no evidence of this opportunity existing for Harborough girls early in this century. After the First World War it was usual for apprentices to receive junior rates of pay. The quality and security of apprenticeship positions varied widely. At one end of the scale the chosen heir to an established family business might be sent to a firm in another town to learn the trade. More commonly the low costs of appprentices and juniors laid training posts open to abuse as a source of cheap labour. Charles Wimlett was an apprentice at Webb Bros, a gent's outfitter's in Church Street, in the mid-1920s:

> I served this apprenticeship for three years; and at the end of the three years they didn't want to keep you at all, because you'd get more than the stated amount. It went up half-a-crown a year, to 15 bob [a week]. That was too much for an apprentice. They just said, well now, look, go and get a job somewhere else, right away, we'll give you a good reference.[6]

Of all the people we talked with who had served in shops between the wars, only two had taken formal studies to help them. One went to night-school as part of his chemist's training in Coventry; the second took evening courses in grocery and commercial arithmetic at a Leicester Technical College. The latter was hardly typical as he was the son of a private grocer and was being groomed to go into the business. Most assistants had no opportunity for formal study. Cecil Copson started work as a 'shop-lad' at the Co-operative Society's Kibworth branch in 1924, aged fifteen, and he recalls how studying was frowned upon :

> We made arrangements, another young chap and myself, to go to Leicester on Monday evenings to a course at the technical college there. And Monday was always a busy day, and we always said that the manager put difficulties in our way so that the first two Mondays we attended this class we were late. 'Course we had to push-bike to Leicester. And the third time he put difficulties in our way, so we withdrew our application and packed the lot in. He could have helped us then, but he didn't believe in that sort of thing. There was only one place where you learned the job, that was in the shop itself.[7]

From before the Second World War some of the established multiples began to offer intensive training courses for their staff away from the workplace. Boots the Chemists was one firm which was keen to train its staff in this way. Carol Dainty got a job at Boots in Market Harborough in the late 1950s after leaving school.

> First duties was just a sales assistant, just serving on the cosmetics counter, which I was interested in. And then after that they sent you to Leicester, to the Boots training school, which . . . only lasted a week but it was quite tough.
>
> [We learnt] the beauty side of it, on 'No 7' beauty products, how to cash up at the end of the day, how to cash up at the end of the week, and how to look after the customer.

Organizations like Boots and W.H. Smith were large enough to provide special training on a regional basis:

> W.H. Smith's was the same type of firm, because they send you on courses for various things. . . . They were the first ones [in Harborough] to do training in the new [decimal] coinage. . . . Now I could do that, oh, a long time before it came out, 'cos they sent us to Leicester on a course.[8]

However both W.H. Smith and Boots were firms which took a pride in looking after their employees. In most companies non-management grades were, and still are, expected to learn on the shop-floor.

A major feature of shopwork in our century has been the growing number of women employed. National censuses have captured this change: in 1911 38 per cent of all shop assistants were women, by 1951 women accounted for 67 per cent of assistants. The gender balance had tipped from one side to the other. This trend started in the late nineteenth century, as the expansion of the retail sector demanded the employment of more shop assistants, both female and male. Before this expansion women were as likely to be owners of small shops as employees.

Contemporaries noted the supply of young women workers and linked it to the national provision of elementary education. In demand terms, employers were able to pay women shopworkers lower wages than equally skilled men. At first the employment of women was concentrated in certain trades – drapers and women's clothing retailers, bakers and confectioners, shops selling dairy produce, tobacconists, stationers and florists. There was a marked scarcity of women workers employed by jewellers and wine merchants, by some food retailers, such as grocers and butchers, and by men's clothing retailers.[9]

Although women were drafted during both world wars in larger numbers than ever before to both counter service and work in the warehouse, major employment gains were made in peacetime too, which was not the case in many other expanding industries. Shopwork, like office work, came to be regarded as fit work for the growing number of women in the labour market. The importance of shopwork to women's paid employment opportunities increased during the 1920s and '30s. While jobs in textile manufacturing declined, the number of women shopworkers in England and Wales went up from 500,000 in 1923 to over 900,000 by 1938.[10]

Rates of pay remained significantly lower and opportunities for promotion remained less for women than for men. Prejudice against the employment of women in certain types of shopwork, and expectations that a woman would leave her employment if she got married were tenacious and have only disappeared in recent times.

In the Market Harborough Industrial Co-operative Society's Central Stores in the 1920s, the different departments were virtually split on gender lines. Many of the retail and productive departments, including the grocery, butcher's and men's clothing departments, and the Stores' delivery and warehouse sections, were male preserves: 'The only female labour in the grocery, the Central Grocery shop, was the cashier'. Women were employed in the Co-op's confectionery, drapery and womenswear departments and in their offices. In Market Harborough during the 1920s, as in most towns, it was only in a shop like Wood's the draper's, where the staff was predominantly female, that you could find women as department heads and buyers.[11]

Symington & Thwaites, a high-class grocer's in the town, consistently employed 'half a dozen women' from the end of the First World War. This represented between a quarter and a third of their staff over the next two decades. Their small branch at Great Bowden was managed by a Miss Wall before she moved to the main shop to become cashier. Gladys Sharpe, who had joined Symington & Thwaites in 1917 aged thirteen, left her job in 1932 to get married. In her time she had worked at most duties – serving behind the counter, making up orders in the despatch department, and staffing the cash desk – before progressing to clerical work in the office. As a woman she was paid less than her male colleagues, and started work an hour later at 9 a.m. instead of 8 a.m. Her wedding presents from the shop staff included, 'a dinner service from Mr Thwaites [one of the partners] and cut-glass bowls from some of the workers there – the fellers – bedspread, pillowcases and all sorts'.[12]

Olive Bland joined Symington & Thwaites shortly after Gladys Sharpe had left in 1932. Then in her late twenties, she already had some experience of running a small shop in Lincolnshire, and when Symington & Thwaites opened a new 'fancy' department (table decorations and biscuits) she was put in charge of it.

> I had all the fancy stuff. I carried 100 large tins of biscuits, and 50 half-tins, and just a few packets, not many packets in those days, just Crawford's Cream Crackers and Jacob's Cream Crackers and Popular Assorted in Jacob's. All the others were loose biscuits, there was quite a problem to keep all those fresh. . . . Then I had all the fancy boxes of biscuits and chocolates, and, as Christmas came round, the crackers. We had a wonderful sale of these: used to get all different colours for people's tables to match up with their tea services.

It was at Symington & Thwaites that Olive Bland met her husband, Hubert Reeve, who was an assistant and traveller for the shop. They got married in 1937, and Olive kept her job in the fancy department, setting a precedent for the firm. 'When I got married Mr Thwaites said, "I will still call you Miss Bland. I hope you won't mind."'

The hours of women workers in the shop were eventually made the same as those of the men, but the differential in wages remained. Olive Reeve spent the rest of her working career at the shop, under various managements, retiring after thirty-eight years.[13]

Between 1951 and 1966 almost two million women joined the paid workforce in England, Scotland and Wales. Women were not only more likely than previously to have paid jobs, but they were also staying in their careers longer. This was reflected in the large numbers of women in employment in the 1950s who had started their careers between the wars. In the late 1950s a woman shop assistant was still only earning on average 65 per cent of the pay of a man in the same job. Her relative earnings had improved little on the state of affairs in the first decade of the twentieth century when a woman shop assistant might expect to take home around 60 per cent of a male assistant's wages. However this was better than the situation for other 'semi-skilled' women workers, where the gap between women's and men's wages was actually widening dramatically through the 1950s and '60s.[14]

Mr F.W. Lee was an apprentice at C.F. Lea's, an independent grocer, from 1937 to 1941, and then moved to Symington & Thwaites after the war. He exaggerates the increase of women workers that was taking place: 'I mean it was unheard of to see a woman behind the counter, or not very often, before the war. We had one [at C.F. Lea's]. But after the war, there were all women in the grocery shops. In Symington's there were women there – they were quite good too'.

Others were less willing to praise the abilities of working women. A near contemporary of Mr Lee's remarked to us that after the Second World War, 'Ladies with no grocery training at all were serving in the shop'. Undoubtedly the grocery trade was being deskilled at this time, but the employment of more women was a symptom not a cause of the change. The old grocery training, the knowledge of foodstuffs, and packing, weighing and blending, was becoming obsolete, and apprenticeships were no longer offered to new employees.[15]

The late twentieth-century pattern of shops with large staffs, predominantly women, and often part-time, was now emerging. A good example of this was the

Boots' sales assistants, *c.* 1960. All but three of the staff at Boots then were women. From left to right are: Carol Dainty, Dorothy Hutchinson, Cynthia Hardy and Julie Wainwright

local branch of Woolworths which had been in the town since 1927. 'It was very popular, I mean, if you went to Harborough, you went round Woolies. It was a bit like going round the market now – you might not buy anything, but you like to see what they've got. . . . It was a very colourful shop with all these things laid out.'

In the mid-1950s the staff comprised a manager (male), a supervisor, a couple of office workers, stock-room staff and a cook, and a dozen or so shop assistants. The supervisor, office-workers and assistants were all women. A sixteen-year-old assistant could expect to get £2 *2s 6d* for a five-day week, including either all-day Saturday or half-days on Wednesday and Saturday, working 9 a.m. to 5.30 p.m. The shop also took on part-time 'Saturday girls'. Vivien Panter started work at Woolworths when she was still at school to help with the family finances:

> The day I turned fifteen I went into the old Woolworths on the High Street and I got myself a job working Saturdays only. I didn't work in Woolworths for pleasure – I worked there because I needed the money, and I remember it [being] very, very tiring work even then – because we were on our feet all day, and we were running up and down the counter, answering to the calls of people who wanted to be served. And Christmas Eve in particular was absolute hell, because the counter would be surrounded by people . . . calling out 'Miss, Miss, Miss!' A few of the men whistled, and we ignored them totally – we hated being whistled [at].
>
> I earned 12*s* *6d* for working all day Saturday. We had to pay 3*s* *3d* national insurance . . . I then paid 1*s* *6d* for a return fare on the train from Desborough, and 1*s* *6d* bought us a hot lunch in Woolworths. The management gave us a cook, who did rather a nice, fairly simple, basic meal at lunchtime. . . . That left me with 6*s* *3d* for working all day.
>
> [The manager] was around, we knew he was around, and we were very much in awe of him . . . he wasn't a supervisor, so he didn't have to walk the floor and keep an eye on us girls, but if you saw him you shot past fast and looked busy!
>
> We had maroon overalls, which were provided by the shop. It was a little bit sort of 'first come best dressed', particularly for the casual girls. You . . . went and took one off the hooks and wore it, and they weren't particularly smart of course.
>
> I remember the summer day Symington's [the corset factory] had their big anniversary in 1956 – it was a very hot day. And all the girls came in buying jewellery and lipsticks to make themselves look pretty, and they all wore roses in their buttonholes.
>
> Woolworths was not considered the cream of jobs for older women . . . really it was about the lowest paid of all shop work. There was a lot more kudos attached to, say, working in a chemist – although I had a friend who worked in a chemist and got less than we did. . . . It was the sort of thing that at High School – where we were probably a little bit snobby, 'cos we passed exams to get there – we used to make a bit of a joke in the end-of-term entertainment about how we'd have to leave school and go into Woolworths because there was nothing better for us.[16]

Since the 1950s the main trend in the nature of women's employment in shops has been the continued increase in part-time working. This reflects a general feature of lower-paid women's work; by the end of the 1970s over a third of all working women in the United Kingdom were employed part-time.

One of the largest retail employers in Market Harborough in the late 1980s was Tesco. In 1986 their Harborough branch employed eighty-eight workers, full or part-time. This complement equalled sixty-two full-time equivalent jobs. From the company's point of view the employment of part-timers was and remains a vital means of covering extended opening hours. Ted Ashby, then general manager of the branch, explained how the system operated:

> Without part-timers we would not be able to exist, and students, basically for the late evenings, are our life's blood. We have a nucleus of full-timers, but because of the 69 hour trading week which we do, obviously it would be impossible to even work shifts for full-timers that would be acceptable to their social and domestic life, and we just wouldn't get the staff. So we find we get a lot of mums that work for us from 9 [a.m.] till 2 [p.m.], and then we get ladies whose husbands are milkmen – things like that – that like to come in from 2 till 6 [p.m.]. The students coming from college . . . like to come in from 6 till 8 [p.m.]. And that way we seem to schedule pretty well.

Recruitment was through the job-centre and 'where the young people are concerned mainly by word of mouth'. There was a fairly high turnover among the part-time staff, especially in summer as students moved on to further education or jobs. 'Every two years we normally try to recruit sixth-formers, where by the time we've trained them we know that we're going to get two years' service from them.'[17]

The trade unions have never had a large presence in the retail trades, except for the Co-operative Societies. It is thought that by 1914 only some 13 per cent of retail and distributive workers were in a trade union.[18] Even in the 1980s, when some of the large retail corporations had recognized the usefulness of dealing with one body which represented their workers, it was still not the norm for a shopworker to be in a union.

The most important trade union in the retail sector in the 1980s was USDAW (Union of Shop, Distributive and Allied Workers) with 400,000 members. The GMB (General and Municipal Boilermakers Union), who had a membership agreement with the Asda chain, and the TGW (Transport and General Workers Union) had smaller memberships among retail workers. In the 1980s USDAW prided itself as having a 'community responsibility' to all retail workers and not just its members. This worked in practice through USDAW's representation on regional Wages Councils which then set rates of pay and conditions of work for workers over twenty-one in the retail industries. Another aspect of USDAW's community responsibility was the union's lobbying of parliamentary legislation. For instance it took part in the opposition to the 1986 Sunday Trading Bill.

The organization of existing members and recruitment of new ones have always been fraught with difficulties because of the nature of retail employment. Shopworkers are scattered in small groups and many are employed in businesses that are hostile towards unions. The problem of effective representation means that many shopworkers are not convinced of the benefits of union membership. Inevitably part-time workers are the hardest to recruit, yet these are the people who historically have had the minimum of employment rights.[19]

Such problems have dogged attempts at unionization in the retail sector for a hundred years. The major union for workers in the 'private' trades (private firms as opposed to the Co-operatives), the National Amalgamated Union of Shop Assistants, Warehousemen and Clerks, or NAUSA, founded in 1891, grew slowly before it was made an approved society for administering the National Insurance scheme in 1911 (a separate union existed for employees in the Co-operative retail societies).

In Market Harborough the local paper recorded the setting up of an apparently short-lived NAUSA branch, with twelve founder members, in 1904. There were no further mentions of this branch in the newspaper. Apart from this episode, and for at least the first half of this century, trade unions might as well not have existed as far as the great majority of Harborough shopworkers in private firms were concerned.

> None of the private firms had – the only trade unions were the Co-op. . . . If those people [i.e. the owner/employers] didn't agree with trade unions it was more than anyone dare do to join. (Despatch department assistant, independent grocer's, mid-1930s)

> No. I'd never heard of them!' (Draper's shop assistant, between the wars)

> Not until the 1950s, and no one joined it. They came round and tried to recruit a few people. One or two did join and then fell out. It wasn't popular. And it wasn't popular to be in a union with the firm either in those days. . . . I never belonged to one. You had to look which way the cat might jump. They didn't say they couldn't join, they were allowed to, but – I always thought that if you kept out of the union you were a lot better off. It all depends how the firm treated you – I mean Burton's paid more than the union rate, always, well over the union rates and nobody bothered. What was the point? (Assistant manager at Burton's the grocer's (part of a chain) in the 1950s)

> They tried to start a union once, and the union fee was 10*d* a week. I couldn't see the fun

of paying 10*d* a week for nothing. That's how it struck me, because they never did any good for the grocery trade, not for donkey's years. (Traveller and shop assistant, Symington & Thwaites/Burton's, grocer's)

The attitude of employers, whether stated or implicit, was significant in discouraging workers from joining unions. Boots the Chemists, for instance, has always had a non-union policy, seeing this as part of a paternalistic strategy. Of all the shopworkers we spoke to who had worked for private firms in the town before the 1960s, we found only one who had been a union member. The union in question was the specialist Retail Book, Stationery and Allied Trades' Employees' Association, or RBSATEA. This association, which was affiliated to both the TUC and the National Federation of Professional Workers, was the recognized union for W.H. Smith's staff throughout the country. Gwendoline March (later Parke) worked at the Harborough branch of W.H. Smith from the late 1920s to 1950. She ultimately became deputy manageress. 'We used to pay a subscription of about 5*s* a quarter. Like when you wanted a rise, or asked for a rise you had to prove, show your union card, to say that you were a paid-up member'. The union had social and professional aims as well as a protective purpose; a 1944 circular that Mrs Parke had kept was full of articles on the book-selling business, and kept members informed of news about their colleagues.[20]

Although trade union organization was far more advanced among the Co-operative retail societies than the private trades, the Market Harborough Industrial Co-operative Society was not unionized until the 1930s. But, then, uncertainty about their jobs and the union's claim that they were being 'grossly underpaid' made the workforce anxious for protection.

The union involved was the National Union of Distributive and Allied Workers (NUDAW), which had started life in 1895 as the Amalgamated Union of Co-operative Employees. By 1920 the AUCE represented just under half of all Co-op workers. It joined with the National Warehouse and General Workers' Union in 1921 to form NUDAW. The union was admitted to the Harborough Co-op in 1933–4. Memories differ as to who took the initiative. 'Mr Heighton came, a Labour man, on the [general management] committee, and he started to talk about unions.' 'Mrs Martin, from Kettering . . . she was a union representative, and she came into Harborough once or twice, and met employees, and at different times met the committee, and it was agreed that we should be allowed to join this union.'[21]

What did this mean to the workers? Geoff Johnson was employed in the Co-op's drapery department. Shortly before his twenty-first birthday he had been given his notice as part of a drive to save money. But as soon as the union was introduced, he was told, 'My work had vastly improved; I would be kept on and my wages increased'.

Norman Marlow was a provision hand in the Central Grocery. He had been twenty-one the previous year, but 'at that time things were supposed to be bad' and the general manager had given him the 'option' of either staying on at the junior rate of pay or finding another job. It was the middle of the Depression and there were no jobs going in Harborough, so he stayed: 'And so I paid *6d* to join the union, and about two weeks later I was called into the office. . . . The committee used to meet there, and they said, 'We've decided to give you the man's rate'. I was getting *23s*, and [the man's rate] was *49s* I think – more than £1 a week difference, which I'd been underpaid for twelve months. So I was very pleased with the union'.

Wages were regraded from the scales for a rural area which were 'the lowest grade as far as the union was concerned' to 'Provincial Grade B'. Other new benefits included longer holidays and entitlement to overtime pay 'which you hadn't had before'.[22]

'About 97 per cent of the employees joined.' The 'one or two' who stayed out of the union did so according to one non-member because they disliked the extra deduction from their wage packet or because they were sceptical of the union's strength: 'Men was afraid them days of losing their job if they joined a union. . . . If you struck for something and got the sack, you was finished'.

The decision by a few not to join was 'a sore point' with other employees, since the non-members got the pay increases negotiated by the union regardless of membership. 'About the same time as the union's arrival the society's employees also formed a self-help Social and Welfare Fund. They paid a penny a week and received benefits from the fund when they were ill. This was very useful since the small sum due from the National Insurance (which became less the longer the worker was sick) was only made up to full wages by employers for the first fortnight.[23]

In 1947 NUDAW joined together with the major union for private shopworkers to form the Union of Shop, Distributive and Allied Workers (USDAW). USDAW continued to represent Co-operative employees. Unlike the Co-op in Leicester, the Market Harborough Society did not have a strong tradition of union activity: 'We never had a local committee or anything like that; it was all done from Kettering'. Attendance at local meetings varied, and in one former member's opinion there was a general feeling that the union couldn't do much for them.

After the formation of the Leicestershire Co-operative Society in 1969, the union was in a stronger position and 'got more sway politically'. It now represented a combined workforce of over 2,000 employees. Wages were also levelled up to those of the Leicester Society: 'They paid Grade A, Metropolitan Grade A wages, which was quite a bump up for we people in Harborough'. 'We had a number of girls come from other shops to get into our place, into the Co-op, because it was better conditions, a lot better facilities and better money.'[24]

Alongside the unions' trials to represent members in the workplace went improvements resulting from new legislation. The shopworkers unions were one of the interest groups campaigning for restriction of working hours and minimum standards of pay and working conditions through legislation. However, such laws appeared relatively slowly for the retail trades, compared to manufacturing industries, reflecting the weak organization of shopworkers. It was not until 1963, for example, that the Offices, Shops and Railway Premises Acts laid down standards of health and safety for shopworkers similar to those enjoyed by factory workers.

The 1911 Shops Act, weakened after lobbying from the retail trade associations representing the major employers, allowed shop assistants a half-day a week off and gave them official meal-breaks. In the First World War compulsory closing hours for all shops were brought in for the first time as an emergency measure designed to save fuel. After the war these restrictions were renewed annually until the 1928 Shops Act made them permanent. However restricted opening hours did not limit all shop assistants' hours: there was plenty of work – making up orders, preparing goods for sale, and stocktaking – which could and did take place behind closed doors. The first laws to limit assistants' hours significantly came into force in 1932.

Union pay scales and working weeks had most impact in the Co-operative movement, where a number of retail societies adopted them before 1914. But again it was the state that was to widen regulation of working conditions. Between the wars Trade Boards were set up for some of the retail trades, and these boards fixed minimum levels of pay. And from 1945 all shopworkers were brought under minimum wage legislation by the passing of the Wages Councils Acts. This system remained in place to protect all shopworkers until its powers were dismantled in the 1980s.[25]

Since the 1960s some of the larger chains have changed their attitudes towards trade unions. A good example is Tesco. Ken Wylie, who was general manager of Tesco's Harborough branch from 1971 to 1976, and who still works for the firm, described this change to us:

> It must have been about 1976–7 that we came to an agreement that people could openly join a trades union with the blessing of the company. . . . It [Harborough] never was a very militant shop – never had that many problems that you would need to get involved with trade unions. . . . In the old days if somebody didn't do as they were told it was 'You're fired!' . . . but now of course we don't do that anymore.

In 1986 Tesco had a corporate membership agreement with USDAW. The majority of its full-time staff at Harborough were in the union and they were entitled to their own shop steward. At that time however there was no steward, and the manager claimed this was because of good industrial relations: 'Normally if we have any problems in the store it never gets to union level anyway. It's either sorted out by the departmental head [on the shop-floor] or it comes down to this office and it gets sorted out quite amicably. Unions, really, are a last resort, when we've got total failure to agree'.[26]

In the 1980s and now in the '90s shopworkers have faced difficulties which reflect the changing patterns of shopping. Work studies identify shopwork as a stressful job, particularly for checkout operators. Financially the work is undervalued, and low pay is often allied to part-time working and few employment rights.

These criticisms raise the question of whether the status of shopworkers has altered during the last hundred years. There has certainly been a decline in the prestige attached to the work. In the early part of this century getting a junior's position in a shop was an achievement, and a source of pride as well as income for his or her family. For the generation brought up in Market Harborough between the wars, if you came from a working or lower middle class family, shopwork might realistically be your highest aspiration. The kudos of working in a retail business was slow to fade as Vivien Window, talking about the 1950s, pointed out: 'I suppose the shop was considered a cut above the factory, but the factory paid a lot better'.

Shopwork has never been well-paid. Its prestige came from the idea that it was a 'respectable' job, from the expectation of learning a trade, and from the hope of climbing to a management grade. In many of today's large shops, the workers on the shop-floor are employed to carry out narrow repetitive tasks, while more and more managers are recruited from a graduate intake. As large shops have come to resemble factories in scale and lack of job fulfilment, much of the gloss of shopwork has worn off.[27]

## The Management Grades

> You can't be a popular manager, not with everybody, or else you don't manage – A manager's job is to look after the firm. (Co-operative Society manager, 1930s–'70s)

The rewards for those who made it into the managerial grades were better pay and higher status. There was more responsibility in the job, but a manager was also more exposed to the diktat of the company or private proprietor. If the shop was part of a large organization, it was likely that promotion would mean moving away to other branches.

Pay varied between different shops, but national averages at least give a good idea of the going rate for a shop manager. In 1924–5 for example the averages were £230 a year for men in management jobs and £157 a year for women. Allowing two weeks' unpaid holiday these averages work out at £4 6*s* a week for men and £3 3*s* a week for women. At that time average pay for a male shop assistant was £2 8*s* a week, and for a female shop assistant £1 8*s* a week. Large differentials persisted. In 1960 when the average wages of shop assistants were estimated at £487 a year for men and £315 for women, a grocery branch manager might expect a minimum of £1,000 a year and a maximum of over £2,000 a year.[28]

> The managers and the proprietors of businesses were all on the same footing. . . . They were regarded as shopkeepers. (Son of a multiple shop manager)

Good pay also meant a better standard of living. In the 1930s Charles Wimlett worked in a gentleman's outfitters in Leicester and lived at home in Market Harborough. His father was a shop manager for Eastmans. 'There was always a reward on a Saturday when I got home [after late night closing]. [From] my father, being a butcher, there was always a piece of steak weighing about ¾ lb – a slice of fried bread with the steak on it, just underdone (I can taste it now!) – and a bottle of Guinness!'

Ken Wylie was general manager of Tesco's Market Harborough branch from 1971 to 1977:

> I've got a manager's rate of pay dated January 29th, 1975. I actually didn't realize we had so much – probably in those days I was earning in the region of £100 a week. It was a lot of money; I can remember my old boss saying to me, 'You earn more than that bank manager up the road, boy. Earn it!' And on a turnover of £25,000, which is nothing compared to what we take nowadays, I was paid £5,000 a year. . . . I know I lived very, very well in 1975, I can remember going out for meals was a common thing.
>
> [By 1986] a small store manager would earn something like £14,000 a year. Normal pay, I suppose, £20,000, top stores £25,000, then you've got a company car to take into consideration – all the various things like that which didn't happen in those days.[29]

A retail business only needs a shop manager when it reaches a certain size and the owner is no longer the shopkeeper. The Harborough trade directories list no shop managers before the 1880s. Shops in the town were owned and run by the proprietor, with help in some cases from a senior counterhand. As businesses, Harborough shops were too small to be financed by an absentee owner. The one local exception was the Market Harborough Industrial Co-operative Society store, managed by Thomas Scott. The society was owned by its members, and therefore needed an employee to run its shop, under the supervision of an elected committee

Families waited upon daily for orders
Our Noted Beef Sausages a Speciality
EASTMANS LIMITED
High-class Meat Purveyors,
Prime Ox Beef, Canterbury Mutton
and Lamb
2, CHURCH SQUARE,
MARKET HARBOROUGH
C. WIMLETT, Manager

Advertising card for Eastmans

(see Chapter Six). Only when chain stores started up branches in Harborough did outside capital pay for managers to look after their shops.

Chain stores, also known as multiples, took off in the last quarter of the nineteenth century. By 1900 multiples had made a major impact on several retail sectors. These brash new organizations included shoe shops, grocers, frozen meat traders, books and stationery sellers, menswear retailers, and chemists. The Singer Manufacturing Machine Company had a tied outlet in Market Harborough for its sewing machines by the late 1880s. Then in the 1890s Freeman, Hardy & Willis, the London Central Meat Company and London & Midland Stores were three out of a handful of retail firms which opened branches in the town. The multiples had come to stay.

Many of these multiples were sizeable organizations. At one extreme was the large grocery conglomerate Home & Colonial Stores Ltd (later Allied Suppliers Ltd) which by 1931 encompassed Home & Colonial, Lipton's, Maypole Dairy Co. and Meadow Dairy Co. as well as other smaller companies. This combination of firms was estimated at the time to have 5,500 shops in Britain employing a total of 40,000 staff.

The early multiples prospered on a large volume of sales at low profits, usually carrying a very narrow range of products in branches which were tiny by modern standards. They were well known for running tight shops with little in the way of frills. Each organization had to ensure that decisions taken at the centre were carried out in all their outlets up and down the country. Final responsibility rested with the shop managers.[30]

Mr W. Ingram started as an errand boy, straight from school, at the Kettering branch of the Maypole Dairy Company in 1925. He eventually worked his way up to relief manager, standing in for the managers of the various local branches. In his own words, the method of selling at Maypole was 'push, push, push' all the time. The employees were pushed too:

> With things the way they were, every now and again an assistant would get the sack, and they'd put another errand boy in, and bring one up, to keep the wages down. . . . I've seen more than one at the manager's desk on a Friday night – 'Get your money!' – finished, just like that. No warning.
>
> Apart, I should say, from the fishmongers, the Maypole shops were the coldest shops you could possibly work in. There was no such thing as heat, and in the winter – we wore white jackets and apron, and we used to wear them on top of your [own] jacket. It was so cold . . . all tiles on the floor, all marble on the counters, the only wood was just the floor you walked on at the back of the counters – everywhere it was bitterly cold.
>
> You could never pick your holiday: a list would come round and you had your holiday when they stated. And you had ten working days, which means you finished Saturday night, and you could either go away on the Sunday or the Monday. . . . You had a full week – Saturday was a working day – and you had four days [to take] the next week and started back on the Friday morning.
>
> But the one big fear really was when they got 'short sticks' [at cashing-up], somebody under suspicion. Things were so tight. Even say you had an accident, which happened occasionally, perhaps a piece of butter or a piece of marge might drop on the floor, you'd got to clean it up . . . and that would be weighed every Saturday, and when you'd got enough it all went to the sweet manufacturer.

The staff even had to provide their own uniforms and see to their laundry.

> We just wore the white jackets and aprons. The managers wore the jacket outside the apron. And we always had to wear white stiff collars, starched collar, always. Woe betide you if you wore a soft collar. . . . This [was] changed about twice a week, and we changed the uniform at least once a week – every Friday you had to have your clean uniform on.
>
> Well in 16 years I went from 10*s* a week to £3 3*s* a week when I got married. Managers usually got about either 10*s* or £1 a week more. I got an extra 10s a week on relief work. And one year everybody had a 2*s* a week cut, when things were so bad.

The Maypole organization treated its managers and its workers equally strictly. The firm employed 'inspectors' who went round the shops checking up on the staff. Since head-office sent out stock and decided the 'specials' (sales promotions), the shop managers had virtually no scope for initiative.

Some of them [the shop managers] were afraid: it's this pressing for trade – you must do more you see. And it used to come down to the chief inspector, he'd get onto the inspector, and the inspector'd get onto the manager; then the manager would get onto us.

They'd pass it onto the managers what they wanted them to do to try and increase sales of this, or if sales were lagging in any shape or form. And then bank holidays and Christmas we had what they call specials – that was all over every Maypole. Tinned fruit specials . . . you'd got to sell as much tinned fruit as you possibly could. It was push, push, push.

I went all round the shops [at the beginning of the Second World War] doing relief work, and I was at Corby for a time. This week I were there on the Saturday – what we used to do, the first hand and manager used to start taking stock Saturday afternoon, one at a time, all the things in boxes and crates. . . . This Saturday I was out in the warehouse, and blow me the inspector and chief inspector walked into the shop! And I didn't know, and they stopped there 'cos I wasn't in the shop . . . they wouldn't let anybody go and tell me they were there. And they came out and asked me what I was doin'. I was caught red-handed really – I didn't half cop it – and you know what they did? They got hold of all the stock-sheets and [tore them up]! But it was done, every shop did it. You couldn't stop there after 8 o'clock at night and take all the stock of a shop! But that's what we had to put up with.[31]

It is worth comparing Maypole's inspector system with a similar system used by another centrally minded retail firm, Boots the Chemists. Carol Dainty worked for Boots in Harborough in the late 1950s. She was a sales assistant on the surgical counter and on cosmetics, and she did a lot of the shop's window-dressing.

The hours for opening were from 9[a.m.] till 5.30[p.m.], but you had to be behind the counter for 8.45[a.m.] promptly – should have been. But on the odd occasion if we were late arriving at the shop – got behind the counter about a minute to nine – that was the day Mr Prentice, the Territory Manager, would be there waiting . . . and if you weren't behind the counter at 8.45[a.m.] you was in for a good ticking-off.

[The Territory Manager's] head-office was at Leicester. He would come in about once a fortnight . . . . We were all very frightened of him, very strict he was. He would check the windows at night : he'd come by Christmas Eve and have a look!

I didn't know about trade unions; but as I said if you'd got any trouble or anything to do with Boots or our own personal life, we either went to see our senior or we made an appointment to see the Territory Manager. So when he came to the shop, if you had any problems . . . he would then take you upstairs and you would discuss your problems with him. Of course the manager wasn't very pleased about this: the manager would rather you go to him. But sometimes if the shop wasn't running quite right . . . then if you'd

> already taken it to your senior and she'd passed it on to the manager, and the manager says 'Leave it with me' – well if it was serious enough you had to take it higher, so we always took it to the Territory Manager.[32]

A personal and authoritative supervision, whether the accent was on profits or staff relations, marked any large firm's attempts to keep a check on its widespread shop staff. The other main check was through the accounting systems, which demanded a constant flow of paper to head office. Looking after the shop's accounts was a headache for any manager. Inevitably it meant an amount of unpaid overtime: 'Father, while he was with Eastmans, his Sunday morning was spent in making up his returns'.

The duties of a shop manager were fairly similar across the trades, and would have varied more by size than type of shop. They included staff supervision – allocating work, setting standards and taking care of discipline – and responsibility for the money side – keeping stock, doing the books, usually the buying of goods, and paying out of wages.

Frederick William Lee was assistant manager at Harborough's branch of Burton's the grocer's in the 1950s. He explained to us how he and the manager divided the running of the shop between them. The manager 'oversaw the whole lot and the buying side'. The assistant manager was responsible for the staff and the shop-floor, including the window displays. 'That was how Burton's used to work it – two-man team.'

Mr Lee's training had been in a high-class independent grocer's before the war. There he had learnt the skills of his trade, which stood him in good stead in a management position. His knowledge of food and drink allowed him to buy continental specialities and wines and spirits for the branch. He also displayed goods in the windows of the shop, which had a large corner frontage: 'There were about eight windows: I spent a week window-dressing, changing them all round'. Conversely his skills as a shopman and storeman became less important, as Burton's went self-service and more and more goods were bought ready packed.

All Burton's managers and assistant managers received a commission on sales plus a percentage bonus twice a year; junior staff were simply given the bonus. 'The bigger the turnover of the shop, the bigger bonus you got. . . . It paid everybody to push sales as much as they could – from the lowest to the highest, you all got something.'

> Burton's had got the family touch still, and they looked after you. A director from Burton's would come down every month to every shop [the firm had about 100 branches], he'd speak to every member of staff from the junior to the manager. If there were any complaints you could take it direct to a director and get it put right straightaway.

The personal touch was a very useful management skill. Even in a large shop it was important to be seen on the shop-floor: 'I used to make it my business to walk round the shop two or three times in the morning – have a word with people that was in'.[33]

Sometimes managerial responsibility could be more onerous. Cecil Copson was a relief manager for Harborough's Co-operative Society in the 1930s, having been groomed in the Central Store's grocery department.

> I used to do a lot of relieving; at some branches it was real hard graft, but at others it was not quite so rough. . . . I remember I was at [Medbourne] branch; the builders had been repairing the chimney on the bakehouse. Somehow or other a brick had dropped down in the flue which meant that they hadn't got the draft. I got there about 8 o'clock on the Saturday morning and there was the baker and all in a terrible state. The dough was rising out of the top of the bins and he couldn't use it. So we bundled the dough into the van and brought it into Harborough here, and got some bread from Harborough to start on with, while this builder came out and put the oven right.

Saturday was late-night opening as usual:

> . . . well with that delay and everything it was 12 o'clock when I left the shop. And of course we used to send the cash through the Post Office. Post Office people had all gone to bed so I couldn't do that. So I wrapped all the cash up and tied it round my body, [and] pushbiked to Kibworth. And during the afternoon it had been some snow: I got as far as Ashley station and the snow froze under the mudguard of my bike so that the wheel wouldn't turn round. . . . So I had no option but, I took the belt from me mac – underneath the saddle and over me shoulder – carried the back wheel and walked to Kibworth. I got to Kibworth about half-past four, Sunday morning. Then on the Monday morning, instead of going straight from Kibworth to Medbourne, I came to Harborough and went up to the General Manager's house and left the cash with him. Went on to Medbourne.
>
> Later in the week the Secretary [the head-man of Harborough's Co-operative Society] rang up. He said – he was a North Country man – he said, 'They tell me you had a bit of bother last weekend,' he said,' You did a bit of overtime'. I said, 'Yes, I did some overtime . . . I was here late on Friday, and I was here later than that on Saturday'. . . . 'Well,' he said, 'when you do your wages this week, take an extra half-a-crown for yourself but don't tell anybody!'[34]

In line with the general loss of craft skills in the retail trades, the modern shop manager, at least in the larger shops, has become essentially an office administrator, more familiar with stock returns and work schedules than bacon, books or bathroom suites. The target of centralized control, which early multiples like Maypole were striving for, has been achieved with the aid of new technology.

We came across a good example of this at Tesco, a firm which until the end of the 1970s had allowed its shop managers a fair amount of leeway in how they achieved their sales. Ken Wylie started with Tesco in 1967 when he got a job in their Lee Circle store while staying with relatives in Leicester. In 1986 he was manager of one of their large stores in the West Midlands, and explained how his job had changed over the years:

> I had been to college and hadn't actually intended to do or even thought about shopwork as a career, but I was a General Manager within two years of joining Tesco's. My first promotion was to warehouse manager . . . checking all the goods in through the back door, looking after the general condition of the warehouse, which you'd got staff to obviously do that – stocktaking every week, every day, for the following week's orders.
>
> I then went as trainee manager, which meant that you sort of went round all the shop and did all the various departments. In those days the company was very much [learning] on the job, very much get in there, learn the business. Then got made Assistant Manager of the smallest store in Leicester, in those days, which was Uppingham Road. I then went as Assistant Manager to Oadby store, and then General Manager of Market Harborough – which I went to in January 1971 . . . twenty-one years of age – I should think it was [stressful], and you really weren't a manager. You were just a young lad who had taken on the responsibility and you had to learn very fast, and grow up very fast, and really it was a matter of 'Sink or swim, boy!'
>
> Nowadays there's a full training programme from the minute they start with the company. There's graduates who come from university – there's a set twenty to thirty-five week programme and they have to follow that to the letter. An induction programme, an introduction to the company and then an introduction to their own job – and even to the jobs of other people, because we're trying now very much to make people multi-skilled, which is another thing that didn't happen years ago. The company are not necessarily looking to graduates for all their jobs, but they are looking at a type of person that they feel will be their management of the future, and one of their criteria will obviously be their educational standards.
>
> You see, when you run a supermarket, you've got to know how to look at a product, how to know if it's cut properly, if it's presented properly – and that's the sort of thing we learnt. In those days it was the old gut feeling of selling things – priority space to certain things. Nowadays there's layouts which tell you where to put [them]: there's Marketing Departments at Head Office that tell you exactly what lines sell, why and how and where to put them, so really all we do is make sure these policies are carried out nowadays, which is what the role of the manager is.
>
> [When I started] suppliers would say 'Buy ten, get one free' – and you would end up buying a hundred cases and stacking it in the corner. But you see that was how money was made in those days – the company weren't having the influence on it, you were the person having to make the money for the company.

> Market Harborough [in 1971] had an assistant manager, provisions manager, meat manager, greengrocery manager, home'n'wear manager, warehouse manager – I was the interviewer, I was the staff taker-oner, I was everything like that. Once again every store now in the company has got a staff manageress, who looks after the staff welfare and employs staff, and people go to see her for their problems. She's basically the equivalent of an assistant manager, I look to her as the same way I look to my assistant manager.
>
> It's far better, I'm a much happier person working nowadays than I was in those days, in the sense that I know what I'm doing, and you know exactly where you stand, how you're progressing. In the old days you were only as good as the day before, 'cos if something went wrong – you'd be gone, unfortunately, so you were always under a lot of pressure.

There is another more sceptical reaction to modern management training methods: 'They call it Pre-Management Courses now, where the guys go through the complete range of departments. There's no way they could buck the system or bend the rules because they've been washed in one colour and they don't know anything different'.[35]

The range of a modern shop manager's job still depends largely on the size of shop where he or she is employed. Only in the supermarkets and hyperstores is the specialized shop administrator found. In smaller shops the manager still has to muck in filling fixtures and serving customers. But in any multiple organization managing a large store is the prized job which carries a large salary. Above the store managers lies the territory of distribution, marketing and policy making. Whether today's training for managers on the shopfloor is designed to produce tomorrow's company directors or to keep them in their place is an open question.

## PRIVATE AND COMPANY OWNERS

> Old John Wood used to invite us up: we used to have tennis and that once a year up at his house. (Draper's employee, 1930s, discussing the staff's annual treat)[36]

The owners of larger private shops had a high status in the town. They played correspondingly large roles in the community and were to be found on the committees of most religious and secular organizations of any importance or influence. The Market Harborough Urban District Council, and its predecessor the Local Board from its birth in 1880, always included a significant number of retail tradespeople. In the first year of the Local Board there were three shopkeepers and two wholesale distributors among the twelve members. The Urban District Council of 1937–40 boasted one retired and six practising shopkeepers in a council of twelve. These included the chairman, H.H. Pickering, the town's leading

Cllr. H.H. Pickering officially opening Roman Way, Market Harborough, 1936, watched by other leading town councillors, most of whom were shopkeepers

independent butcher and a local magistrate, and John Wood, proprietor of a draper's store which was one of the town's largest private shops.

Among these top proprietors there were few 'sleeping partners', (people who invest in a business without working in it). Most of the working proprietors served behind their shop counters, although in the larger concerns there might be a division of labour, such as at the high-class grocer's Symington & Thwaites where different partners took care of shop-work and office-work.

For successful owners there were material rewards. Until 1922–3 John and Grace Wood and their family lived in 'quite a big house' in Northampton Road, with other substantial tradespeople as their near neighbours. Then they moved to another large house, newly built, in Burnmill Road. Joyce Dexter, the Woods' second child, describes their situation: 'There we had five bedrooms and a bathroom. . . . Yes, we had a maid – we always had paid help . . . 'Cause my mother played golf and tennis and bridge'. John Wood also ran a car, which was used in his drapery business for order rounds. Away from the shop he enjoyed a range of sports and was Vice-Chairman of the Urban District Council.

As leading shop-owners the Woods had to be careful where their own custom went:

> Things were 'put down' [i.e. credited] to my father. There was the Looms' shop, a shoe shop in Adam and Eve Street, there was Mr Falkner's [in High Street], we used to have my shoes from there. . . . I think as far as grocery's concerned, I think Symington & Thwaites was the main one, but she would go and give orders to other shops every so often. Being a tradesperson in the town, she had to go one week to one shop, one week to another shop.

The family's clothes were bought through the shop: 'When I got a bit older I used to see the travellers, and perhaps have something that he wasn't going to have in the shop'.[37]

Even though there was some competition, the links between private traders were often stronger than their differences. Partly this was a question of mutual interest and mutual defence – there was a distinct fear of the threat posed by the multiples and the local Co-op – and partly it was due to other bonds. Some of the leading families were closely related. Ronald Hodby, a former grocer in Nelson Street, explained to us:

> My mother was a Gardiner; Mr Pickering [the butcher] married a Gardiner. Emerson's shop was another brother, Roland Gardiner. At one time they used to say that Harborough shops were nearly all controlled by Gardiners! There was a Gardiner the furniture shop down St Mary's Road, that big double-fronted shop, and there's a John Gardiner the milkman up Lubenham Hill – eventually I think he sold his business to Kirby & West.

In this case the connections spread wider and among smaller shopkeepers through the Gardiners' membership of the 'Top Chapel', the Congregationalists:

> One thing that did happen was traders traded with each other. In this way Looms the shoe factory also had a shop in Adam and Eve Street and we would perhaps go to Looms and buy shoes. They in turn would come to us with an order perhaps once a month, once in six weeks. And later on we'd deal with Foster [who was a Methodist] who had a boot shop, and they came to us. You sort of supported those who supported you, and I suppose it created quite a lot of business. I suppose you were tied; you felt you'd like to go somewhere else, but if you wanted a suit you must go to Remington's say, or Elliott's, because they go to the chapel.[38]

Networks among private traders were created by shared religion, community service, friendship, social life, masonic ties or financial interest as well as by family relationship. These networks could act as a support service and even provide financial help in the time of need. There are two documented cases of independent shopkeepers between the two wars putting up capital to set someone up in business in Market Harborough. One trader had a new start this way: 'They clubbed together and there was a shop two door away or one door away and it was Gardiner's, carpet people. They were using the top floor for furniture storage, and they talked to [Mr —] and said, if you'd like to take this other shop on, they'd help him out'.

All the private shop owners in the town, except for a handful of 'sleeping partners', exercised a management function within their shops and came into close contact with their staff. This encouraged them to have a paternalistic attitude towards their employees, which was meant to produce, and often did, a personal loyalty from staff to owners. Symington & Thwaites, for instance, which was a strict shop and paid comparatively low wages, was nevertheless regarded by the staff as a good place to work where they received proper training. Gladys Sharpe worked there from 1917 to 1932, first in the order room, then on the cash-desk and later behind the counter:

> Thwaites had a bowls green and a tennis court made for us. . . . Yes, he had it specially made for the staff. We used to go up there in the evenings and either have bowls or tennis, very popular. Dad [James Sharpe, manager of the order room] was a big bowls player and mother used to help with the teas when we had Thursday afternoons – the half-day used to be spent up there.
>
> My father used to get a turkey and I got £1 Christmas box. Never varied. Mind you, you put in a lot of extra time for that, working so late Christmas week, often until midnight'.[39]

A 'fatherly' style of management was very much in evidence at Wood's the draper's where the brothers John and Stanley Wood employed a workforce of about twenty, most of them women. John Wood supervised the running of the shop and the staff: 'And they had to be very polite to their customers, otherwise my father was very strict and would tick them off. But they, I think they all respected him very much'. As an ex-employee of Wood's put it, 'He was a good old boss, bit strict, but there you are'. The staff were given a 10 per cent discount on clothes they bought from the shop, and once a year on a Thursday half-day they were invited up to the Woods' house in Burnmill Road for tea, and tennis on the family's courts. 'My mother used to do a tea for them. . . . The ice-cream man, "STOP ME AND BUY ONE", pedalled along . . . and I can remember it coming up the road, and my father buying all these girls [i.e. the shop staff] ice-cream.'[40]

Paternalism was not confined to private owners. The local Co-operative Society,

Staff of the Market Harborough Co-op about to depart on a works outing into Northamptonshire from the front of the central premises, High Street, Market Harborough, *c.* 1920

which was the largest retail institution in the town throughout its independent existence, was also concerned to treat its staff well and provide opportunities for entertainment and social life through the society. From the 1890s the staff enjoyed annual outings at the Co-op's expense, and these became elaborate day-trips by rail between the two world wars. At this time the Co-op also had its own cricket team and a tennis court for employees in Coventry Road.

As at the Maypole Dairy Company, some multiples in the inter-war period ruled by a system of management based on fear. But a more positive attitude to employees did exist in some of the large chains, especially those run by philanthropic capitalists. One such firm was W.H. Smith, owned and directed by the Hambleden family. W.H. Smith had one shop in Market Harborough in St Mary's Road (Croft-Wingates in 1994). It was a small shop in the 1920s, with only a manager and an assistant, as well as the paper-boys. Gwendoline March started work there as general assistant in 1927. During the war she became deputy manageress. In her opinion Smith's was an 'extremely good firm' to work for.

The Harborough W.H. Smith branch was part of the Nottingham regional area: 'We used to have these sort of social get-togethers and dinners and that . . . at

Nottingham usually'. She remembers vividly a national social event for employees which was organized in 1938:

> There was one celebration, I've still got the brochure somewhere – it was for the sort of junior members if they'd been there so long – at Henley, Lord and Lady Hambleden's house at Henley, on the Thames. I went, I was the only one from Harborough.
>
> And we had these passes come . . . free rail-ticket to London. . . . And then, there was a special train from London, I think was from Paddington, to Henley. And you were met at Henley with the launches, went right up the river to this 'Greenlands' at Henley. . . . Gosh, there was never such a do in all your life: it was beautiful, really it was, and it was a beautiful day.

The party included bands and lunch and afternoon tea in marquees. The grounds of aristocratic 'Greenlands' thronged with W.H. Smith employees, gathered from all over the country. Each wore the appropriate badge with W.H.S. initials – white on green for the company's shops staff, white on yellow for bookstalls staff, while the addition of a red star identified management grades. Lord and Lady Hambleden graciously circulated to meet their retainers. 'And then [we] came back, and the launches took you to Henley station. . . . They did us well, Smith's did, really.'[41]

Other national chains have realized that good wages and conditions and staff-perks are an investment which fosters workers' loyalty, especially in companies where such conditions are part of a non-union policy. Two of our respondents remembered affectionately working for Boots, a non-union firm, in the late 1950s and early '60s:

> It was a great time working at Boots . . . they really train their staff, and they looked after you as well. . . . Boots is a company that take great care of their employees. And you go to Boots on a trial basis for six months, and then if you're suitable you're allowed all the privileges. . . . You have a discount card, very excellent discount. . . . You only had two weeks paid holiday, but when you'd been there two years you went to three weeks paid holidays, which was quite a thing in those days.[42]

In the 1980s Tesco was a good example of a company where a relatively recent concern for employees' welfare existed alongside an active union organization, although staff benefits varied with the size of the store. Ken Wylie had worked for the Tesco organization since 1967 and eventually became a manager in a superstore:

> Now every store in the company has got a staff manageress who looks after the staff welfare and employs staff, and people go to see her with their problems. . . . That's probably one of the bigger changes, they're very much into caring for the staff and looking after their needs and seeing if they can offer various things; staff discount, hair-dressing, chiropody, even cancer screening. . . . I think what they're saying is, 'If we're

going to keep our standards, we want to keep our staff', because it costs a lot of money to train staff nowadays. You've got to keep somebody, train them, look after them, so they're going to be a vital part of the company, and that's their attitude now towards staff, which has changed dramatically.

The manager of Tesco's Harborough branch in 1986, Ted Ashby, pointed out a recent staff perk:

> The company [also] has a 'Save as You Earn' scheme. Any member of staff who's been with the company two years can make a commitment to a building society to save a maximum of £100 a month, which will be converted into company stock in five years time at today's price. . . . Next year anybody who has been with us for two years [will be included in] the profit-sharing scheme, either paid in shares or in the salary. With profit-sharing, the only thing the company can do by it is benefit ; everybody starts treating it as their own business.[43]

By the 1960s and '70s, Market Harborough had few substantial private owners remaining in the retail trades. Where did they go? The high-class grocer's founded by Samuel Symington and George Thwaites was run by two partners, Mr Allen and Mr Sumpter, until 1950 when the shop was sold to Burton's the biscuit manufacturers. The Woods, the Pickerings, and even the numerous Gardiners all left retailing, and their places were taken by the managers of multiple stores. Although there were still independent owners in the town who had local influence, none of them ran shops which matched the scale of a Symington & Thwaites, or a Wood's.

Following local government reorganization in 1974, Market Harborough in administrative and political terms changed from a three-parish urban local authority to being a minority part of a larger district council spread across a broad swathe of rural south Leicestershire. The politics of the new authority are inevitably less parochial and the town's interests are outvoted by the rural constituencies and Lutterworth. While it is thus less easy for local shopkeepers to have an influence on local affairs, there are anyway far fewer independent retailers to be represented. Most high street shops are now part of multiple chains, with managers who rarely stay long enough to become involved in local affairs and who often do not live in the town. Of the thirty-seven members of Harborough District Council in 1988, only two were involved in the town's retail trades.

In the second half of this century large private shops have gradually beeen displaced by the outlets of expanding national multiples. Small branches that were once ranked in the town's second division of shops have confidently moved into the first division; the supermarkets, including the Leicestershire Co-operative Society, and high street chain stores are now the largest retail employers in Harborough. These companies play a key role in the town's retail provision, a role once occupied by the family businesses of independent owner-occupiers. While the multiples continue to attract the allegiance of their customers through presentation, service and advertising, and of their staff through training and welfare schemes, their connection with the town is far more tenuous. With policies and strategy decided at a remote head-office, and with successful managers moving away for promotion, those in charge of the main retail businesses play little part in the social and political life of the town.

## *Chapter Five*

# The Small Shopkeeper

*The thing in a village . . . everybody knows where you go, what you do and knows every bird that flies across the street.*
(Son of a post office manager and general shopkeeper, 1920s[1])

For much of this century, the small independent shopkeeper, in both town and village, has been in decline. Beset by the irresistible march of the multiple stores, stripped of customers by the motor car and hedged around by government legislation, the demise of the small retailer has been repeatedly predicted. Despite this gloomy prognostication, ownership of a small shop remains a widely held aspiration, however unrealistic or romanticized a view of the shopkeeper's life this may represent, and the small, privately owned, shop has proved remarkably resilient. The small shopkeeper whether located on a suburban corner or behind the archetypal rose-decked frontage on a village street does have more freedom of action and a more direct satisfaction with his job than his counterpart who manages the multiple store. Indeed the entrepreneurial spark was encountered in researching this book not so often in the high street as in the independent store. In this chapter we examine the life and work of the small independent shopkeeper in both town and village since the last century. While there are important distinctions to be drawn between such types of shop, more in the past than the present perhaps, their independence gives them much in common.

Despite the focal role of Market Harborough, the villages of south Leicestershire and north-west Northamptonshire had shops of their own. By the late eighteenth century, shops were to be found in at least eleven of the twenty-three villages in Northamptonshire thought to be within the market area of Harborough. Clipston, for example, in 1777, had one grocer and three butchers, and Stoke Albany, one chandler, a baker and a butcher. The retail occupations listed in the villages at this date were predominantly butchers and bakers, with little evidence for grocers or general stores. It seems likely however that at least some of those listed as butchers were graziers in the business of livestock rearing rather than retailing.[2]

Until the nineteenth century, comprehensive sources for village shops are notably lacking and it is impossible to chart the growth of village shops in the area. Certainly by Victoria's reign, when the earliest reliable trade directories for the villages appeared, there already existed a comprehensive network of village shops throughout the district. The middle of the century appears to have been a high point for the village shop, when all but the smallest of villages had at least one shop. The roadside village of Welford (population: 1,074 in 1841) boasted no fewer than twenty shops or retail tradesmen in 1849; three butchers, four bakers, four grocers, one druggist and eight tailors and drapers. Even small villages such as Kelmarsh (population: 163) and Haselbech (population: 194) had a grocer and a baker respectively. In all, the villages within Market Harborough's ambit in 1849 had 207 shops or retail businesses, one for every 95 inhabitants. The overwhelming majority of these were general shops, butchers or bakers although the two directories appear to differ over their definitions of 'shopkeeper', Hagar's Directory recording forty-nine in the Leicestershire half of the area and Whelan's locating only eight south of the Welland in Northamptonshire. The tendency towards a broad range of stock across two or more specialities is however evident in both sectors, shopkeeper and carrier, baker and flour dealer, grocer, draper and hatter, to name the more common combinations. Some unusual bedfellows are also to be found under the same roof, such as Great Easton's J. Everett, 'ironmonger and draper', Lubenham's T. Perkins, 'shopkeeper, silk plush man and beer retailer', and Naseby's Eli Adnitt, 'wheelwright and grocer'. This suggests that to establish and maintain a village shop it was necessary to spread wide the range of goods offered and to be opportunist to demand and circumstance. The combination of shop and a trade or craft may reflect a husband-and-wife business: the man running the workshop, the woman the shop.[3]

The Scrimshire family shop in Husbands Bosworth was an example of the village shopkeeper's perennial readiness to grasp any retail opportunity. George Scrimshire spent most of his working life running one of Husbands Bosworth's several general stores. His father was a tailor and drapery was the original speciality of the shop. His account is witness to the importance of the hunting season to village economies in south Leicestershire and the strengths of the village store, service, credit and a diverse stock:

> When he started, my father was a tailor. He used to do all the hunters' clothes. . . . He took two rooms in the thatched house. One he started as a little sweet shop and the other he did his work in. It grew from that, he stocked different things. . . . My brother was estate plumber at Sulby Hall. They must have had fifteen or twenty grooms and three or four chauffeurs. They wanted groceries for the bothy, so we started supplying them. That's how we got into the grocery line. We grew on from that. I helped my father then. Later on we had two girls and myself and my wife. We used to run it and he ran his other business. We used to milk six cows. I used to take the milk around the village in a bucket with a lid on and the two measures in it. I think the dearest it got in the winter was about 1*s* 8*d* a quart, 10*d* a pint but it used to drop a lot in the summer.

My father bought the shop for £250. . . . When I came in [about 1928], I more or less took over. Father kept on with the tailoring. He'd help me if I was busy but we weren't in such a big way then. We kept growing all the while. The main thing then was cigarettes, sweets and chocolates. He used to get up, my father, at six o'clock and go across to serve all the people going down to the station for the BTH train [British Thompson Houston, major employers in Rugby], because that was a very busy time of day. Very busy Kilworth station was . . . . As people asked for stuff, we got it, until we sold practically everything; boots, shoes, drapery, cartridges, greengrocery. We had split the shop into three, it was a long one; drapery at one end, greengrocery in the middle and grocery at the other end.

The different sorts of customer there are, you have to 'molly' them, whatever they say or do. . . . When we had the shop turned into three, we kept the fireplace in the middle shop and we used to have a nice open fire in there and a couple of chairs. Some of the old ladies didn't mind going and sitting there for ten minutes against the fire, especially if it was cold weather. We'd take them around there which was away from the bustling part of the shop. . . . A lot of these old ladies, they'd like to come in to have a little chat. That's why they didn't like the supermarkets. They don't like to wander around and help

Scrimshire's tailor's shop in Husbands Bosworth, *c.* 1885

themselves. They like to have a little chat and be served, tell you all their troubles, and aches and pains. The shop was open from eight in the morning until eight at night and nine o'clock on Saturdays, and an hour after lunch on Sundays. We were open every day of the year except Christmas Day. [The busiest time] was Saturday, at that time of day, because a lot of the people weren't paid until Friday night. We were always busy Sunday dinner. That was only, more or less, sweets and cigarettes. But we could take up to £10 on a Sunday dinner in an hour. That was good going in them days. My father used to say that was a good start for the week anyway, to put that in the till for Monday morning.

We used to make ice cream. Tye Miller used to run a bus to Leicester and he used to bring us a hundredweight of ice back every Saturday from the ice people there and we used to have that in a bucket and stand there and turn the old handle and make ice cream on a Sunday morning, ready for after lunch. There was a lot of credit, a lot of bad credit. It was very bad at that time of day. With a little village shop I think it's worse than in a town shop because everybody knows you and they think you won't refuse them. . . . A lot of it was booked until the weekend until they got their wages. There was not a lot of cash in the week really, only for just oddments. The bulk of the grocery was paid for at the weekend. They'd pay for one week and go into debt again for the next week. It was very difficult because you used to keep scrabbling a bit after them if you could because you didn't want to lose the custom.

They [the 'big houses'] were very full for the hunting season. I used to deliver to them on a bicycle with a big basket on the front . . . Symington & Thwaites [see Chapter Seven] used to come here. They used to come for orders one day and deliver the next with the horse and van, so they took one or two of the big orders. . . . The old cook would order once a week. Of course, they only wanted groceries because they'd got all the vegetables and all that they wanted in the gardens. You'd give her [cook] a commission or you'd have to give her a tip at Christmas or something to keep in with her.[4]

By 1885–8, the population of Harborough's rural hinterland was 17,704, spread across fifty villages. They were served by 157 village shops, representing one shop for every 113 people. Only fourteen communities, the smallest villages – West Langton (population: 60), Shangton (population: 74), Brampton Ash (population: 120) – were without a shop of any kind. The general store was the most common type of village shop, followed by the bakers (36) and butchers shops (29). In the Victorian period, larger villages in the area were well-provided with shops. In 1888, for example, Hallaton (population: 716), boasted no fewer than nine shops, including three drapers or clothiers, and Great Easton (population: 540) had ten shops, including a tailor/grocer, a clothier and draper and a blacksmith/shopkeeper. Shops in larger villages served neighbouring settlements as well as their own residents and the range of shops was sufficient for every day-to-day need.[5]

For the next half-century, the population of Harborough's hinterland declined steadily, as did the number of village shops. By 1936–7, the rural population of 11,993 supported 107 shops, which still represented one shop for every 112 people.[6] It has only been the spread of car ownership in the past thirty years that has really affected this ratio. While the availability of cars has reversed the decline in village population, it also made the town shops, and latterly the hypermarket, easily accessible to the car owner, providing the majority of village shops with unbearably strong competition. In 1987 there were just twenty shops in the villages around Market Harborough, one shop for every 420 people.[7]

Mr Charles Kirby's mother ran a small village shop and post office at Slawston in the 1920s. Village shops were commonly run by widows or otherwise single women of slender means, being almost the only trade open to them with limited capital. His account of her shop touches on the importance of the post office to the village shop's business, which remains a significant if vexed question today, and on the problems of eking out a living in a community comprised largely of farm labourers:

> She sold post office and most [other things], bacon, flour and tea, sugar, all that sort of thing. She done very well, but it wouldn't have paid without the post office you see. At one time she had to deliver the post from Harborough, it come with a horse and cart, delivered all the letters to her for Slawston and some of the surrounding farms, you know, across fields and she had to deliver the letters. The post'd go onto the next village and somebody'd do the same there. The postman, he took the letters but he didn't deliver them, only to the post office and whoever kept the post office would deliver them. You made a sheet out every week and they'd bring them [pensions, stamps etc.] out with the mail in the morning.
>
> They'd deliver [shop supplies] from Leicester. Some of the big firms used to run big wagons out, steam wagons, I remember seeing these old Foden wagons about. She used to sell corn and barleymeal for pigmeal. They used to deliver it from Leicester, not ever so often, they used to deliver about once a month. Me sister lived in the village and she used to help her what she could. . . . No, no clothing or boots or anything like that.
>
> The biggest thing in a country village was your debts. Well, take farm labourers, I mean at that time of day they was only getting about thirty bob a week. Well, I mean, if they got behind one week it was a job to pull up. It was getting your money, that's what done the little shops in villages. You couldn't blame them, because they didn't earn it so they couldn't pay out, could they? You know as well as I do, if some people can get something for nothing, they're going to get it, that's what done little shops in villages, debt.
>
> The thing in a village, everybody knows everybody. Everybody knows where you go, what you do and knows every bird that flies across the street. They know everybody's business.[8]

Mr William Gardner is the proprietor of a long-established grocery and hardware store in the large village of Welford. His father ran the business before him, having bought it from the previous owner, and his former employer, Mr G.W. Bird in 1924. This was a large and well-appointed village shop, with much in common with independent grocers' shops in Harborough itself:

> Father went to work there straight from school, as a boy, and continued to work there until about 1912, when Mr Bird sent him to be apprenticed in Southport, to a company grocer's, Seymour & Meades, and father was there until war broke out. Then when he came out of the Army, Mr Bird asked if he would like to come back, as he was thinking of retiring and he wished to give him the first chance of taking the business over. . . . He bought the shop in 1924. Mr Bird lent him half of the money. I think it was £960 for the business [the property was rented]. The wholesalers who supplied us with groceries lent the other half and father paid it back gradually. That was a lot of money at that time.
>
> It was a general grocery and quite a lot of hardware; paraffin lamps were the vogue in those days and he sold vast amounts of lamp glasses and lamp fittings as well as the general groceries and paraffin . . . groceries to wine and spirits, hardware; you name it, we sold it.
>
> I think he began with a horse and cart but he had an early bull-nosed Morris car which he used to do deliveries in, because at that time we did deliver to seven other villages in the neighbourhood. . . . There was a big order trade. Times were different then, not many people had cars and they did rely on us for delivering large boxes of groceries. . . . He did have a [hand-]truck which on Thursday nights and Friday nights was loaded up with orders and this old Mr Grant used to push round the village.
>
> There was a long counter at the back with mahogany shelves behind and quite ornate bins which held tea and rice and that kind of thing, and then above those were more mahogany shelves on which there were smaller canisters, black with gold chinese lettering in which were dry goods. . . . There was a biscuit stand on the side which held tins of biscuits with glass lids from which you weighed out biscuits in bags. On the other side there was another counter but it was more or less covered with glass showcases. Round the other side there were rather biggish shelves on which canned goods were kept and the front wall was mainly hardware, pots, pans and brushes.
>
> The greater part of [trade] was in orders to other villages because at that time there were seven or even ten shops in Welford, now there's only two. The main competition was the shop next door, Goodfellows, who were also the post office, and they were quite good grocers too and also did delivery. Most of the others did sell some grocery. Actually it was a bit of segregation in those days because Goodfellows were staunch Chapel supporters and we were Church of England supporters and the customers seemed to be a bit divided that way.[9]

From the late nineteenth century, Market Harborough began to grow rapidly, with R. & W.H. Symington's corset factory going from strength to strength, similar progress at W. Symington's Coffee Mills and new factories established: the Harboro' Rubber factory, Looms boot and shoe works, Haddon's Type Foundry, Hearth's the hosiers. The town well deserved its title of 'manufacturing market town' in a descriptive guide of 1902. The population of Harborough and the new suburbs of Great and Little Bowden doubled between 1871 and 1911, rising from 4,364 to 8,853. For the first time, the town began to expand significantly beyond the constricting boundaries of the medieval chapelry, the 60-acre site laid out in the twelfth century. A previous period of growth, earlier in the nineteenth century, had been accommodated in the backyards, in rows of small terraced cottages built along the backs of medieval burgage plots. From the 1870s, new housing was begun to the west of Fairfield Road and along Coventry Road, known as 'New Harborough', to the south along Northampton Road and a small area immediately to the north-east of the old centre in Heygate Street. Much of this development was undertaken on the initiative of the Market Harborough Freehold Land Society and the Market Harborough Building Society. From the dateable houses and the style of many terraces, the pace of new building appears to have quickened around the turn of the century. It was in these new suburbs that many small shopkeepers were to flourish and, indeed, flourish to this day.[10]

Miss Ann Brooke's general store was one of the first suburban shops, established around 1880 in the recently built East Street. New Harborough developed westwards from the triangle where Nelson Street, East Street and Goward Street converged. By the turn of the century several shops had been established at this focal point, past which most people from the new streets walked on their way to work in the town's factories, shops and railway yard. Another early suburban shop was Gardiner's, a grocer and baker's (later Hodby's), established at 30 Nelson Street by 1881.

> I was born in the house attached to Mr R. Hodby's shop. It had just been built. . . . At that time it consisted of a house, shop and bakehouse. Standing at the shop door, you could see both Nelson Street and East Street. These houses were surrounded by fields. Looking up East Street, there was no house beyond the bakehouse until you passed the back road to houses in both Nelson Street and Highfield Street . . . but in front and at the top again stretched fields as far as the eye could reach.[11]

By 1900 there were eight shops in New Harborough and a further five in the new streets leading off Northampton Road. There had also been a significant turnover among the proprietors of shops in St Mary's Road, probably in response to opportunities offered by building in the Connaught Road area. From 1900 to 1912

Nelson Street, Market Harborough, *c.* 1910. This stretch of Nelson Street formed the southern boundary of the Market Harborough Freehold Land Society's third and largest estate. George Gardiner's shop on the right occupied the important property on the corner with East Street.

the number of suburban shops nearly trebled to thirty-five, and by 1922 a peak of thirty-seven had been reached. This number stayed roughly constant through the decades between the wars. Gardiner's, a suburban general store dating back to 1881, was a landmark in New Harborough until Mr Ron Hodby retired in 1971. The business had been established by his grandfather, George Godbehere Gardiner:

> He seemed to have a multiplicity of trades. There was this grocery, bakery and post office and he also ran a carting business opposite to the shop. He was also one of the founders of the Land Society which developed all of New Harborough from Nelson Street.
>
> When I was a boy [there was] fetching butter and eggs from the farmers and fetching it from the ostlers' rooms at the pubs. That would be a weekly thing on a Tuesday. . . . The problem with farm produce was you either had a lot or a little. With butter in particular, we would have more than we could sell in spring and then in the wintertime have about a tenth of the quantity. We had so many farm butter customers, we'd have to try and ration it out amongst them. With eggs we had whatever the farmer could bring and in spring we'd have three times as many as we could sell and so we just had to pickle

> them, put them down in the cellar in big tins in water glass and bring them out in winter to supplement the few fresh eggs that there were. The farmer would come eventually to the shop before going home to have some grocery and it would be putting one thing against another. We would have to pay out in most cases.[12]

The great attraction for most people who run small shops is the opportunity to be their own boss. But owning and running a small shop has always been a great tie, impinging on almost every aspect of family life and demanding a great deal of enthusiasm and commitment from all concerned. 'I chucked it and started a new life . . . it was a sub post office. The first day I was there, I think people came to see who I was. I think I took £3 10*s* and the second day, the Tuesday, I took 15*s* and sold one tuppeny stamp. But I was happy because I was me own boss.'[13]

This smart turn-out belonged to George Godbehere Gardiner, grocer of Nelson Street, Market Harborough, *c.* 1910

Mr and Mrs Murkitt ran a combined grocery and bakery in Church Street. They lived over the shop and also offered bed-and-breakfast. Their daughter's account of home life in the 1920s and 1930s demonstrates how much hard work this meant for all the family and how intrusive the business was on family life and living space:

> We never employed anybody full-time in the shop. . . . My mother worked in the shop. We'd have maybe Fridays and Saturday some casual help but we certainly didn't have any other help. My father would pop in from the bakehouse if my mother was doing something whereby she couldn't go in. We as children helped after school to give her the break after four o'clock time.
>
> I can't really remember a time when I wasn't helping . . . as soon as I could add up money I suppose. . . . He actually did have a catering business as well as the shop, because we used to be bed-and-breakfast for lorry drivers. [We] had all sorts of people passing through. We were in the Cyclist Touring Club handbook, so that sometimes we got cyclists who were going through. We quite often had, being a hunting district, grooms who worked for different stables in the area. I can remember us having tailors a time or two.
>
> On the left of the shop as far as you could go, was a doorway that led into our living room; so that we didn't always have to be in the shop because there was a bell. Our living-room was at the side of the shop which we also shared with whoever came for bed-and-breakfast. And then the rest of the house above we lived in, with the bedrooms at the top for the catering part of it; two very big ones on the top floor, three on the next floor plus our own sitting room.
>
> And then his bakehouse downstairs [on the ground floor at the back] with a scullery beside it where my mother used to do the cooking . . . . Eastman the butchers, their back door was into the alleyway between our two houses. We didn't have to keep meat like steak or chops or anything like that in, because if anybody turned up we only had to whip to the back door and get a piece of steak or a couple of chops or whatever.

Dorothy Murkitt had a younger brother who also helped in the shop. There was also a lodger who did 'general rough jobs about the house' in return for his keep. Mr Murkitt worked in the bakehouse while his wife ran the shop and looked after the paying guests. The children helped in both areas, although Dorothy preferred working in the bakehouse:

> He was always up very early, but I don't think he started to bake before about six o'clock in the morning. . . . It used to take him the rest of the morning to do the bread, two or three batches of bread . . . I always remember he had a sort of rest for about half-an-hour after lunch and then he would start again in the afternoon. That would be when he did his cakes and pastry. He wouldn't be finished before five o'clock.
>
> [I helped] preparing the tins for him when he was doing the bread. Now and then I would help him weigh off the dough. I would weigh off while he moulded up. This of

Mr and Mrs Murkitt outside their bakery and shop in Church Street, Market Harborough

course would have to be in the school holidays, because at that time of day I would be at school normally. But Saturdays I would do that. It was just really generally being on hand for the odd job that wanted doing. Certainly I had to do my stint in the shop. That was the thing that sometimes I used to be a bit fed-up with.

It was always an understood thing that a portion of what they charged for their bed-and-breakfast went to my mother, which she paid the laundry out of and what was left over was then her perks, and the proportion that they considered was the food had to go back into the business. I can remember that she charged 1*s* 6*d* for the bed and the food depended on what you had. . . . She would never stand any bad language in the house. That was another thing she was very down on, no drinking; being a Chapel girl she was very anti-drink.

The Murkitts had an eye for extra trade and, like many private shopkeepers, supplemented what they retailed with home-made 'specials':

When the market was on the Square, before it moved to the Market Hall [1938], we used to cook dinners and take them to the market holders, actually carry them down on trays. . . . And he also made up cheese rolls which he supplied to the Working Men's Club, so again he would carry them down.

> Summertime my mother used to make fresh lemonade which she kept in a big glass, barrel-shaped, container with a tap on it. It really looked super with slices of lemon floating on it. . . . At one stage she used to make ice-cream. . . . I do remember having to help to turn the handle.

The Murkitts had no recreation apart from Mr Murkitt's allotment, 'which he took on in later years because my mother thought he wasn't getting out of the bakehouse enough', his occasional game of billiards at the Working Men's Club and their Sunday attendance at the Congregational Chapel. 'I think work must have been their whole existence really.' The family enterprise was dealt a severe blow by Mrs Murkitt's death. Dorothy was fourteen and still at school, her brother was twelve and Mr Murkitt's health gave cause for concern:

> Well, he found it very difficult then. He employed a housekeeper to start with and that didn't work really. And then my aunt who had been in domestic service, she joined us and she stayed with us. But obviously she didn't work in the same way that my mother did in the business, because, well, it was in my mother's interest to put in sort of all hours.

In the late 1930s, Dorothy started work at Stewarts and Lloyds' steelworks in Corby. She continued to work in the shop on Saturdays, unpaid of course, 'you just did that because you were part of the family'. She left Stewarts and Lloyds to get married:

> I think my father did less baking and concentrated on the shop more. He never employed anybody full-time in the shop. I had more time to help him in the shop . . . I did a job during the war which took me only about three days a week, so that I'd have the rest of the time then and I helped him in the shop. . . . He started to have asthma very badly – he could cope in the shop when the bakehouse got too much for him. But he still kept on with the bakehouse until he retired, but not doing as much. Towards the end we bought some of our bread in and he only did the cakes and pastries and that sort of thing because of his health.
>
> Before Roman Way was built, there was all these little alleys and loads and loads of families. Well they were the people we used to serve. It was in fact when they started building the council houses in Welland Park Road [1933] and moving the people out from these little alleyways that really our business began to go down.[14]

Around 1946, Mr Murkitt gave up baking altogether on account of his health and retired. The family themselves then moved to Roman Way, which had been built on the site of the narrow courts and yards which had been home to so many of their regular customers.

Such family commitment was a common factor in many of the town's small shops. Mr Michael Kelly ran a fruiterer's and florist's business in St Mary's Road until 1969. The shop had been in the Kelly family since 1934 and after working there as an errand boy just before the Second World War, Mick Kelly returned to the business as a partner in 1950. The shop opened long hours and was generally able to undercut the more expensive fruiterers on the High Street such as Plowman's, Brook's and Norbury's: 'They used to get so worried about prices that we used to see them – at night we could look down and see the pavement – see these people with notebooks taking the prices. They used to worry'.

As small traders, the Kellys had to work hard to make a living from the shop and a stall in the weekly market. In the fruit and veg trade profit margins are low and the trade highly seasonal. One of the main problems was maintaining sufficient cash flow:

> Our bad times were always July, August, September. Many, many people had a garden then, their own garden and allotment, and your biggest job was refusing people coming in wanting to sell you produce. Soft fruit, you could buy that, but there used to be an abundance of potatoes, cabbage, runner beans, broad beans . . . too much of everything. Then towards the end of September it starts building up good again and we used to have some really excellent Christmas trade.

The large amount of stock bought and sold at Christmas caused financial strains on the business and called for careful budgeting:

> They were always difficult times, if you knew that you were going in the red at the bank a bit, to lay out all this money. I mean to lay out £1,000 is nothing now, but it was quite an experience in those days. And if you didn't pay for it [the stock] within a week you didn't get it and that was it. Sometimes pay on delivery. So you had to be as kind as you could to the bank manager. Mine was very, very good, and he would say, 'When can you pay it back?' Well it was always about the first week in the New Year, you got straight again. You could only borrow so much you see, so you had to try and work within that budget.

Christmas was the high point of the year, when the shop could 'shift well over a thousand Christmas trees, nuts by the hundredweight, citrus fruit, apples and even strawberries and something a bit different like pineapples and a bag or two of coconuts. . . . Trade was just wonderful [on Christmas Eve]. People were queuing up, and especially after lunch they'd been and had a little snorter somewhere and it put them in a good mood and everybody was happy and spending their money and got the Christmas feeling. And we used to have one long laugh in the old shop then'.[15]

The successful small shopkeeper is invariably more than just a retailer. The small shop, in village or suburb, is a focal point in the community, the hub where news and gossip is exchanged. Mick Kelly explained the tendency to build up personal relations with customers:

Kelly's fruiterer's shop at 16 St Mary's Road, Market Harborough, 1960

They go where they got value for money and, I think, courtesy and of course cleanliness. You look upon them as friends coming in. My late wife, she was a great diplomat in that field, she had many friends from the shop. They used to come to her for all sorts of questions. At one time we had a spate of filling in forms. I used to have a little office at the back and help people with forms.

There was a wonderful camaraderie among the people up the old St Mary's Road then and some of the customers too. They got their problems with illness, bereavements and things, and they'd come in and tell you, and come and sit down in the back in the old kitchen and tell you all their problems.

Mick Kelly was fortunate in getting financial help from his father to go into the business run by his uncles and aunts, and thus overcame the problem of raising capital to get started. Thereafter the shop and a market stall was the Kellys' way of life for twenty years.

We could never get a holiday – you just don't dare do it. Once we had a relief chap in, provided by an organization I belonged to called the Retail Traders Association. They sent this chap, and of course you provided him with accommodation and his food and you paid him. But for a week away and to come back, and every thing all upset and the customers upset and the takings down, it just wasn't worth it. So we never did it again. We used to have our holidays separately if we had one at all.[16]

As Mick Kelly put it: 'You can't expect anyone outside to put the same amount of effort in that you'd do yourself, as your own living, your own business'.

The final economic decision faced by the independent shopkeeper is when to leave the trade. The situation can be forced, through ill-health or financial failure. Otherwise judging the right time to sell out, whether for retirement or to move on to a better prospect, is difficult. In 1969 the Kellys' shop still had a large trade although profit margins were falling as overheads rose. Mick's accountant advised him to sell while the going was good, and warned him that small shops would be squeezed as supermarkets came into the town. One offer fell through, but then the Kellys received another offer from people who wanted to turn it into an antiques shop, and so they closed their doors. 'I didn't come out a millionaire, but I came out with my head held high – I didn't owe anybody anything and I had enough to buy a house, and we had a new car at the time.'[17]

The challenge of the new supermarkets and their price wars to the small independent shops was a serious one. Small retailers had always had to make the most of their particular brand of personal service which distinguished them from the larger stores, whether private or multiple. Long opening hours, stocking a bit of everything, a readiness to extend credit, good personal relations with customers, and 'social services' were features of many a self-owned retail business. After the collapse of price maintenance in the 1960s, private shops could no longer rely on the high profit margins which protected prices guaranteed. The convenience of the corner shop or the suburban parade and the benefits of personal service, long opening hours and 'basket trade' have become all the more important. Today the small shopkeeper has not been totally squeezed out of existence, despite the gloomy predictions of the 1960s and '70s. However, many of those who keep small shops are now on the margins of the retail trade, picking up the crumbs left by the big stores. Located in villages lacking other facilities, and on residential estates and city suburbs away from the centre, these shops survive because of an 'on your doorstep' trade. Much of their custom is at odd hours; during the daytime a main part of their customers are those nearby who lack transport or mobility. We talked to the owners of three shops, one in a village and two in the suburbs, who discussed the kind of living that could be garnered from the small retail business in the mid-1980s.

Geoff Bonnett ran the village shop and post office at Great Easton, a large village on the edge of Market Harborough's area of influence. Shopkeepers' views of the benefits or otherwise of having a post office are subject to great variation:

This is always the thing that used to sell – a post office in a village shop. It's the sub post office that brings people in, yes and no. It can be a terrible bind as well because, whatever you are doing in the shop, if somebody wants the post office, you have to drop that, change hats and go and do it. . . . I would sooner have a thriving shop standing up in its own right than having a post office in the corner. The post office is very restricting . . . the books have to be balanced every Friday regardless, even if you are on holiday. . . . Yes, I suppose it brings in certain people but I think on balance it's a nuisance really. It's a very difficult job being a sub-postmaster because the Post Office give you no training before you actually take over the job. They train you on the job and if you can imagine the situation back in August '76 when here was a completely green shopkeeper taking over a shop with no stock in it and a little man trying to train you to do the post office in amongst all this . . . . You don't even start becoming confident of knowing what you're doing till you've done it for about three years and even then you still get things crop up that maybe happen once every four years. There's this terribly embarrassing situation of, 'Hang on a minute, while I look up the rule book'.

It's a very demanding job where you have to learn an awful lot and it's not terribly rewarding financially in itself and it's getting less all the time. There is a move by the Post Office to review our salaries yearly. This was always done three-yearly in the past, so that they can get the salaries down quicker. You may have noticed ads in the paper for Savings Bank business, fill out this coupon here and do it by post whereas it should be saying go into your local post office. Of course, a great number of village shops are only viable because of the combined income of the post office salary and the profit from the shop. Anything the Post Office chips away at means the endangering of that whole operation, the removal of a rural service altogether.[18]

The post offices at both Hallaton and Medbourne in the late 1980s were full offices in their own right, whereas those at Great Easton, Cranoe and Horninghold were essentially extra counters of the Market Harborough post office. Alan Clayton at Hallaton reckoned the post office an important part of his business, despite the diminishing salary from the Post Office. He had strived to build up the post office business although he found it difficult to quantify its significance in his shop's total business:

The only thing I know is that the shop has got busier and the post office has got busier at the same time as the shop. Which is influencing which I don't honestly know. The way you behave towards your customers makes a lot of difference. You've got to work at that, so that customers feel they want to do business with you in the post office. They feel they'd rather come to our post office than go to say Market Harborough post office. People don't wait here generally and they get chatted to as well. They don't just get, 'Thank you very much, goodbye', they come and tell me their problems, sort out their difficulties and that all helps; people feel they can trust you. The post office used to be in the front of the shop and was [next to] the counter that is generally served over . . . people tend to come and buy a stamp and they've got to walk through the rest of the shop to get to the post office so they notice that you're there.[19]

The post office is regarded as an important source of trade not only by the village shopkeeper, but also by the urban corner shop proprietor. In 1986 Mr Ramesh Radia had run the Northampton Road post office in Market Harborough since 1980. Situated only a five-minute walk from the town centre, the shop relied on the populous surrounding area, passing traffic on the busy Northampton Road, family labour, long opening hours from 6.30 a.m. to 6.30 p.m. and Sunday mornings, and the enterprizing enthusiasm of its owner:

When we first bought it, it was only a small shop about 12 by 10 [feet] . . . a very small shop and a small post office. Because of the post office I get all Southern Estate people and most of Little Bowden. I see people living on St Mary's Road, Nelson Street, Roman Way, they're all my customers because all these people can't cope with long queues at the main post office, they prefer to walk just a little bit further and get served and then walk home. Thursday on average about 700 to 800 pensioners come into my shop and then between Monday and Tuesday, half of Wednesday and Friday, about another 500 or 600 customers, women who take their family allowances and pensioners who draw their pensions on other days. . . . It is the people coming into the post office and thinking I'll get this and that, yes the post office is an important part of the business.[20]

The urban corner shop follows its rural counterpart in many respects. Its appeal is based on customer service and on being in the heart of a residential area or on a busy road. The urban shop must however be there when the supermarket competition just down the road is closed. In the 1980s, supermarkets adopted late-night opening until 8 p.m. on most nights of the week. The Spar organization espoused the cause of 'eight till late' for its members. The Leicestershire Co-op also moved in this direction with its village stores, the Co-op store at Great Glen being one of the first to offer daily twelve hour opening.

In larger urban centres, the independent store had been given a considerable shot in the arm by Asian proprietors, particularly since the expulsion of the Ugandan Asians by the regime of General Amin in 1972. Working as family units, Asian shopkeepers turned the clock back for the independent urban shop, living over the shop and opening twelve hour days or longer. Mr Radia, in 1980, became the first shopkeeper of Asian origin in Market Harborough. His father had run a catering and grocery business in Kampala before losing everything in the harrowing days of 1972. He fled from Uganda and joined part of the family already in Britain and in 1980 became the owner of the Northampton Road post office. In 1988 there were

Leicestershire Co-operative Society's store at Great Glen, 1986. The interior had just been refurbished as an 'Eight to Eight' store

four other proprietors of Asian origin in Market Harborough, three involved with general or corner shops. The Radia shop was very much a family affair, with the family living in a large extension to the rear of the shop:

> I am in partnership with my brother, we've got split jobs . . . in the [early] mornings, I like doing the papers and magazines. Then I do all my post office work between nine and half-past five. Between that I do my book-keeping and my cash account. My brother works in the shop, he looks after all parts of the shop, makes sure there is stock available etc. We close the shop at half-past six. We have dinner at night. We then sit down and discuss the day's ins and outs and I do my book-keeping which will take me to about half-past eight or nine . . . my brother's wife comes in part-time, probably a couple of hours a day, to sort of give us a break in between the business and I've got one full-time staff.[21]

A major issue arising out of the independent shopkeeper's concern over the competition of the multiples is that of price. The buying power of the supermarket chains is so strong that small shopkeepers complain that they can't even buy goods at a wholesale price that can compete with the retail prices of many lines in supermarkets. The large grocery chains concentrate their pricing policy on items which shoppers buy regularly and of which they might be expected to know the price. These are the 'KVIs' or Known Value Items: tea, sugar, baked beans, instant coffee etc. The multiples sell huge quantities of such lines and are able to negotiate low prices with suppliers. Own label items are almost invariably KVIs as well. Small shops, even though buying most of their goods from cash-and-carry warehouses, often themselves large, nationally based organizations, cannot compete with such loss-leading or low margin prices. It is on the basis of the KVIs that most people consider small shop prices to be greater than the supermarket. As noted already, price is not the prime factor for customers of the village shops:

> I think you can get paranoid about prices. I compare quite favourably [with supermarkets] given the buying power I have. . . . Generally we find we do compare quite well. It depends what you're buying, no one's cheap on everything, they can't be. . . . Look at the cough mixture, that's always the thing, because that's retail price maintained . . . you can't sell it below that price. You'll find in supermarkets it's always way above that price, whereas the smaller people always sell it at RRP [recommended retail price]. We keep an eye on prices. We have a booklet called *Shaw's* [Retail Price Guide] which is a sort of bible. It's issued monthly and they give you in there the price of the vast majority of the goods you sell. They give a fair and reasonable price and I always try and keep either on Shaw's price or below. I never go above Shaw's price. On some things we are cheaper than anybody else, whisky particularly at the moment because I am able to buy it at a very good price. If I can buy it cheap, I'll sell it cheap, I suppose, is my philosophy. I've got to have a return on my money, as long as I get a reasonable return.
>
> You never make a fortune in a village store; the man who sets out to will not be in a village store very long! You've got to set your price at a level which gives a reasonable return and enables you to stay there. The income tax people set the margin. They say officially there are no guidelines and they treat everybody as an individual case but in fact with a shop like this they look for you on your yearly takings to take 20–22 per cent. If you don't they assume you are taking money out of the till and putting it in your pocket. . . . That's the sort of margin you've got to look at because if you don't your accountant's going to say you only took 16 per cent. Now in town or in a multiple, particularly in my supermarket [in Northampton] 15–16 per cent was the norm. Having said that, you couldn't charge everything at 15 per cent because obviously cigarettes are so low you've got to compensate with something else. It's getting the mix right, that's the trick, one of the tricks of the trade. That's where you go bankrupt if you go wrong.[22]

Geoff Bonnett's experience at Great Easton demonstrated a similar pattern:

> My main consideration is that I should get a reasonable return on the product. That differs from product group to product group. You obviously do not make much money on . . . Known Value Items. These are things that the supermarkets have hammered over

> the years to the extent that if you sold them at what you thought was a reasonable profit margin you would never sell any so you have to accept that you're going to make perhaps 5 per cent when the taxman expects you to turn in something in excess of 15 per cent. You have to balance these up with items of hardware or stationery where you can perhaps have a profit margin of perhaps 40 per cent. There's a vast middle-of-the-road section of grocery where you can usually work on a 15 per cent margin. Supermarkets spend a lot of time hammering KVIs home to the general public and their object is to get them into the store. Once they have, of course, they will buy other things without taking into account the price and we have to accept that this is part of their marketing and it works.[23]

In the 1980s, as today, the independent shopkeeper used a combination of cash-and-carry and direct delivery from the supplier to obtain goods. We found that shopkeepers in and around Market Harborough had to use a variety of cash-and-

The conclusion of the traditional Easter Monday 'bottle kicking' at the Cross, Hallaton, *c.* 1910. The main shops of the village are situated in High Street, on the right at the rear of the scene.

carry warehouses in both Leicester and Northampton to obtain coverage of the varied stock they carried in their shops. The shopkeepers who spoke to us tended to shop around between the different warehouses on the lookout for special offers and promotions. All business with such suppliers was done on a strictly cash basis. Storage space in a small shop was strictly limited and the sell-by dates important to observe, so our shopkeepers made a weekly visit to the cash-and-carry.

The introduction of own label brands by the cash-and-carry also offered some hope for the independent grocer in the Known Value area: 'If you look around the shop, you'll find a thing that I thought was going to be absolutely disastrous when they announced it but I've been proved totally wrong . . . it's called "My Mum's". It's been a huge success and that is our own brand if you like which competes with the branded goods'.[24]

Only in the large multiples or more specialized areas such as catering is any training available for the retail trades. For the small shopkeeper it is usually either a matter of following in the family's footsteps or picking it up as you can. Belonging to one of the voluntary groups such as Spar or APT was recognized as a useful way into the business. Geoff Bonnett learnt much about the retail trade from members of his family and from a local shopkeeper but signed up with Spar shortly after moving into the shop in 1976:

> I'd done quite a bit of homework before I actually took over the shop and decided that belonging to a voluntary group was a good idea. It gave an image to the shop, it gave you a respected own-label, an alternative to the brand name in the shop. It had certain advantages for me in that I didn't have to go to cash-and-carry, the orders were delivered to the shop, far less hassle and for many years it worked extremely well. . . . But then the actual Spar group has changed . . . not really interested in the small independent village shop [any more].[25]

The issue of the convenience store, to open all hours or not, highlights the way in which small urban general stores have diverged from their village equivalents. Through the voluntary groups such as Spar and APT, small shops attempted to put themselves on a par with the multiple giants by national advertising, own labels brands, corporate identity and special offer posters in the window. As we have already suggested, the service offered by the village shop is now widely recognized as being much more diverse than the multiple store and shopkeepers such as Geoff Bonnett and Alan Clayton play to their strengths of stock flexibility, friendly personal service and availability and leave the multiples to compete among themselves for the weekly bulk shop. The range of things which is now regarded by most people as essential has increased steadily with the standard of living in recent years and taken with the gentrification of many villages, this means what is left over from the weekly shop now provides an adequate return for the village shopkeeper.

> When I started [in 1980], people were very much looking to go to a multiple and they saw Spar as another multiple, although it was your business, basically you looked as though you were a branch of a multiple. And for a newcomer, it does help, because they offer you their expertise and if you have no knowledge of the business it does help. . . . But I'm more independent. I didn't like it that Spar, for instance, treat you as one of their managers, although it's your money they're risking, so I left.[26]

Here we have arrived at the heart of the matter, the motivation of the independent shopkeeper. They work longer hours and at greater financial risk than their multiple equivalents, but they do it their way:

> The village [Hallaton] for a start; it's a bit special. It's very historic and that is of interest to me. The business is exactly the right sort of business; very mixed, very general, that was very much what we wanted and it had a post office. I didn't have contact with the customers in the supermarket. My wife's a good seller, I'm not. Doing the post office is exactly the sort of thing I thrive on. The combination works very well. I enjoy being with people, talking to people. . . . Basically I didn't fancy staying in research for the rest of my life. Very boring really, doing the same job each and every day. I really looked for something that I could do with my wife and this was the logical thing to do, to run a shop.[27]

## SECTION THREE

# THE TRADES

*Chapter Six*

# The Harborough Co-op

*Supply yourselves with the necessaries of life, and share in the profits.*
(Market Harborough Industrial Co-operative Society's, 1912 Jubilee Calendar)

For much of its independent existence the local Co-operative Society was the nearest thing Market Harborough had to a general department store. From the beginning of the century it sold clothes and coal, hardware, fabrics and footwear in addition to grocery and provisions, bread, and animal feed. It also had a separate butchery department. By the 1950s the Co-op was offering nearly all the 'necessaries of life' to its members. You could even have your eyes tested or your house decorated by the Co-op.[1]

The Market Harborough Industrial Co-operative Society had started humbly in 1862. The founder members subscribed £40 of capital which enabled them to open a shop in Church Square selling grocery and provisions. Thirty years and three buildings later, the society bought premises from a local grocer and wine merchant, and moved into 4 High Street.[2]

The society added more lines of business, and then in the late 1890s opened its first branch-shop, in the adjoining village of Great Bowden. Increasingly the society looked outside the town and sought to meet the needs of existing and potential customers in the surrounding district. By 1913 it had established four outlying branches: at Kibworth to the north-west on the road to Leicester, then at Husbands Bosworth to the west, Medbourne to the north-east, and finally at Lutterworth, a small market town twelve miles west of Harborough. The branches were general shops, concentrating on grocery and provisions, but also selling household goods, animal feed and bread. The society's success was reflected in its membership, which had risen from 808 in 1899 to 2,595 by the end of 1914.[3]

## CO-OP MEMBERS

Who were the regular customers and members of Harborough's rapidly growing society? 'Co-opers' came from the working classes and lower middle classes.

The Market Harborough Co-op's first branch shop, on the Green, Great Bowden, *c.* 1908. The shop boy, William March stands with the manager, Harry Rose who wears a frilled apron as his symbol of office

Although there was some unofficial giving of credit, members were generally those who had sufficient regular income to pay cash for their goods. The Co-op saw itself as a respectable institution, encouraging thrift and self-sufficiency in its members. It catered for the families of factory hands, clerical workers and employees of the two railways in the town, and for farm labourers and small farmers in the country.[4]

The expanded central premises at 2–4 High Street were the headquarters of the society. Mr Cecil Copson and Mr Norman Marlow both worked there as junior staff in the 1920s and described it to us. In the central premises on a Friday they waited for the five o'clock rush of workers from the corset factory across the way. Many picked up orders which had been left at lunchtime, but it still took two people to serve them. 'They always wanted . . . to have their groceries all in a hurry.' These were working women who had to get home and prepare the evening meal.[5]

The Co-op did have poorer customers too, 'real poor people' from 'the old Commons . . . where the leather factory was'. Bits of 'the rough stuff', pieces 'off the bacon counter or the cheese counter' were kept for these customers, but behind the counter, not on display. Competition for the Co-op's working-class trade came from two sources – the multiples with their cheap lines, and the small shopkeepers who gave credit to their regular customers.[6]

The Market Harborough Co-operative Society's Central Stores at 2–4 High Street, 1920s

Harborough was, and still is, a fairly prosperous town in an agricultural area, with its share of middle-class professional and managerial employees, landowners and large farmers, as well as blue-collar factory workers, male and female. Unlike the dense concentration of workers in local industrial towns such as Coalville and Desborough, the Market Harborough Co-op's clientele was dispersed; this probably encouraged the society to spread itself over a large geographical area. In the early twentieth century average spending per member was lower for the Harborough Co-op than for the societies in Desborough and Coalville. This made it more difficult to offer a full range of services. At the end of the nineteenth century the Desborough Industrial and Provident Co-operative Society, which never expanded beyond this small Northamptonshire industrial town, was building houses for its members, and the Harborough society was criticized for not following their example. Similarly in the 1950s Desborough Co-op had its own chemist's and funeral service, neither of which Harborough could then boast.[7]

Nevertheless, in the 1920s and '30s the Market Harborough society enjoyed a large share of the trade in the town. The society offered life assurance for the first time, and more departments were created at the central premises – confectionery, a chemist's (until 1935), millinery, a café and a bazaar selling crockery and hardware. These two decades saw a second phase of expansion, with four branches built in ten years inside the town to ease the burden of deliveries from the central store and to provide for the growing suburbs. Two more village shops were also opened, one at

Dunton Bassett just north of Lutterworth, and the other at Clipston, to the south of Harborough. The Clipston branch cut down on the long country rounds which were being done from Husbands Bosworth and the central store.[8]

The idea behind trading in new departments and having more local branches was to provide a comprehensive and convenient service for Co-op members, so that eventually they would not need to shop anywhere else. In their report at the beginning of 1933 the Co-op committee stated, 'Our progressive trading policy of the last few years has placed the society in a strong position to meet all the demands of our members'. But in a competitive retail centre like Market Harborough this ideal was a long way from being realized: the Committee felt sure 'that members are shopping outside the society to their own disadvantage' and appealed to them to trade 'loyally' in all departments.[9]

## THE MEMBERS' SHARE – THE 'DIVI'

The main reward for loyal shopping was the members' dividend. Paid twice a year, this '. . . was a big draw . . . because, if they on divi day had a pound or two to draw, it was a bonus . . . it was a big fillip to a housewife's economy'.[10] To become a member of the society a customer had to pay an entrance fee of 1*s*, and take out shares to the value of £1, though this could be paid in quarterly instalments of 3*s* 3*d*. 'There was very few members that were not trading members. Some societies had a lot of members, especially in towns, where they invested cash but didn't trade; but . . . we had quite a good percentage of trading members.' Until 1920 non-members also received a dividend on their purchases, but at a reduced rate.[11]

The profits of the Harborough Co-op, once wages and other overheads had been met, were divided between reserve funds, a broad range of educational activities, and dividend and share-interest payments. A tally of each member's purchases was kept by the shop assistants who wrote out a ticket, or check, for every sale. One copy was given to the customer as a receipt, a second was sent to the offices in the central premises, and a third was kept by the shop.

> I would say 50 per cent of Co-op members at that time used to save all their checks. . . . And they used to put them on a spiked file and then it was a job for the family at the end of the twenty-six weeks to reckon up . . . they'd await until the dividend was fixed at a special meeting the committee used to have. And as soon as it was posted up in the shops . . . these people used to get the old spike-file out, and the family used to get out at night and . . . reckon them up, and they knew thereabouts how much they were due for in dividend.[12]

Each member received a dividend voucher sent to the branch where they normally shopped. 'On that voucher would state how much that person had spent during the twenty-six weeks and then it was worked out at the office here how much she was entitled to. . . . The staff from the office came to each branch in turn at a certain time and paid this money out, to the customer who presented a signed voucher.' 'They had the option of either leaving it in the number, in the share number, which would go into the share account, or draw it out as dividend. And when they drew it out some would spend it back and some would probably use it for paying bills.'[13]

Cecil Copson who started his Co-op career at the Kibworth branch as a shop-boy in the 1920s remembers that many of their customers used the dividend to pay off their rates:

> It was always a big day, the divi day. . . . Saturday afternoons at Kibworth . . . they used to queue up outside. And the rating people from Market Harborough used to ring the office up in Coventry Road and ask what day they was paying the dividend. Because they knew that . . . on the following Tuesday, market day, there'd always be an influx of people coming to Market Harborough to pay their rates.[14]

Otherwise the money might be used to buy items such as clothes which unlike food and other weekly essentials were readily given up if money was tight. 'So that drapery would do very well, or shoes would do very well when it came to dividend time.' This enforced saving through the payment of 'divi' continued to be a useful extension to family budgets in the 'better times' after the Depression, when ' people would save for a holiday'.[15]

Because the dividend came out of the trading surplus, it varied with the fortunes of the society. In the early 1920s the dividend rate dipped to 1*s* in the pound (5 per cent), as the society began to spend its profits on opening two major new departments, confectionery and a chemist's. But thereafter sales and dividend steadily increased. The most stable period for the 'divi' in living memory was the 1930s when the society made enough profits to finance continuing expansion and pay out a constant 2*s* in the pound (10 per cent) to the members.[16] During the Second World War the dividend went into decline again, and never really recovered. It was down to 1*s* 1*d* (5 per cent) by 1950, and eventually fell as low as 4*d* in the pound (1 per cent) in 1968–9. The society experienced the same economic problems as other shops in the post-war period. The rising costs of wages, national insurance and fuel, and, from the 1960s, higher utilities and rates charges, all ate into the society's profits.[17]

Two factors peculiar to Co-operative Societies also worked to reduce the dividend. Previously the Harborough Co-op had received a considerable effective subsidy from the Co-operative Wholesale Society in the shape of the dividend it gave on purchases to its society customers. In the 1930s over three-quarters of the society's stock had come from the CWS. After the lifting of rationing restrictions in the 1950s the

Harborough Co-op bought more branded goods from private manufacturers, on which they received no discount. The CWS subsidy fell correspondingly.[18]

At the same time the Co-operatives were caught up in a revival of price competition among retailers, culminating in the official end to resale price maintenance in 1964. Price cutting, especially on food, encouraged the Co-operatives to offer lower prices instead of regular dividend returns, and in 1961 the Leicester Co-operative Society opened the first 'instant dividend' store in the Midlands. Other stores of this type were soon added, but the traditional dividend was retained for the time being in the rest of the society's shops and on non-food lines. The Harborough Co-op followed suit at its central food hall in the High Street in 1967.[19]

After Market Harborough became part of the newly formed Leicestershire Co-operative Society in 1969, trading stamps were introduced which represented a small dividend at the time of purchase. But 'in the end they finished with the dividend completely and started with . . . the price-cutting instead'. By the mid-1980s the 'Passport to Value' vouchers which gave reductions on selected lines were the only remaining economic incentive for paid-up members.[20] The triumph of 'instant dividend' in the form of lower prices across all its goods brought the Co-op into line with its competitors, but it also ended the attraction of short-term and long-term saving (through dividend or investment) that the Co-op had traditionally provided.

## 'HELP ONE TO ANOTHER'

Constitutionally every paid-up member had the right to attend the society's quarterly (later six-monthly) and annual meetings and to vote in the elections for the committee. The Co-operative Society was organized in the same way as a local council: it had a general committee of elected representatives who supervised the management of the society, and permanent paid officials who ran the society on a day-to-day basis and advised the committee. The general committee was split into a number of small sub-committees to superintend the trading departments such as the grocery and coal together, and the butchery, farm and dairy as another unit. There was also a separate educational committee from 1896, and a committee for the local branch of the Women's Co-operative Guild which was formed in 1899. Those who served on the last two committees were elected.[21]

The members of the general committee were 'working men', men from the upper-working and lower-middle classes. 'The committee was a mixture of all ways of life; there was housewives, there was factory people, there was railwaymen.' Surviving records show no women on the general committee before the First World War, although they did serve on the educational committee. The first woman member of the general committee to appear in the society's records was a Mrs Foster, who had been a member of the education committee and secretary to the Women's Co-operative Guild in Harborough.[22] 'Of course when it came to elections for the committee's vacancies, a member of the women's guild, or a member of the committee who was a prominent member of the women's guild, always had the backing of the guild.' From the 1920s there were frequently 'one or two ladies on the general committee' and perhaps 'six men'. No woman was ever elected president of the society.[23]

Mr W. Carter, the society's president at the beginning of this century, was employed as a departmental manager in the local corset factory. His successor, Mr J. Coe, 'kept an outdoor beerhouse, which was where the Bell is now, in Northampton Road'; and the president in the later 1920s and '30s, Mr J.T. Gibson, was a signalman on the railway.[24]

The Co-op was a local institution, like the Working Men's Club, where ordinary men (and a smaller number of women) could hold responsible positions. As one committee member said at an official dinner at the Cherry Tree in 1900: 'It was a grand thing that working men, like themselves, should be entrusted by members to carry out a business that amounted to something like £4,000 or £5,000 every quarter, and it was beneficial to themselves in fitting them to undertake the duties that devolve upon the citizen and the townsman'.[25] The general committee met weekly, in their spare time and were paid minimal expenses for their attendances. They took their duties very seriously and were anxious that the society should expand its services to the membership. Part and parcel of this outlook before the Second World War was the feeling that profits should benefit the members, by giving a large dividend, rather than the workers. Their background did not guarantee that they were any more sympathetic to the Co-op's employees, as a deliveryman remembers:

> They was men as worked in here [the corset factory], men as worked at Hearth's hosiery or, well, one of them worked for Pugh's the saddler . . . . You see they didn't work those hours we were working. They had a set eight o'clock till perhaps half-past five, quarter to six at night . . . and knocked off at twelve o'clock on a Saturday. We had all these hours to work. They didn't realize what it was like for us. And it was like, to get any extra money, it were like getting blood out of a stone.[26]

As amateurs the committee had to rely heavily on the general manager and the secretary for their 'information and guidance'. 'The general manager was the businessman of the firm', the secretary 'dealt with all paper and cash'. These two officials always sat with the committee at their meetings, and their recommendations carried a great deal of weight.[27]

In theory the members' meetings were the membership's chance to call to account their elected representatives on the general committee. The turn-out for these meetings, held in Harborough's Co-operative Hall, varied from 'not much more than a dozen or fifteen' to a 'full house' of perhaps 120, 'it all depended on the state of the business'. If the committee decided on a drop in the dividend, or if there were grievances among the employees, there would be a large attendance and plenty of questions from the floor. 'But generally speaking it used to be you knew what was coming off and who was to be voted on . . . it was just a show of hands and that was that.'[28]

When Market Harborough merged with the Coalville, Leicester and Melton Mowbray societies to form the Leicestershire Co-operative Society in 1969, it became part of a much larger organization with over 196,000 members. Membership of the Leicester society was already falling before 1969 and this decline accelerated after amalgamation: within two years of the merger the membership was down to 147,000. The removal of dividend from the Society's 'Trendsetter' food shops meant there was little incentive for customers to be members holding shares in the society. The closure of smaller 'uneconomic' grocery and butchery branches was also unpopular. In Harborough 'a lot of people probably came out when it joined Leicestershire'. 'Perhaps 80 per cent were for it. Some, one or two of them, didn't entirely agree. They thought it was . . . killing the small society.' Membership in the Harborough area dropped from 8,534 to 8,087 during the first year of the newly formed society. By the end of 1986 the membership was 6,863.[29]

The Market Harborough 'division' of the Leicestershire society was now supervised by a local regional committee, under the central committee in Leicester. One major change was that employees were allowed to stand for election to the management committees after the amalgamation. The manager of the central grocery in Harborough at the time was Mr Cecil Copson. He was elected onto the regional committee for four years, and then onto the central committee, where he served for two years.[30]

There were still half-yearly members' meetings for the Harborough division, but they suffered from poor attendances. The first one five months after the merger only attracted seventeen members. In October 1972 to 'encourage member participation a Mock Members' meeting was arranged for Market Harborough Young Wives Group in the Co-operative Hall . . . divisional board directors acted as advisors and member relations committee members acted as "Mock Officials".' Perhaps members were less interested because the power to make decisions no longer rested with Harborough.[31]

## 'Learn to Labour and Wait'

The Market Harborough Co-operative Society was an important local employer for the whole district. In the early twentieth century working for the Co-op offered job security and working conditions which were slightly better, for the shop staff at least, than most other shops in the town. In the 1930s the society's labour force became unionized and both pay and job security were improved. Long before the

1969 amalgamation the Market Harborough society was a large enough organization to require a differentiated workforce. As well as the shop assistants and managerial staff, there were clerks in the office, productive workers such as the bakers and dairy employees, and a delivery and warehouse staff ranging from lorry-drivers to boys on trade-bikes. Until it was overtaken by the expanding Tesco supermarket in the early 1970s, the Co-operative Society was easily the biggest retail employer in the town. There were just over 100 people working full-time for the Harborough society immediately before the Second World War. In December 1986 there were 31 full-time and 47 part-time staff employed by Leicestershire Co-operative society in the town, with a further 18 full-time and 59 part-time staff at Lutterworth and Kibworth; Tesco employed 88 staff in the town at this date.[32]

In the office, between the wars, the secretary, assistant secretary and eight or nine clerical workers 'dealt with the day-to-day trading and the cash'. Because the Co-op operated on a shares and dividend basis there was a lot of work handling share deposits and withdrawals, and filing the 'checks' and calculating the returns to members. There was also the Penny Bank, the Death Benefit Fund and the various trading clubs to look after. 'They used to have about four girls in the office here which did nothing else but do checks.'[33]

On the dairy side there was 'a lot of hard graft' before bottling machinery and pasteurization were introduced. Separating the cream from day-old milk and churning butter for sale in the grocery department all had to be done by hand. Even after the plant was modernized there was still a lot of lifting and carrying of churns involved.[34]

Other workers at the central premises in the 1930s included bakers in the main bakery and the confectionery bakehouse, and butchers in their separate department on the Coventry Road. There were staff who worked in the warehouse and the order-room, as well as a groom and a motor mechanic. The local society also ran two farms, a 100-acre mixed farm at Naseby and a smaller dairy farm off the Farndon Road. The latter stretched from 'Farndon Gosse back right to the top of Bath Street' by the side of the Rugby railway line. This land was sold by the Co-op in the early 1930s and is now a council housing estate, opened in 1951.[35]

At Lutterworth, Kibworth, Medbourne and Husbands Bosworth the branches all had their own bakeries. Kibworth and then Lutterworth also had separate butcher's shops added, replacing the travelling butcher's shop which served the outlying districts in the 1920s. The branch bakeries closed one by one after the Second World War, and bread was delivered from Harborough instead. In Lutterworth the George Street butchery was no longer needed when the main shop was modernized in 1959; but Kibworth kept its own butcher until the mid-1970s.[36] Extra departments were added to the society in the 1940s and '50s, and some taken away, but no new branch-stores were opened after Clipston in 1938. The society was now servicing an area of some 200 square miles on both sides of the Leicestershire-Northamptonshire border, and a membership which rose steadily from 6,709 at the start of 1940 to a peak of 8,561 in 1968.[37]

By this time the society's success had become a weakness, as small branch shops were increasingly uneconomical to run and delivery costs escalated. The first of the closures was the Medbourne branch in January 1969, shortly before the society merged with the new Leicestershire Co-operative Society.[38]

## 'SELF-HELP, NOT SELFISH HELP'

Originally the town's Co-operative Society was much more than the largest retail operation in the district. For some of its members it was also a way of life. In 1912 when the society was celebrating its fiftieth anniversary it published a list of 'Objects of the Society'. The first object of the society was 'The Social and Intellectual Advancement of its Members'. The Co-operative commitment to raising the standard of living of the working classes went beyond providing cheap unadulterated food and an opportunity to put by some savings. Members were also given the chance to be involved in the society's affairs through the quarterly meetings and to learn more about the Co-operative movement, at home and abroad, through events and special classes.[39]

The society's educational committee was founded in 1896, and was financed by a percentage of the trading profits. It had two functions: to offer educational activities for existing members and their families, and to encourage new members to join. These 'educational activities' ranged from lectures on Co-operative affairs, children's classes on co-operation and practical courses (gardening lectures, sewing classes) to members' teas and sports fêtes.[40]

The other part of their work was the 'propaganda' meetings, which were held in the Co-op Hall in Harborough and all round the villages to drum up more members. The meetings were a deliberate mix of fun and persuasion. Before the Second World War a concert-party would be engaged to provide the entertainment, with the local artist Ernest Elliott and his marionettes 'one of the most popular' turns. During the interval 'the president and the secretary or the general manager used to have a few words and state his cause, and give the particulars of the society', quoting figures for each branch's trading.[41]

In the 1950s and '60s the committee booked a CWS film unit from Leicester to show films as the evening's entertainment. Since the films were commercial releases this proved very popular. One series of films coincided with the promotion of a new CWS washing powder: 'We took a case, which was eighteen [packets] in a case, to these film-shows . . . and as the people came in we gave them a cloakroom ticket. And at the interval, after somebody had been spouting and putting his part over, we used to make a draw. . . . And you'd be amazed, the people used to go out at night with these packets of soap powder . . . under their arm as though they'd won a motor-car'. These meetings did 'a lot of good' in gaining new members, but they were also a big attraction, especially in the villages, because of the free shows.[42]

The local branch of the Women's Co-operative Guild, which was started in 1899, also put on concerts as part of its activities. Designed to interest women co-operators in the wider work of co-operation, the guild held meetings and talks, and sent delegates to local Co-operative conferences. Market Harborough's branch of the guild thrived for a long while, 'they perhaps had forty or fifty members at one time', but then faded in strength as its membership got older and younger women failed to join. After amalgamation the Leicestershire Co-operative Society encouraged the setting-up of young wives' groups to attract this age-group. Market Harborough had also had a branch of the Men's Co-operative Guild, but this 'didn't last for long'.[43]

Unlike the general committee, employees were allowed to sit on the education committee of the old Market Harborough Society. So on this body, and the social and welfare committee, employees were able to participate in the running of the society's activities.[44]

## 'None of those Socialistic Ideas'

Despite its initial avowed neutrality in both politics and religion the Co-operative movement was inevitably involved in politics because of its concern to improve working-class living standards. Co-operation was seen as a form of self-help for the working classes: 'If ever we are to rise in the social scale, it will be by our own efforts alone,' wrote a Kettering supporter of the movement in the 1860s.[45]

Political activity was never as important for the Market Harborough society as it was for the larger societies such as Leicester. But political considerations still had a part to play. During the second half of the nineteenth century there was a general debate in the movement over whether the well-being of Co-operative workers in productive and retail societies should be a priority, or whether co-operation should aim first and foremost to benefit consumers. This debate was reflected at conferences held in the Kettering and Wellingborough district, which included Market Harborough. Viewpoints naturally overlapped, but those who put forward the claims of the workers looked to co-operation to achieve 'the re-organization of labour' and to fight the 'sweating' or exploitation of workers. Their opponents objected to these 'Socialistic ideas' and emphasized that co-operative trading was to 'the benefit of the great masses of the people'.

This second view was dominant in the local Co-operative leadership, as it tended to be in the national movement at this time (1898–9): 'Co-operators should be supplied by their society with everything they require and in the conduct of business generally what they wanted was none of those Socialistic ideas, but more brotherhood, more of the gentlemanly element'.[46]

Within the Market Harborough Co-op in the 1890s there was lively discussion as to how it should progress in the future, especially since they were building up a large amount of capital. Crucial decisions to expand the number of departments, join the CWS and the Co-operative Union, and open the society's first branch shop were taken in this decade.[47]

Outright political activity by the Harborough Co-op was usually a response to threats against it. The society was concerned, for example, at British governments' attempts to increase the Co-operative Societies' liability for taxes, as in 1917 and 1933. In 1933 the National Government proposed that any Co-op profits placed in reserve funds should be taxed for the first time, and 'all Co-op societies right throughout the country organized a petition . . . objecting to this tax'. A shopman who was relieving at the branch in Great Bowden recalls canvassing the members in the village after work, helped by one of the dairy roundsmen. With its mixture of staff from the Fernie Hunt kennels and the horse-racing stables, and workers from the Harborough factories (a lot of them employed at the rubber company just down the road from the village), Bowden was a 'very good Co-op place' and the canvassers got a good response. Nevertheless the Government imposed the tax, Harborough's Conservative MP voting in favour. The Co-op committee, in their next report, were so annoyed that they called on their members not to vote for him in future![48]

Anti-Co-op feeling in Market Harborough amounted to latent antagonism rather than open opposition. The society's managers were on good terms with most managers from the larger grocery firms in the town – Symington & Thwaites and the multiples – 'it was a job you were doing and that was that'. [49] Some of the small independent traders felt less warmly towards the Co-op, which was competing with them for their working-class customers. The daughter of one prominent private tradesman told us, 'I was bred never to go in the Co-op . . . because of course . . . they were a multiple and they were Labour'. One pre-war retailer in the west end of the town was mildly paranoid about the Co-operative: 'We felt our greatest competitor was the Co-operative Society because it had so many branches. . . . My uncle . . . had a plot of land in Wartnaby Street, and my father was very cross because he sold the land and eventually the Co-op built a shop on it'.[50]

In the 1930s snobbery towards the Co-op was often based on assumed political differences. 'Oh, they didn't hit it at all with the Town Councillors you know. The Co-op was a bit black, because it was dead Labour.' Bias from local landowners was also to be expected. 'They used to have . . . horse-shows, where the cricket field is now. . . . We put a milk-float and a horse [in the show] . . . and it was beautiful, but

. . . they didn't look at the Co-op. . . . Couldn't see Major So-and-so and that giving the Co-op a prize.' In fact the story of the local society's involvement with political parties was quite complicated. 'It was a sort of acknowledged thing that in those days if you were a Co-oper you were a Labour person; that's what everybody seemed to think, but that was a fallacy.'[51]

At the end of the nineteenth century the Liberals regarded themselves as the champions of the minority of working-class men who had the vote. Therefore they were keen to back respectable working-class organizations, such as the Co-operative Societies. From 1891 up until 1922 Harborough returned Liberal MPs, and at this time there was a noticeable connection between the Liberals and the local Co-operative Society. Looking at a ten-year period around 1900, a sizeable minority of Co-op committee members were also active Liberals. These included the first president of the society's committee, James Stevens (1896–1900), who became president of the Market Harborough and District Liberal Club. The link worked both ways. Local Liberal worthies publicly supported the Co-operative Society; and in 1897 Harborough's Liberal MP, J.W. Logan, opened the grounds of his house at Thorpe Langton for the society's annual outing.[52]

In the early 1920s the Harborough constituency switched from being Liberal to 'very strong Conservative'. Meanwhile the Co-operative movement nationally had identified itself with the cause of the Labour Party. In 1917 the Co-operative movement decided to seek 'direct representation' in Parliament and on local councils. From 1918 Co-operative candidates fought elections under an electoral agreement with Labour, although the Co-operative and Labour Parties did not become formally allied till 1927.[53]

Regardless of Kettering's success in electing Britain's first ever Co-operative MP in 1918, the society in Market Harborough was slow to affiliate to the Co-operative Party, not doing so before the mid-1920s. During the 1920s and '30s however certain sections of the society, in particular the Women's Co-operative Guild branch and the education committee, gave aid to political causes as part of their work. The local women's guild branch sent donations to the beleagured Poplar Borough Council in the early 1920s and to striking miners in 1926, sent delegates to disarmament meetings and took part in the pacifist white poppies campaign in the 1930s. And though the president at this time, J.T. Gibson, 'wasn't wrapped up in politics at all', a known Labour man, Andrew Heighton, was elected onto the committee. Heighton later became the society's president from 1943 to 1954.[54]

A politically committed minority within the society was always balanced by those whose political beliefs (or lack of them) did not effect their Co-op activities. 'There was people who was on the board of management who were well-known for their political activities.' But 'politics in this area was never strong'.[55]

Staff of the Market Harborough Co-op and their float for the 1948 town carnival

The principal reason behind the Harborough Co-op's ambiguous political identity was the broad loyalties of its membership, which included both committed Conservatives as well as staunch Labour supporters. Close identification with either party would have lost the society many members. After the Second World War, the then president, 'a prominent Labour man', considered displaying election posters in the society's shops for the local Labour candidate. He asked Cecil Copson, by then a shop manager, for his opinion 'and I told him in no uncertain manner what I thought about it'. The proposal was thrown out by the general committee:

> No posters for any election or anything was ever exhibited. . . . It used to be my argument . . . you can't advertise opposition to some of your best customers. As I say, some of the best customers were Conservatives, and known Conservatives.[56]

Another former branch manager agreed that you could not mix business and politics. You had to be 'very careful in shops of saying what you are [politically], because you had to run with the fox and hunt with the hounds. . . . If it was a

Conservative person, you tended to be pleased with their side a bit and if it was Labour you done the other. . . . To keep the customers happy, that was the main thing'.[57]

In more recent times, political involvement and the women's guild branch faded away. Merger with the Leicester society and its much stronger tradition of political activity failed to avert this decline. Only 'one or two people from this area . . . was interested in the political side, especially in the Co-op Party'. In June 1973 the Leicester Co-operative society held celebrations for 'International Co-operation' and asked all social groups outside Leicester to do their own thing. In Market Harborough, the Young Wives Group arranged a disco in the Co-op Hall and 'everyone seemed to enjoy themselves'.[58]

## LOCAL LOYALTIES

While it was an independent society, Harborough was part of the Kettering and Wellingborough Co-operative district. Until recently, much closer ties were maintained with the small and medium-sized societies of north-west Northamptonshire than those of south Leicestershire. Local educational and political conferences were often hosted by the societies at Kettering or Wellingborough, the latter being an active centre for co-operation: 'It was Kettering, Wellingborough, Rushden and that district. . . . Although we were in Leicestershire, we was on the border . . . and the majority of the business was done that side [i.e. Northamptonshire]'.

Before 1969, most of the society's supplies came through the CWS depot at Northampton. Twice a year there was a sales day when 'the managers from this area used to meet at Northampton' and place orders with reps from the different CWS factories. After amalgamation in 1969 Harborough was supplied via Leicester, though the Leicestershire society was itself part of a larger Co-operative buying group based in Birmingham.[59]

The Leicestershire Co-operative Society continued to expand after 1969. In the north of the county Barrow-on-Soar and Shepshed & Hathern Co-operatives joined in 1972 and 1973 respectively. The late 1970s saw the reforging of Kettering's link with Harborough, when that society also merged with Leicestershire Co-op. Rothwell followed suit a few years later. And finally in 1985 the South Leicestershire Society (a grouping of small societies including Wigston, Fleckney and Great Glen) gave up its former independence.[60]

Of the major societies in the county only Hinckley did not join Leicestershire. 'They were very disappointed that Hinckley didn't join them, because Hinckley was a very strong Society.' Instead it went into the East Mercia Co-op.[61] Being part of Leicestershire Co-op meant Harborough could benefit from the buying power of a large organization and draw on their resources for the changes ahead. The 1970s was a period of adjustment for the Harborough area, as the society set about streamlining the divisions to make itself more competitive:

> The idea behind the whole scheme was to close the 'pantry shops' and increase the central premises in the more populated areas to superstores, as we now know them . . . for the simple reason . . . they could retail the commodities much cheaper than they could by keeping the small shop on. Although I don't know whether there was any of the smaller shops were losing money or not.[62]

In the 1970s Harborough shed its village and town 'pantry shops' until only Kibworth and Lutterworth were left of the former eleven branches. Retailing also became increasingly concentrated on food and electrical goods, with the closure of the menswear and ladieswear shops on Coventry Road, and the building of a supermarket on the High Street site in Market Harborough in 1979.[63]

In the 1980s the tide turned once more and smaller stores came back into fashion. By 1986 the remaining branch shops were being remodelled as convenience stores, open from 8 a.m. to 8 p.m. to serve their local communities. 'The idea of "eight-to-eight" is to be open when everybody else is shut.' The system also put more stress on the old role of the small shop being a general store and not just selling food. One store where the 'eight-to-eight' system was run successfully was at Kibworth, which was open twelve hours a day, six days a week. The shops in the Harborough area were also upgraded. A new supermarket was built at Lutterworth in 1986 and the Kibworth store was expanded. Finally, an inevitable move to modernization came when the Co-op in Market Harborough relocated to the Coventry Road superstore after nearly a century at the central premises in the High Street.[64]

## *Chapter Seven*

# The Grocery Trade

*It is food you are handling and you will handle it like fine gold.*
(Instruction to young provisions hand, about 1933)

*Anything you could think of, it was in a tin or a packet.*
(Grocery manager working in the 1950s[1])

Since 1900 the high street has seen two retailing revolutions: the rapid spread of multiple or chain stores in the early part of the century and, from the 1950s, the introduction of self-service and the supermarket. In both cases, national organizations were to have a profound effect on the town's shops and shoppers, and both revolutions have been felt nowhere more acutely than in the grocery and provision trades.

In 1881 there were only six grocery or provision dealers in Market Harborough: five independent retailers and the still small Co-operative Society. By contrast, there were thirty-one grocers' shops in the villages within a ten-mile radius of the town. In the later years of the nineteenth century, country people relied on the village shops for the necessities of life. The arrival of multiple stores was to begin a process of greater dependence on town shops that has been completed in the last twenty years by widespread access to a motor car.

Of the five independent grocers trading in the 1880s, the longest established was T.G. Goward at 18 High Street (Gateway supermarket in 1994). Goward's had been in the same premises for at least fifty years, since T.G. Goward's father established the business there in 1810. In 1871 Goward lived over the shop in a large household that included his wife and three daughters, three of his shopmen and two domestic servants. In common with many other prosperous shopkeepers, he was later to move out to a villa in Victoria Avenue.[2]

Thomas Goodwin Goward was typical of the Victorian grocer and provision merchant. In a warehouse behind the shop, his staff blended tea, ground coffee, chopped sugar, ground spices, and washed and polished dried fruit for sale in the shop. He was also a wholesale supplier to smaller shops. Goward's trade was principally with the middle and upper classes of the town. A description of his trade in 1892 stressed the grocer's knowledge of his wares and his buying skills:

> The premises consist of a double-fronted shop in High Street, with extensive warehouses behind . . . tea takes the lead with its many qualities adapted to many tastes and its many

prices suited to many means. Mr Goward's teas are highly appreciated. He himself is a connoisseur, and his selections are decidedly good value and excellent in flavour; the other beverages, coffee and cocoa, are from the best houses and full of richness and fragrance . . . we cannot overlook the fine display of foreign [dried] fruits, the choicest varieties of which appear to be on hand . . . this is a speciality of the establishment . . . Huntley and Palmer's biscuits, H. & A. Gilbey's wines and spirits, the finest tinned and potted delicacies, all prove that the proprietor makes it his study to be abreast of the times by having on hand the best of everything which comes within the compass of his business, thereby commanding the satisfaction and confidence of his customers. (*Market Harborough Illustrated*, 1892)

Fred Tuffs worked at Goward's while still at school in 1908, when the shop still appears to have been run in very similar fashion:

When I was 12 years old, a boy said he was leaving Goward's. He got half-a-crown a week, so I went and applied for the job and got it. . . . I was errand boy, just errand boy . . . picking grass out of the cobbles up the yard and rubbing currants, coffee grinding. . . . I used to be there from eight o'clock in the morning until about ten minutes to nine, just get up to school for nine o'clock. Then from twelve till one and I used to nip home for dinner and then

Goward's grocery shop, High Street, Market Harborough, 1892. Goward's were one of the leading grocery and provision dealers in the town at the turn of the century and boasted establishment around 1810

> I went from about five till seven and on a Saturday night I was there till ten o'clock. . . . They used to get big boxes of oranges come in, which we used to have to get unwrapped and put out for show. We always used to roll two big cheeses out, one either side of the doorway, just in the doorway on the top of the step. . . . Christmas time they never rolled the cheeses in from the front door until twelve o'clock [midnight]. . . . They had to be [well turned-out] because they used to get a lot of the posh people of the town would deal with Goward's.[3]

The other grocer of consequence in the town towards the end of the century was Symington & Thwaites, on the corner of St Mary's Road and Adam & Eve Street. This was to become the 'Fortnum & Mason' of Market Harborough in the first half of the twentieth century, the town's premier grocer and provisions dealer until taken over around 1960 by Fine Fare, by which time it had become part of the Burton chain.

Symington & Thwaites was founded by Samuel Symington, the third of the entrepreneurial Symington brothers to make their way south to Harborough from Scotland by the middle of the last century. Samuel Symington worked as a commercial traveller for his brother William's tea and coffee business until 1877, when he struck out on his own with a wholesale and manufacturing concern in premises behind 7 Adam & Eve Street (Hamblin Racing in 1994). He took over the premises of Thomas Flavell, grocer, druggist, tallow chandler, tea and coffee dealer, who had occupied the shop until his death around 1858. In 1892 Samuel Symington's business remained in existence as G. Thwaites & Co., manufacturing baking powders, egg, custard and blancmange powders, ginger beer powder, bread crumbs or 'raspings', and the 'Aesthetic' rinsing powder for fixing colours to printed materials.[4]

In 1877 Walter Symington, Samuel's son, entered the retail grocery trade and took the shop at the front of 7 Adam & Eve Street. The following year he entered into partnership with George Thwaites, the son of a Norfolk parson, and founded the business which was to be, as Symington & Thwaites, an enduring feature of the town for over ninety years. In its early years, like other grocers, the shop carried a broad range of stock, including groceries, provisions, patent medicines, tinned goods, fruits and brushes. In 1892 it was likened to the Army and Navy Stores as a general supply warehouse:

> The great object Messrs Symington and Thwaites keep in view is to provide the community with a good article at store prices. To this end they maintain a big and comprehensive stock of goods, embracing everything that is likely to be enquired for in the way of groceries, provisions, patent medicines and general domestic requisites . . . the internal arrangements of Messrs Symington and Thwaites stores are so complete and their counter assistants so well up to their work that 'waiting' is practically unknown at this establishment, whilst orders are received, made up and dispatched to all parts of the town by regular deliveries. (*Market Harborough Illustrated*, 1892)

In 1894, Symington & Thwaites moved down to the corner of Adam & Eve Street and St Mary's Road, into new purpose-built premises designed by George Isaac of Coventry. These comprised a large L-shape, a three-storey brick structure on the street frontage which housed the shop and a warehouse at right-angles to the rear. This included a bacon drying room, packing room, mixing room, stock room, lift and tea room. The shop was entered from a door on the street corner. The shop front itself was divided into six large display windows, four of which faced onto Adam & Eve Street. It was moulded, faced with raised decorative panels and headed by a deep fascia on which ornate back-painted glass signs proclaimed it as 'Symington & Thwaites', 'Family Grocer' and 'Consumers Stores'.[5]

Symington & Thwaites moved upmarket in the early years of this century, presumably in the face of growing competition from the multiple stores by then arriving in the town. For many years the shop traded on high quality, a remarkable service and a large and varied stock. Mr Hubert Reeve started with Symington & Thwaites as a shop assistant in 1923, after previously working at the Star Supply Stores, an early multiple in Church Street:

> Symington & Thwaites [had] a mahogany counter top, always clean and polished. Everything about the place was first-class. We used to wear an apron and later years we had a white jacket.
>
> I was serving in the shop, five-and-a-half days a week on the grocery counter. I think I was paid 32*s* 6*d* . . . there must have been twenty of us in the shop, twenty-four. . . . There was eight of us in the shop [itself]. There was two on the bacon counter and then six getting orders upstairs – they did nothing but get orders up – then there was two men permanently in the warehouse . . . then there was two men on the vans delivering continually.
>
> When I first went there everything was weighed; sugar, tea, butter, lard, dried fruit, glacé cherries – that was a nice job – and of course we had our own blends of coffee, blended for us by the coffee people but to our blend. They roasted it and we had it fresh every week and we ground it as people wanted it.
>
> A bit later I used to go out travelling in the town. I used to go out two, three days a week getting the orders, then I had to come back and get them up and then a bit later on still I started on the country round. First off it was just round Dingley. I used to go up to Dingley Hall when Earl Beatty lived there. I had an order from there that filled the big van and I had to take it up specially. Then there was all the village and Brampton [Ash]. I used to push-bike, then I went to Arthingworth and Oxendon. . . . It was always 'Good Morning' or 'Good Afternoon'. They were all regular customers, there was no patter at all but I just went in and sat down and they paid the bill for the past fortnight's groceries . . . then they told us what they wanted and I kept suggesting other things, anything I thought they might want. No sales patter, we didn't need that. You got to know the people, you'd talk about their children or something like that you see.[6]

Symington & Thwaites, on the corner of Adam & Eve Street and St Mary's Road, Market Harborough, with shop and staff alike decorated for the coronation of Edward VII in 1902. This shop was the 'Fortnum & Mason' of the town for the first half of the century. Note one of the shop's horse-drawn delivery vans on the left and the six gas lights illuminating the windows

Mrs Gladys Wimlett (née Sharpe) left school at thirteen in 1917 and started with Symington & Thwaites. The firm had been obliged by the shortage of men during the First World War to take female assistants into what had been largely a male preserve up to 1914:

I went on my own, saw the bosses and got the job . . . father had worked there. . . . I worked there for about fifteen years. . . . The head was Mr George Thwaites and then the next in charge was Walter Symington, then Mr Allen; he had worked since he was a boy in the business and he was made a partner, and he and Mr Sumpter were in the shop. Mr Thwaites just came in the office daily, you know, just to see things were OK. . . . Mr Allen, he would take the first customer, then we'd go for anyone else that came in.

My first duties were everything had to be marked off in those days, the cost and the selling price. Even on the cans of sardines we used to have to scratch the prices on those, that was an awful job, the cost price and the selling price . . . they were a bit oily. . . . The customer wouldn't know what the cost price was because it was a special one in code.

Then I was in the Order Room. . . . It was quite a big place. We used to go up in the lift . . . and bring the stuff down with us. Did some heavy work really, filling fixtures, filling drawers with rice and all the cereals, and brought them down in the lift. About half a dozen women worked there and I was the youngest. . . . They had a big order trade in those days, family orders and, as I say, the big halls, and women mostly worked on the orders. When my father came back from the wars, he worked in that room as manager.

Miss Sharpe later worked on the cash desk, which stood centrally at the back of the main shop:

The orders were taken over the counter, but the money was paid at the desk. . . . Giving the change, taking the money and cashing the cheques and when people came in to pay their monthly accounts, I used to take the money for that. . . . Well you sometimes had a little queue, especially on the Tuesday when they came in out of the villages. They'd make out a bill for them or they usually had monthly books, particularly the farmers. They had monthly books and they'd bring their order in, in their monthly book, and it would be done in the shop if they weren't too busy. If not it was sent upstairs [to the Order Room] to do. . . . The farmers were always trying to get discount off you when I was in the desk. 'How much are you going to take off?', knock off, you know. Don't think they were lucky though.[7]

Mrs Olive Reeve started with Symington & Thwaites in 1932 when Lennard's shoe shop next door on St Mary's Road was taken and knocked through into the main shop to create a 'fancy department':

I had all the fancy stuff, I had all the biscuits; I carried a hundred large tins of biscuits and fifty half tins and just a few packets. Not many packets in those days, just Crawford's Cream Crackers and Jacob's Cream Crackers and Popular Assorted in Jacob's. All the others were loose biscuits. . . . Then I had all the fancy boxes of biscuits and chocolates, and as Christmas came round, the crackers. We had a wonderful sale of these. . . . One end of my shop was all stacked with tins of fruit. . . . We had Andy's Candies, a beautiful selection of sweets and chocolates . . . and we had Quality Street, all those different ones and all glass cases to show them in.

It was a long shop and all one side were fixtures; half of it was full of biscuits, five or six tins high. . . . Then in front of these biscuit fixtures was two long glass cases, the first with a small narrow counter at the back and scales, and I had all the slab cake inside and all the packet stuff on the top, and the next glass case I had all chocolates and sweets and all fancy bits. On the right-hand side were two long cases where I had all cake decorations.[8]

Mr Les Buswell went to work in the order department at Symington & Thwaites in 1933:

At that time, Symington & Thwaites was *the* grocery and provision merchants of the town. They used to supply – not so much counter customers you get now – they were nearly all delivery . . . so the biggest part of their trade was done not in the shop but upstairs where there was a despatch department. . . . It was reckoned to be a good trade to learn in those days and to learn a trade the best place to do it, they said, was at a place like Symington & Thwaites.

In those days we used to weigh all our sugar up by hand, so we had two hundredweight bags of sugar to manhandle into the department from downstairs in the lift, weighing up sugar for hours on end, weighing up rice, weighing up fruit. All the fruit was loose and it was all cleaned, currants, sultanas, prunes. . . . The man who cleaned the fruit used to get his boxes of fruit and put it all through a sieve to get the stalks off . . . moisten the hands with syrupy water, you know, to polish them, polished, all the fruit was done like that to make them shiny. . . . All the tea had to be wrapped in a special wrapper in a certain shape in a certain way with string, same with coffee. Lots and lots of different blends of teas were all loose in big japanned containers and they all had to be weighed up.

They didn't just go to a big hall and collect the order . . . often they would have the housekeeper or the butler come to the shop and they'd be taken down the cellar with a cheese-iron – they'd bring their own cheese-iron – and go down in the cellar. The firm used to buy all the prize-winning Stilton cheeses . . . butlers and so forth would come and choose their wines.

There were certain things laid down: everyone had to wear an apron with a frill, white apron with a frill and the directors wore black alpaca jackets and the other staff wore short white coats, and we had to do our own laundry.[9]

The traditional grocer, dealing in a broad range of goods and undertaking some manufacture, processing and packaging, for both a retail and wholesale market, began

Symington & Thwaites' branch shop on the Green, Great Bowden, *c.* 1938

to come under pressure from the competition of multiple stores from the end of the nineteenth century. A steady rise in real wages due to a fall in food prices had taken place in the last thirty years of the century. This brought a great increase in the effective demand for foodstuffs. Agricultural markets around the world had been opened up to British buyers. The development of effective refrigeration and the greater bulk of cargoes had resulted in a lowering of freight charges. Food manufacturing and processing had developed in response to the growing market; jellies, jams, relishes, pickles, ketchup, sauces, canned milk, meat extracts, canned meat, fruit and fish, and margarine all came onto the market in the second half of the last century.

The development of a food processing and packaging industry can also be illustrated through an example local to Market Harborough, William Symington, tea dealer and coffee roaster. The first of the Symington brothers to make his fortune in the town, William came south from Sanquhar, Dumfriesshire in 1827 and by 1835 was established as a grocer and tea dealer in Church Street. In the 1840s, William Symington appears to have concentrated on the wholesale tea and coffee trade, after briefly going into partnership with his brother James, then a clothier and stay maker in the same street. In 1846, William Symington was described as a travelling tea dealer and by 1850 he had established a small tea-blending and coffee-roasting business in Springfield Street, or Billy Boys Lane as it became known, presumably following the factory's steady growth on the site. The development of a patent process for preparing peas as pea flour and contracts to supply the War Office during the Crimean War (1853–6) with this means of making a thick nourishing soup from dried ingredients, proved the beginning of steady success.

Coffee roasting and blending remained William Symington's staple product. By 1870, the original Billy Boys Lane premises had been considerably extended and in 1881 the three-storey brick mill on the corner of Springfield Street and Northampton Road was built. It is still known today as 'the Coffee Mills', even though Symingtons have not produced coffee for many years. The 1891 edition of Mrs Beeton's *Everyday Cookery* advertised Symingtons' products as pea flour, pea soup, 'Egyptian Food' (a lentil preparation for invalids and children), 'Arab's Coffee' and 'Dandelion Coffee'. Both brands of coffee included chicory. By 1904, ten different branded coffee lines were advertised, together with patent prepared groats, barley, oatmeal and flaked oats, although tea would seem to have been dropped from the product range by this date.[10]

This range of dried and instant preparations continued to expand in the early years of this century, including table creams, a granulated gravy improver, custard powder, table jellies, blancmange mix and lemonade crystals. Symington table creams are still made today. By 1907, Symingtons had thirty-five commission agents covering the country and were heavily engaged in national advertising of its lines. In 1919 coffee production ceased and the firm henceforth relied upon

Bill head for W. Symington & Co.

powdered soups and its other dried products. Symington's still occupy much expanded factory premises on the original site in Northampton Road and Springfield Street. In 1987 they were part of the Imperial Foods group and made a range of powdered soups, table creams, gravy mixes, most of which were sold as own-label brands by major retailers such as Sainsbury's.

The growth and success of William Symington's dried and prepared branded products was a modest part of the nationwide development of food packaging and processing in the second half of the nineteenth century. In effect the grocer's traditional skills in buying, preparing and packaging raw materials for the shopper were transferred to the factory. Here the maufacturer mechanized some processes, gained price advantage by buying in large bulk and made steady inroads on the seasonality of goods through canning, salting and drying. Combined with a real rise in working-class wages as the century progressed, the new branded packaged goods brought about a revolutionary change in the organization of the grocery and provision trade. This was to be manifested in the creation and rapid spread of the multiple store.

From around 1880, the number of firms operating multiple stores grew in number rapidly, as did the number of stores in each chain. Several very large firms catering for a national market came rapidly to prominence. By 1890, the International Tea Company had over 200 stores, Home & Colonial passed 200 stores in 1895, closely followed by Lipton's, the Star Tea Company and the Maypole Dairy Company by 1900. By 1910, each of these companies controlled over 300 stores and by 1920, together with the Meadow Dairy Company, each had an empire of over 400 stores. Beneath these large national organizations were also to be found smaller chains of stores with a local or regional coverage.

The early multiple chain stores were of two main types. The International Tea Co., and Hunter's Stores, for example, stocked a fair range of standard grocery items. Other stores, such as those of the Maypole Dairy, Lipton's and the Home & Colonial, quite deliberately specialized in an extremely limited range of tea and provisions: coffee, butter, margarine, bacon and eggs. Both types of concern bought in great bulk, especially from importers, but were also involved in food manufacture and processing. The Maypole Dairy, for example, had their own creameries and margarine factories and their stores stocked originally only tea, butter, margarine and eggs. Just before the First World War, over three-quarters of the trade of the Maypole's 800 or so branches was in margarine alone. The early national multiples, with the exception of the International, 'specialized in distributing a limited range of products in bulk through a large number of outlets and at an absolute minimum of cost and service'.[11]

The first multiple stores were small, characterized by a single counter, standard fascia and the company's name over the shop-front. They sold goods strictly for cash, backed by national advertising campaigns. Service rarely extended to home delivery. In areas where the Co-op was strong, the multiples were obliged to offer a dividend to compete. Multiple stores' customers were drawn almost exclusively from the working classes.

Selling cheap food at low prices for cash was a potent strategy which the new multiples exploited sucessfully in the late nineteenth century to meet an increasing demand from working-class consumers. Price competition (or 'price cutting' as it was pejoratively known) in the grocery trade thus spread from town to town on the heels of the regional and national multiple grocery stores.

Multiple stores came relatively late to smaller towns such as Market Harborough. The first grocery multiple to open a branch in the town was the London & Midland Stores. In 1898 the firm, which had over a hundred branches nationally, acquired Belton Bros' shop in Church Street (in 1994 the Harborough Gas façade still retains the Belton Bros' shop-front). Competition soon became rife among Harborough grocers. The dividend paid by the local Co-operative Society fell steadily as a result and by 1901 the society's officials were complaining bitterly of reduced grocery profits: 'Our Grocery Department having to compete against some of the most cutting traders we find in existence in any town has not been able to make the profit we anticipated it doing'. The Harborough Co-op's predicament

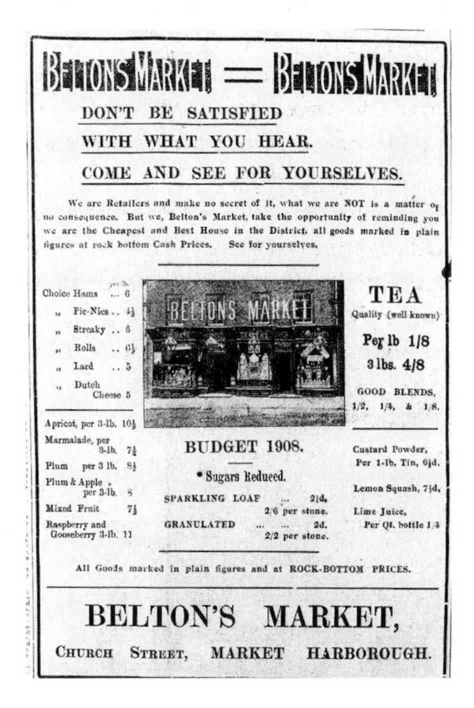


Newspaper advertisement for Belton's Market in Church Street, Market Harborough, 1908. This was one of the first grocers in the town to adopt the chain stores' retailing methods, with elaborate shop-front and competitive prices on a relatively limited range of lines. The shop prided itself on being the cheapest in the area

was more than a touch ironic since their own trade had been built up partly through the attraction of the discounts that their dividend represented.

The London & Midland Stores did not stay the course, disappearing from Market Harborough after only a few years trading. Price competition continued however and by 1903 Belton's were back in business and making the following promise: 'Belton's Market is the People's Provider. No Advance in Prices. Goods Marked in Plain Figures. Why Pay More?' It would appear that Belton's, like the multiples, was competing on price across a limited range of lines – teas, hams, lard, cheese, butter, sausages and pork pies. By 1915 there was also a Belton's Market in nearby Rothwell.[12]

Price wars have been a recurring feature of the British grocery trade in the twentieth century. Multiple firms established themselves in the national market by selling cheap and growing in size. As they grew they found it necessary to stock steadily wider ranges of goods and to give better service until they in turn became vulnerable to competition from newcomers who undercut them on price. Successful firms were also prone to takeover by larger competitors.

This characteristic business cycle has been reflected in the history of Market Harborough's grocery stores over the past century. Successive incoming multiple firms: Star Supply, Melia's, Premier, Fine Fare, Tesco, Kwik Save, all sought to undercut existing grocers in the town, whether multiples or private traders, with varying degrees of success. Tesco for instance was supreme at piling it high and selling it cheap in the 1970s but moved steadily upmarket in the 1980s. Kwik Save arrived in the 1980s and proved that low prices could still generate a sufficient turnover. Operating out of the former cinema in Northampton Road, the shop resembled a cash-and-carry warehouse rather than a modern supermarket.

The distinctive methods of the 'company stores' in their early days were explained by a former employee. Mr Reeve was apprenticed at Smith's in St Mary's Road, an independent grocer, before going to work at the Star Supply Store, one of the huge Star Tea Company chain, around 1920:

> It was different. It was what you might call a poor people's shop, and they cut prices, but they cut quality as well. That wasn't what I should call a good shop. And it was quick profits, extra profit, all they could get: 'If you cut a pound of bacon, give 'em a little bit short and charge 'em a penny too much', that was the idea. Because you see, all that stuff was charged to them [the shop] at retail price and there was no allowance for waste, so he'd got to make money to keep himself clear.
>
> [The Manager was a] man named Flint. . . . He was all right but he'd always been in company shops and he'd got company shops' ideas. There was only three of us, the manager, I was on the bacon counter and there was a girl on the grocery counter. It wasn't a big trade. Bacon was from Latvia. In those days, it used to come very cheap. Lard was

> all imported; you could get home-rendered lard but not at Star Supply. . . . There used to be a lot of Canadian cheese and then New Zealand cheese.[13]

The Star Tea Company had arrived in Market Harborough around 1902, opening a double-fronted shop on The Square (No. 17, a YMCA charity shop in 1994). Towards the end of the First World War, the company moved into the former Belton's premises in Church Street. This move may have been the result of a takeover, since the Star Supply chain achieved quick growth through the acquisition of smaller regional and local firms.

> The firm was a big one, but it wasn't a particularly big shop. Of course, before Star Supply, it was Belton's Market and he [Mr Belton] was a local man, lived at Farndon, and he was a proper go-ahead chap, and he had everything fresh and nice and good quality, but when Star took it, well, they had their own methods.[14]

Multiple stores began to affect the retail pattern of grocery and provisions in Harborough substantially only after the First World War. Home & Colonial opened

The Star Supply Stores on The Square, Market Harborough, *c.* 1902. This was one of the first grocery multiples in the town. Note the model window displays and their emphasis on prices

at 63 High Street and Lipton's at 8 High Street. By 1932 there was also a Maypole Dairy at 1 Church Square (Lord's in 1994) while a smaller chain, Melia's, were briefly at 6 The Square, adjacent to Wood's the drapers. A former Co-op employee remembered stiff competition from Melia's:

> That was a cheap shop, a real cheap shop. They were selling cake, I think it was a seed-cake, at *4d* a pound, it was unbelievable! And the fruit they had, like the currants and prunes and those sorts of things, was so much cheaper than what ours was. Mind you, they wasn't the quality of other people's. They were a real cheap shop, but they didn't last in Harborough . . . didn't last for long.

In the face of competition and falling food prices in the recession years after 1921, the well-established multiples were obliged to compete on service and facilities to win custom. Improved shops with tiled floors, marble-topped counters, bacon slicers, cash registers and display windows were introduced, a broader range of lines offered to the customer and dividends, deliveries and even credit thrown in too. More home-grown produce was sold to escape the poor quality which for the middle classes had stigmatized 'foreign' food.

Mr W. Ingram worked for the Maypole Dairy Company for sixteen years from 1925, mostly in their branch at Kettering but also as relief manager at Market Harborough. When he started, the Maypole stocked only five products, butter, margarine, tea, eggs and condensed milk. Like the other specialized multiples, the Maypole was obliged to broaden its range between the wars, to include jams, cheese, tinned fruit, cake, marmalade and sugar. Mr Ingram remembers trade in the 1920s and '30s at Kettering being so poor, that they took on country rounds and home deliveries to bring in orders. His experience was typical of practice in specialist multiples between the wars:

> First job that came up was errand boy at the Maypole at Kettering, 10*s* a week and that's how I started. . . . All the Maypoles were run on exactly the same line. . . . They were nearly all the same, green and gold, and green tiles on the front underneath. . . . The main speciality was Maypole butter, which was Danish and then the margarines and tinned milk, and as they gradually introduced the other things . . . 'May Queen' [margarine] was I think a shilling a pound, that'd got butter in it, but at one period when things were so bad they even introduced a margarine at *4d* a pound. That was for the benefit of people in poverty. There just wasn't the money, shoe factories were on short time.
>
> It was mainly New Zealand butter. It used to come in boxes about 56 lb and then the Danish butter used to come in like casks, hundredweights [112 lb]. They used to be all cut up in the warehouse [behind the shop]. You'd tip it out and you'd have these cheese wires and you'd wire it like you do cheese. Tea always came packeted. There was different prices of tea. 'Red Label' was the Maypole tea, the popular tea and we used to have one a

little bit dearer than that, 'Mikado' in a silvery packet. 'Red Label' was *7d* a quarter I think and then we had some cheaper at *6d* a quarter and *5d* a quarter. . . . The only thing we used to weigh up was the butter, margarine and the cheese. We used to have a cheeseboard and wire the cheese, according to what kind of pieces people wanted, and you might wire a few pieces up spare, you see, and put a bit round them and try and tempt somebody with a piece of cheese.

We opened at half-past eight but you had to be there a few minutes before, get upstairs, change, and you had to be on the counter in your coat and apron ready for your first customer at half-past eight. The first thing you'd do, you'd clear the blocks and start getting butter and marge, get it all into the blocks, and beaters and shears, get them in and all ready to start. . . . Get a little bit of a lull, you'd get one or two pounds or half-pounds ready and then if a customer came you'd have some ready.

We called them 'blocks'; like very thick slabs of slate, with marble sides, a marble front and a marble top, and you used to knock the marge and butter up on there. We always used to have a bottle of water, because every now and then you'd got to sprinkle a few spots on the slab, otherwise you'd have it stick. That's why the tools always had to be in cold water and then when you handle it, it never stuck to anything. . . . At Kettering we had four blocks, one for one butter, one for the other butter and then two for different margarines. There'd be three or four sets of scales. There'd be like a porcelain plate and then you'd got your weights on the other side. The greaseproof paper was very, very thin. You cut the butter and marge out and put it on the scale and it had got to be exactly right; you'd put a bit on or take a bit off. If you didn't do that, you'd never get your weight, you might get a few ounces or a quarter pound to spare, because every block that came in, when it was taken out of the case it was always weighed and you had to get it exactly right. Woe betide you if an inspector came along and weighed it. What we always used to say was 'just but not generous'.

But the first thing, every woman that came in, you always greeted them, 'Serve you madam please?' Nobody was allowed to be kept waiting. You'd got to give first class service. . . . People would know what they wanted, they'd come in, they'd ask for half a pound of butter and they'd mention one or two things, and when the customer had finished then you'd suggest . . . . You never refused a customer, even if you had to take half the window out, and that's been done many a time! If you got so low on goods, a certain line, and there were still one or two in the bottom of the window, you'd take half the window out to get it. You never missed a sale if it was possible.

I did a lot of window dressing. We used to have half hundredweights standing in the window and we used to make up 'fancies', there'd be the imprint of a swan or something else. . . . But the summer was awful. Get a heatwave and sometimes you might get one start collapsing, but you always had to show it in the window. We had to do a lot of heavy lifting. We'd got a box to stand on to lean down into the window, it was all marble.

Bob Shaw, First Hand, outside the Maypole Dairy at 50 High Street, Kettering, *c.* 1929

> Head officer or inspectors, they'd pass it on to the managers, what they wanted them to do to try and increase sales of this or that. Bank holidays and Christmas we had what they called specials. That was all over every Maypole. Tinned fruit; you'd got to sell as much tinned fruit as you possibly could. It was push, push, push. Cake used to come in these seven pound slabs and we'd get a big knife and we used to cut it up and put a bit of greaseproof paper round, and we used to stand pieces of cake on pots of jam or tins of fruit; 'Nice piece of cake today madam?', all that kind of thing.[15]

As the number of multiple stores grew steadily between the wars, the number of independent grocers stayed fairly static. Despite fears to the contrary, the independent shopkeeper proved remarkably resilient, although they were to be found increasingly in secondary shopping areas in the suburbs and side streets of residential areas, rather then in prime high street sites.

The independent grocer's principal advantage over the multiple stores was credit. Both the Co-op and the multiples preferred to trade for cash. The independent shopkeeper could offer credit on a monthly or longer basis to his more prosperous or valued customers or until pay-day at the end of the week for those short of money.

The giving of credit was, however, a source of constant difficulty for the shopkeeper and bad debts were the inevitable drawback of the service.

Branded and pre-packed goods demanded less technical skill to present and sell, and they received extensive national advertising from the manufacturers. Between the wars the practice of resale price maintenance limited the numbers of lines in which price competition was possible. By 1938, one third of the total sales by independent retailers were subject to resale price maintenance. This benefited the independent shopkeeper in competing with the large multiples.[16] 'A lot of the prices were more or less fixed. Supposing it was Chivers "Old English Marmalade", that would be advertised in the papers. For years it never altered, at 8*d* a pound and 1*s* 3*d* for two pounds.'[17]

In these circumstances, the rate of decline of the smaller grocer was slowed and the 'differentiation between shops came to be related as much to the range and quality of services provided as to the type and price of goods sold'.[18] As in the example of the Kettering Maypole store, the depressed conditions of the 1930s led multiples to seek to compete as much on service as on price.

There were seven independent grocers in the town in 1900, eight in 1912, six in 1922 and seven in 1941: C.H. Maycock in Abbey Street, F. Murkitt at 18 Church Street, R.A. Hodby at 30 Nelson Street, H.J. Monroe at 24 Leicester Road, Hensley Cobb at 90 Northampton Road, C.F. Lea at 33 St Mary's Road (present day number), Symington & Thwaites on Adam & Eve St and 1 St Mary's Road. Three were still sited in the town centre, with four in secondary locations.

Bill Wood's account of the service provided by C.F. Lea's at 15/17 St Mary's Road during the 1930s illustrates the resilience and high standards of the independent grocer of that period:

> I started there in about 1933. Most of the assistants in Lea's were grammar school boys and most had gone straight from school. I remember shopping as being a social occasion for customers. They would come in regularly, same time, same day. . . . Friday night, I could almost run through the customers now and the time they would come in. Well there was one lady would come in at half-past seven and take till gone eight to give her order and it would be delivered the same night, perhaps at ten o'clock. We had two errand boys and customers would ring up in the morning for one item, our regular customers would get on the telephone: 'I've run out of self-raising or plain flour and I haven't got any to make the Yorkshire, could you let me have some?' and we would send it. It would perhaps be only a shilling.
>
> They'd come into Lea's, they'd sit down on a chair at the counter and they would have an assistant who would take their grocery order – very few had a shopping list when they came in – they had the standard items and when they had given their order to a certain point and could think of no more, that is the time you came up with your salesmanship if you could. You were also expected to make suggestions to the customer, 'What could we have for tea?',

'Can you suggest something for lunch on Saturday?', and we would make a point of knowing the answers to these things so that we could help the customers. But a customer would come, the old Harborians, and perhaps sit there for half-an-hour giving their grocery order. You would show them things, you would let them try a new biscuit; there was always a new biscuit on the market, because biscuits were very competitive. . . . Another thing was they always sat in the same place in the shop when they came in and usually had the same assistant. . . . It seemed to fit into a pattern by itself; I think once you'd served somebody for a few times you naturally went and the other assistants wouldn't push in before you.

I think the first thing you were taught then was that the customer is always right; you would never argue with a customer. We had very few complaints but if we did have a complaint, anything, it was always taken back and changed. Our business was divided into two parts. We had the customers that came into the shop and some would take the things they wanted, but if it was a general grocery order, they gave their order that was assembled later and it was delivered to their house. And then we had, for the country and to a certain extent the town, we had two travellers and they would go to the houses and take grocery orders. These were then brought back and the next day put together in the shop and delivered the following day. At Lea's we went as far as Creaton, Cottesbrooke, Thornby, the Langtons, Wilbarston [approximately 8–10 miles from Market Harborough].

The tea was good. It was weighed out on scales and wrapped in a flat paper. We did have it, in later years, packed. It was a flat paper, shiny blue with a greaseproof paper

St Mary's Road, Market Harborough, 1930s. C.F. Lea's grocery shop can be seen on the corner with Mill Hill Road

lining. Now coffee, that was roasted twice a day and it was ground as it was purchased in an electric coffee machine. You would ask them how they would like it, fine or coarse, and they would select the grade they wanted and you would grind them a quarter of coffee and that would be weighed on these beautiful brass beam scales, all highly polished. There's two things that were impressed upon you from day one. One, that the customer is always right and I always remember the phrase that Ernest Clark used with me: 'It is food you are handling and you will handle it like fine gold'. If we cut a pound of bacon on the bacon machine and put it onto the scale, you put it on the scale, you don't flop it onto the scales. . . . Not at Lea's; you take each slice off and you lay it on greaseproof paper and you pick it up and place it on the scales and you say, 'That is a pound and half-an-ounce, will that be all right madam?', and if she said, 'No, I want a pound', you would say 'Very well, it is a pound'. You wouldn't take it off. Ninety-nine per cent of people say 'Yes it's perfectly all right'.

Well, it was a sort of pride how well you could wrap things. No one was ever allowed to take a bottle out of the shop unless it had been wrapped in white paper. For a lot of things we used to make those little cones out of a flat sheet of paper, pepper and the smaller things, and put an ounce of pepper on, which was weighed on these big scales. You were always respectful to a customer but you were not expected to be subservient. Some we would call 'Mrs So-and-so', but the majority you would address as 'Madam', the gentlemen, if you knew them particularly well you would say 'Mister' and otherwise you would call them 'Sir'. Every customer you tried to make them feel they were the most important customer. Then if they were lucky enough to have a motor car, you would put them in a box and take it out to the car for them. If they didn't, no one would dream, as my wife does now, of walking round the town with a trolley and coming back and lifting it in the car. That would be delivered; no charge for the delivery, it was just part of the service a high-class grocer or any other trade would give. . . . A high-class grocery and provision merchant, their trade was built on service and quality, and once the customer was satisfied, they kept dealing with you.[19]

Relations between shopkeeper and customer were radically altered by the strictures of rationing during the last war. For many of our respondents, things were never the same again, even when rationing was finally removed in 1954. For over fourteen years, from January 1940 to July 1954, customers had been obliged to register with a single grocer, whose stock had been severely limited and whose staff had become progressively less skilled as apprenticed and trained men went away to war to be replaced by inexperienced and untrained assistants. By the time a more normal state of affairs was resumed in the 1950s, the world of shops and shopkeeping had changed. Self-service and supermarket shopping were just around the corner, people were more mobile and perhaps the tradition of mutual trust remembered by Bill Wood and many others had been irreparably damaged by rationing and social change:

During the war a customer was registered with a grocer and that's where you had your supplies from because his supplies were dependent on the number of registered customers that he'd got. When you get this element of compulsion, well, I think it gets taken advantage of doesn't it. You've got to deal with us, but it wasn't like that before the war. . . . Ladies with no grocery training at all were serving in the shop and the relationship with customers had changed. Whereas the customer was always right, in times of shortage the customer was rather in the begging position, 'Could you spare me so-and-so?' A different type of shopping had been born.

After the war you didn't need your skills. You only needed your skills after the war for bacon and cheese. Other stuff used to be all done for you [i.e. pre-packed]. And now you don't need your skills for bacon and cheese . . . I mean, it was unheard of to see a woman behind the counter, or not very often, before the war. We had one. But after the war, they were all women in the grocery shops.[20]

Mr F.W. Lee followed Bill Wood as apprentice at C.F. Lea's and then after the Second World War worked at Symington & Thwaites. He was assistant manager in 1950 when the business was taken over by Joseph Burton & Son Ltd, a high-class grocery and provisions chain of over a hundred shops based in Nottingham and he was later manager when Fine Fare in turn took over the store around 1960. Mr Lee was in an excellent position to describe the radical changes in this counter-service, high-class grocer's shop wrought by the second revolution in retailing:

Symington's was a bigger concern [than C.F. Lea's] and very high class. Burton's took it over in the 1950s and kept it that way and expanded it. When Fine Fare took it, that was it, they ruined it. The 1950s saw the end of high-class grocery firms . . . Burton's were one of the first in the country 'supermarketing'. Their Market Harborough shop became the first self-service store in the town around 1958, with three checkouts. Head office decided on commercial policy, right down to promotions and sale items. They had a fortnightly promotion in each of their stores throughout the country with goods and prices supplied from head office.

The variety of tinned stuff that came after the war was amazing. Anything you could think of, it was in a tin or a packet. You had an order book for Burton's and you'd go round the warehouse filling it in. Send it off on a Friday to Nottingham and deliveries would come on Wednesdays. Everything was stored in that warehouse at Nottingham, you went outside for nothing except the foreign stuff which I used to buy direct from London myself. Our main competition in the 1950s was International [12 High Street]. We were on good terms with them. I knew the manager well, Fred Neville. . . . We used to borrow stuff from each other if we were short. . . . Best of terms really. There was no point in not being. Then you see there was only Burton's and International really, and the Co-op – they didn't count! Burton's were very successful until Premier came, where Gateway now is,

> then the price war started. . . . They started cutting and then of course things changed . . . and Premier were creaming the trade off. People were money conscious in the '50s. They wanted it cheap and of course trade was going downhill [at Burton's], that's when the rot started. . . . Then of course Fine Fare took it over and they competed with Premier, cutting it, International the same. . . . We stopped delivering . . . then Tesco came into the town and that was the end of Fine Fare.[21]

Mrs Margaret Prince worked at Lipton's small store at 8 High Street from 1959 to 1964 and saw the changeover to self-service:

> They'd always had to ask for what they wanted, never been allowed to touch as such and suddenly you were free to pick and choose, and change your mind. . . . If you see something cheaper or better further along, you can put the other back, whereas if you started that in shops [like Lipton's] you were considered a nuisance and we avoided them the next time. I was always on the provisions side and perhaps another girl would be on the other [grocery] side. You really did like people to shop one side and then move on to the other. Sometimes we'd say, 'I'm sorry, Madam, that's on the other side'. . . . You'd get the one [customer] who'd say, 'Well, when I was in last week, she served me, she got it for me', meaning, 'You needn't think you can come that with me![22]

The Tesco chain had grown up in London and the Home Counties, the creation of 'Jack' Cohen. He had started in the trade after the First World War, selling surplus NAAFI foodstuffs in London street markets. The first shop was opened in 1931 and by 1939 a chain of 100 stores had been built up, based on the pursuit of maximum turnover through low profit margins and prices. After the Second World War, Cohen pioneered self-service among the grocery multiples and, once rationing had been completely lifted in 1954, his new style of store made rapid progress, with the chain growing to 185 stores by 1959, of which 140 were self-service. In the 1960s the Tesco organization grew rapidly, mostly through take-overs and mergers. After taking over the rival Victor Value chain in 1968, Tesco was the fourth largest in Britain (after the Co-op, Fine Fare and Allied Suppliers), owning 834 stores.[23]

Victor Value had opened a new purpose-built supermarket on The Square in Market Harborough in 1966 and this became a Tesco store after the take-over in 1968. The store was expanded to its present selling area of 7,300 sq ft in 1973 by incorporating shops and a laundrette which had faced the Commons car-park. Just as the opening of Fine Fare had immediately put pressure on the existing multiple stores, which had been relatively small, so the new Tesco operation once again brought changes, spelling the end for the smaller multiple grocery stores in the town.

In 1967 Ken Wylie started work at Tesco's Lee Circle store in Leicester, then the largest shop-floor space in Europe. He was a general assistant, pricing goods, filling shelves and working at the checkouts. Only four years later, aged twenty-one, he became manager at Tesco's Market Harborough supermarket. He was well placed to describe the rapid rise of the Tesco chain since the 1960s and the changes in the company's approach as it moved away from the 'pile it high, sell it cheap' days on which its early success had been based:

> In those days I did the buying on the grocery, the butchery manager would order the meat, the provisions manager would order the pies and sausage, but that's changed now. We've actually got a stock controller in the business who's employed to look after all that. He'll come to me for guidance at times, but there's a basic formula that he has to follow and it's a matter of replenishing stock on a weekly basis . . . computers work at your weekly sales and replenish it on a daily basis when you go round your shop-floor. They start very early in the morning, they start at six. They scan the shop-floor [using a hand-held computer] before the store opens and the following day that order is in your store ready to put out by the night crew that night.
>
> In those days, it [supplies] was very much [a matter of] buying from suppliers and they delivered to the store. I would only get one head office vehicle a week and that was never full, it was a vehicle going to four or five stores. Now I get something in the region of ten vehicles, which is probably two a day. Nowadays the suppliers deliver into our central warehouse.
>
> Dealing with more reps, it meant that you were dealing with people all day long . . . and really all you did was sit upstairs. You really weren't looking after your business properly in my opinion. You were depending a lot on your people under you. Nowadays I very seldom see a representative. The stock controller would see a few in a week but the majority of it is done through a computer. So the rep's job is another thing that through our policies is a dying breed.
>
> Then [in the early 1970s], I would have said 70 per cent of your time was spent in the office, now it's 90 per cent out of it . . . [We were] carrying in those days an unbelievable amount of stock; our warehouses were always full and never necessarily of the right stock. I would think we probably held within the region of five weeks' stock. If you consider now, we don't hold more than a week's stock in any of our stores.[24]

In 1963, Tesco had followed Fine Fare and other supermarket chains in introducing trading stamps. The use of Green Shield stamps was seen as both a highly successful sales ploy (following American examples) as well as a roundabout way of cutting prices at a time when resale price maintenance limited the chains' scope in this direction.[25] Price maintenance was eliminated on all but books and pharmaceutical products following the Resale Prices Act of 1964. Tesco led the rest in their abandonment of trading stamps in favour of simple price cutting with the highly successful 'Checkout' campaign of 1977. Ken Wylie remembers its overnight success in the Market Harborough store:

> Green Shield stamps came along and that was another incentive to drive people into us. . . .

> You couldn't move on a Tuesday and Thursday . . . they were double-stamps days. It used to be half-day on a Wednesday and you had got to work all day on Wednesday to make sure you were right for double-stamps day on Thursday. . . . In Market Harborough, the week I actually gave up Green Shield stamps our turnover doubled. We took more on the day we opened [with 'Checkout'], a Tuesday, we took more on that day than the store had taken ever on the previous weeks. They came in and found everything was so cheap and they were literally buying not one packet but twelve. We worked from Saturday night when we shut right through to that Tuesday morning, never went home, just washed and put our suits on and opened up the door on Tuesday morning and by dinner time the shelves were absolutely gutted and it was like that for months and months afterwards. Macmarket, now Gateway, was very similar to us and they were charging as much as us but not giving the stamps, so when we took away the stamps . . . it meant we went far lower than any competitor. They had then to really think very quickly and change their whole trading policies. It was the beginning of the cut-price war and it's never stopped since.[26]

Since the early 1970s there have been considerable changes within the organization of large chain stores such as Tesco. Mr Wylie's early experiences as a store manager had in several important respects more in common with his predecessors between the wars than with the present role of the store manager. He saw manufacturers' representatives, ordered most of his stock direct and was in charge of all staff relations. Ted Ashby, his successor at Tesco in Market Harborough in 1987 did a quite different type of job:

> I would say there's as much skill and knowledge required nowadays to run a good fresh food operation as there was fifty or sixty years ago. Obviously it's far more technical now, with the computers in the business. Seventy per cent of our food ordering is now done by computer on a modem unit on the phone at the end of the night, having completed the stock counts and scans with the data unit. My responsibilities are to manage other people, to maintain the company policies regarding range and customer service, standards of cleanliness and hygiene, and a general standard which is acceptable to the public. Direct buying and pricing etc, that all comes under the umbrella of head office. We have ranges and different size stores have different ranges, that's the amount of products we are allowed to stock. The company works on the top 2,000 grocery lines on the market in Great Britain at this moment and that product range group is updated once a month. If something has dropped out of the top 2,000 it goes down in the scale and smaller stores won't end up stocking it. . . . It does have its disadvantages. We are basically a southerly orientated company and obviously the tastes vary from area to area. The only thing in this range is what we call regional options. A good example in this particular area are Pork Farms Pies etc where they sell here but probably don't sell in the south. Pricing is a national policy. The company has a price list and that is the price we sell it at.

> I have a set inspection to do every day which covers every aspect of the store and that would normally take me the entire morning. . . . We start at the front door with the produce department; has he set layouts, set ranges, national promotions, all his legal checks, his country of origins, his point of sale, his description of the produce? All these things have to be checked, because any one of them being wrong, I, and not the company, am liable to prosecution. . . . Obviously we like to think everything is fresh and we would buy it ourselves, and it is in code [i.e. sell-by date]. All these things have to be done daily, otherwise we're going to lose an awful lot of customer confidence.[27]

By 1987 there were no grocers in the traditional sense of the word in Market Harborough. The multiple supermarkets dominated town centre trade. The only exception to this was the delicatessen trade for which none of the grocery chains were particularly noted. Emerson & West's offered an extensive loose counter and packaged selection of delicatessen lines as a complementary part of a restaurant, catering and bakery business. Until closure in 1985, Christopher Stopher, a small independent grocer and delicatessen, traded at 54 High Street (Joules in early 1994). The only other independent outlets for groceries and provisions were modern corner shops, stocking not only food lines but also a wide variety of other goods which might include newspapers, wines and spirits, stationery, confectionery, bread, greengrocery, tights and toys. In 1987 the supermarket trade was divided between Tesco, Gateway, the Co-op and Kwik Save, although they were obliged to look over their shoulders at superstore developments in neighbouring towns.

Even the 7,300 sq ft of Tesco's store, the largest in the town, was regarded as small by modern standards, a 'C' grade store in Tesco's ranking. In April 1987 the company was reported to be looking for a new supermarket site in the Harborough area, expressing an interest in the possible redevelopment of the town's cattle market.[28] This development took place in 1992–3, but with Sainsbury's, a supermarket chain new to the town, rather than Tesco at its heart.

Such has been the pace of change in the food retailing sector, that less than twenty years after opening as the town's largest supermarket, the Tesco store had for some time been regarded as inadequate, particularly with regard to its delivery and storage area. Similarly, the Co-op, only a few years after opening their brand-new premises at 4 High Street, a prime site, moved to a new store in Coventry Road in 1987. While only a 1,000 ft larger in selling area than the previous store, it offered the crucial access to extensive car-parking on the Commons.

The development of out-of-town superstores and their recent establishment in neighbouring centres such as Northampton, Kettering, Corby and Wigston meant serious competition for Harborough's supermarkets. The increase in car ownership, longer opening hours, the convenience of finding everything under one roof and even

Martin Lambeth filling shelves at the Co-op superstore, Coventry Road, Market Harborough, 1988 (Photograph by Mrs E. Lambeth)

the sense of occasion and participation experienced by shopping at bright new superstores combined to threaten the older town or city centre's position as the principal seat of the retail trades. As with the early multiples and then the supermarkets, small provincial towns such as Market Harborough were the last to see superstore developments. The informed question being posed in 1987 was whether the town could prosper without one. Another common response to such a proposal was that 'Market Harborough has enough supermarkets already', demonstrating a reaction against supermarkets by those who have known more personal modes of shopping, rather than an appreciation of the economics of the situation.

Grocery and provision dealers have come a long way since the beginning of the century, leading a radical change in the high street for both shopper and shopkeeper. The modern supermarket manager works for a highly centralized and sophisticated organization, with large-scale bulk buying direct from the manufacturer, computer-based stock control and deliveries, national sales strategies and a hierarchy of staff training and benefits. Traditional qualities of the trade, the knowledge of the goods sold and the skills of buying, cutting and weighing, packaging and selling have all but disappeared from the high street. They are now exercised by central buyers, food processing plants, advertising agencies and management consultants. Despite this onslaught and the success of the multiples in the high street, the service and skills of the independent grocer live on to some degree in the thousands of small general stores to be found outside the town centres: in the corner shops, the parades of shops on modern estates and the modern village post offices and stores. In their flexibility of working hours, location and stock, and entrepreneurial enthusiasm, small shopkeepers have proved remarkably resilient in their response to the march of the multiples and exercise at least some of the skills once essential to the high street grocer.

*Chapter Eight*

# Town and Country Butchers

Since the earliest days of the town, butchers had worked from stalls or 'shambles' in the area now occupied by the Old Town Hall, where the funnel-shaped High Street broadens out. In 1380, Thomas Clypston of Harborough sold one stall in 'Haverbergh', situated in 'le fleschschamelis' (the Shambles), to John Boresworth.[1] Butchers from Harborough and the area around brought beasts into the town on market day and slaughtered, butchered and sold meat from stalls there. A lease of 1644 described 'two oxen stalles thacked [thatched] over standing and being in the Butcher's shambles . . . being by measurement 13 foot or thereabouts in length and 8 feet and a half or thereabouts in breadth, late in the tenure of James Frisby and Nicholas Shreeve, butchers'.

From later entries in the Highway Overseers' accounts we know that the butchers' shambles was equipped with a pump, that the stalls were made of wooden spars and that there was a 'great stone' at the Shambles end, perhaps for slaughtering purposes.[2] These wooden but clearly semi-permanent stalls were replaced by two single-storeyed brick structures in 1737. No known pictorial record survives but they were described around 1764 by Rowland Rouse, the town's first historian, himself a draper:

> . . . at the north end of the little Street [Church St] is the Butchers Shambles which consist of two neat Brick Buildings of equal dimensions . . . their Roofs (which are slated) are each of them supported by 8 Semi-Eliptical Arches on each side . . . having 8 of the Stalls on one side and 8 on the other side of it in each building . . . these Shambles were built in 1737 – a Stone cut Lozenge-ways and having this date engraved upon it being built into the north end of one Building.[3]

These brick Shambles were in their turn demolished to make way for the building of the Town Hall in 1788. Butchers continued in this part of the town, accommodated in the ground floor of the new Town Hall, then an arcaded space open to the elements. The Shambles were not replaced as butchers were by this time becoming established in fixed premises in various locations, of which the present Bates shop in Church Square is a fine purpose-built example dating from around 1820. By the 1790s, three butchers were listed for the town, Matthew Chater, Thomas Green and John Mutton.[4]

The butcher's trade in Market Harborough in the late nineteenth century, with a number of shops stocked with locally raised meat was vividly described at Christmas 1896 by the *Market Harborough Advertiser* under the heading 'Ye Christmas Fayre'. The article described the stock of each of the town's butchers in the week before Christmas:

> Mr Edmund Patrick, High Street [No. 53, Joules in early 1994] has as usual a grand show which would be hard to beat but owing to limited accommodation he is only able to show his stock killed, which includes a polled angus ox fed by Mr W.P. Cowley of Braybrooke, and which gained first prize at Harborough Fat Stock Show . . . ; two fine shorthorns fed by Mr Chater, Great Bowden, one Hereford fed by Mr R. Battams, Brampton Ash . . . 20 Southdown sheep fed by Mr Watson, Foxton, 21 Scotch . . . 10 Welsh [sheep] fed by Mr W.W. Wartnaby, Clipston . . . six porket pigs [young, fatty pigs up to 80 lb weight] fed by Mr Edward Flint, Holt, four others from Berry's sale and two from Theddingworth.[5]

Mr Patrick's stock was the largest of the eight butchers described, with nine beef, over fifty-two sheep and twelve pigs on the rail for Christmas 1896. At the turn of the century the butcher's trade in Market Harborough was dominated by the independent producer-retailer, the butcher who raised and bought locally finished stock, slaughtered it in a private slaughterhouse, dressed the carcass and cut up and sold the meat from his own shop. Edmund Patrick's was a family business; both his father John, born in nearby Maidwell in 1806, and his grandfather had been in the trade. By 1838 John Patrick had a shop in Adam & Eve Street. Edmund died in 1901 and the business was carried on by his nephew Philip Edmund, moving to premises at 31 The Square by 1908 and taking in the next generation as 'Patrick & Son' at the same address in 1922. With three or possibly four generations, the Patrick family were one of the longer-established butcher's businesses in the town. Edmund Patrick was described as a 'butcher and grazier' up until 1900, suggesting that like many other butchers up to that time, he not only killed and sold stock from local farms, but also fattened his own livestock.[6]

At Christmas, 1896, there were seven other butcher's shops in the town. Frederick Dexter's 'brilliantly lighted' shop at 31 The Square (Nolan's in early 1994) carried a stock similar to Patrick's, including 'four very fine shorthorn beasts and two runts fed specially for his Christmas show by Mr J. Ashton, Manor House, Lubenham, two nice shorthorn beast and one heifer fed by himself . . . prize winners at Holloway Price & Sons show the previous week, three Southdown sheep which he claims to be the best he has ever killed which is very complimentary to the feeder, Mr Lush of Clipston' and 'two extraordinary fat lambs'; altogether ten beef, twenty-two sheep and five pigs. The remaining butchers had smaller stocks to show. George Northrop in Church Street had three beef, about twenty sheep and four fat pigs, 'his shop being very appropriately decorated with evergreens etc'. Northrop's stock included a prime fat bullock which had taken first prize at the Leicester show,

This formidable group worked for Dexter's the butchers in 1902. They stand near the slaughterhouse in what is now Miller's Yard

fed by Mr C.E. de Trafford at Hothorpe Hall. Mrs Elizabeth Holt's shop at 69 High Street (Chinatown in early 1994) was 'filled with all kinds of meat of first-class quality . . . and a very large supply of home-made sausages for which the shop has been noted for forty years. Also a quantity of potted beef etc.'.

Another long-established business, Mr Gregory's in Granville Street, offered three fat pigs fed by himself, while A.B. Warner (at 27 Nelson Street from around 1895 until the 1950s) had Scotch mutton and porkets bought at Harborough market. Mr John Garner had run a bakery in Adam & Eve Street for some years and in the week before Christmas 1896 opened a refitted butcher's shop at No. 20, 'commodious and lofty, well adapted to business'. This was later occupied by J.F. Stokeley in the 1930s and '40s. In 1896 Garner's stock included three beef and nine sheep, although his trade was primarily in pork, with twenty-eight pigs on the rail, among them one prime fat pig which had won prizes at no less than six shows including Leicester and

John Garner's shops in Adam & Eve Street, Market Harborough, *c.* 1896. The pork butcher's shop is to the right with a fine display of meat. The pies and cooked meats were sold in the left-hand shop

Market Harborough, ten prime fat pigs fed by W. King Esq., Bozeat Manor Farm and two prime fat pigs fed by Capt. Warner, Langton Hall: 'In other departments will be noticed a very large display of glazed hams, glazed and peppered ox tongues, jelleys etc and a large display of his well-known pork pies and sausages'.

Mr Fortnum's shop in Adam & Eve Street was also stocked with locally finished meat, including cross-bred sheep fed by the Great Bowden horsedealer, J.H. Stokes and four pigs fed by Mr E. Eames of Market Harborough. It was a common practice to display prize beasts such as these live in the shop before slaughtering, to encourage customers to place orders for joints from the prize beast. As noted above, Harborough's shops were generally too small for live display. Mr Charles Kirby from Tur Langton was apprenticed at the age of twelve in 1898 to J. Nichols of London Road, Leicester, where this was usual at Christmas:

> It were all Stoneygate, high-class customers. They used to pull up in horse and carriages. . . . At Christmas he generally used to buy the champion bullock at Leicester market and have it in the shop, deep in straw. People would come in and look at it and say they'd

> have so much of that one for Christmas dinner. I think one year while I was there, the shopman reckoned it up and he'd sold about two ton of sirloin off one bullock and they all got some! That was trade wasn't it? They'd buy it because they'd seen the champion bullock alive and they was beef in them days, great fat beautiful bullocks.[7]

Even in 1896 however, changes were evident both in the nation's eating habits and in the production of meat for the butchery trade, which were to have a profound effect in our own century. Between 1871 and 1939, the population of Britain rose by 52 per cent and as real wages and standards of living improved, the consumption of meat per head also rose, from 104 lb per annum in 1868–9 to 143 lb in 1936, an increase of 38 per cent. During this period the livestock population of the UK failed to keep pace with this steadily growing market for meat; between 1871 and 1939 numbers of cattle fell by 4 per cent, sheep fell by 14 per cent and pigs increased by only 7 per cent. Initially the increased demand for meat was met by imports of salted and canned meat, and by imported live animals.

The introduction of refrigeration opened up the British market to imports of chilled and frozen meat from Australia, New Zealand and Argentina. The first refrigerated cargo from Argentina arrived (in Marseilles) in 1877 and from Australia in 1879. Initially this new product encountered considerable consumer resistance and not inconsiderable hostility from the established meat trade. This prejudice declined as high quality and regular supplies, lower prices and steadily rising demand led to broad acceptance of chilled meat in particular. This came mostly from Argentina as until 1932 it was technically impossible to bring anything other than frozen meat from Australia. The imports of refrigerated meat of all kinds rose in value from £12.5 million in 1882 to £93.3 million by 1939. The proportion of the total weight of meat consumed in the UK supplied by home producers fell from 82 per cent in 1877 to 40 per cent by 1924–7.[8]

Imports from Australia and New Zealand, led by lamb, were generally accepted by independent butchers, being comparatively small and seasonal. The lower quality and less palatable Argentinian product, however, was not so readily accepted. The large firms which developed the imported meat trade needed a wide and rapid distribution for their product and were obliged to open their own retail outlets, introducing the concept of the chain butcher. The chains grew very fast; by 1912 James Nelson and Sons mustered 1,500 shops, Eastmans Ltd, 1,400, the London Central Meat Co., over 500 and W. & R. Fletcher and the River Plate Fresh Meat Co., over 400 each.[9]

These shops were mostly to be found in the larger towns and industrial cities. By 1895 the London Central Meat Co. had opened a branch at 66 High Street, a small single-bay shop (Greenwoods in 1994) which was the first multiple butchery in the town. Eastmans opened a shop in Church Square in 1908. The Empire Meat Co. was at 7a/8 High Street by 1932. Further competition for the town's independent butchers was provided by the Market Harborough Co-operative Society which had opened a butchery in Coventry Road in 1899.[10] Eastmans shop in Harborough was at 2 Church Square, a small single-bay shop (Lords in 1994). The first manager of Eastmans was Mr Charles Wimlett's father:

> In 1908 he moved from Northampton where he was managing the [Eastmans] shop there and opened Eastmans in Church Square. . . . He was an English butcher, [as] they called them in those days. Eastmans were a foreign butcher as they sold foreign meat, Argentinian chilled beef. . . . He put in his order for so many 'ship', as they called them in those days, not 'sheep': 'ship and lambs'. . . . Then he would be open on Monday afternoon to receive that. It came by road. . . . They had Monday afternoon and Thursday afternoon off . . . Tuesday was a very big market day and Saturday would be the next big day . . . all day Saturday: they kept on until 10 o'clock at night regularly. . . . He used to have very good displays because it was a glass window, then open at the sides and he would spend say Monday afternoon cutting up the meat and putting it on show for Tuesday.[11]

Mr Wimlett senior had been trained as a butcher in the family business. As manager of the Eastmans shop, he was required to cut up the meat economically and sell it as quickly as possible before it was unfit for human consumption. He also kept the books and chased up debtors, supervised his staff of two shopmen and a boy, and dealt with customers. While this was a job carrying responsibility and some social standing in the town – 'the managers and proprietors of businesses were all on the same footing' – the assessment and procurement of stock was no longer part of the job, the butchery variant of the 'de-skilling' trend that was to extend through most retail trades with the rise of factory-packed and processed goods, and centrally controlled chains of shops. The traditional butcher, however, remained more typical of Market Harborough, combining the assessment and purchase of live animals, with the skills of slaughtering and cutting to match the tastes and pockets of a broad clientele. His success was based firmly on training, experience and judgement.

The trade of H.H. Pickering, butcher in the High Street between the wars, related by his son Mr George Pickering gives a comprehensive picture of the skills and methods of the traditional independent master butcher. Mrs Holt's butcher's shop at 69 High Street, already noted for its sausages in 1896, passed to a Mr Shore who around 1910 emigrated to Canada. The shop was taken by Henry Halford Pickering, who was to become an influential figure in the town between the wars. He had been born in Lubenham, just outside the town, and apprenticed to the village butcher. He had done his time as a journeyman in Harborough and Mablethorpe, Lincs., and as a shopman in Hornsey, London, before returning to Market Harborough around 1910 to set up in business on his own. In 1918 he moved over the street to the Old Bank House, imposing premises formerly occupied by Barnsley's, a high-class tailors. H.H. Pickering was widely recognized as the town's premier butcher, 'he was a master butcher in the proper concept of the word':

> All the stock was bought alive, either in the local market or on the local farms, or occasionally, in my father's case, stock that he'd got on his own farm . . . all the cattle that were killed in those days were all two-and-a-half years to three years old, whereas today they are one to two years old. They'd had an extra season on the grass in those days . . . They were all shorthorns, which have disappeared completely. They were red cattle with horns or Herefords, there were a lot of Herefords about and there were a lot of Welsh cattle sold through Harborough or fed in the Harborough district. The Welsh breed is black and if you cross those with a Hereford you get a black beast with a white face and those were the fancied ones.
>
> But even buying cattle alive was much different in those days. There were no weighing machines in the market, they were brought in in the 1930s when the Government started to pay a subsidy on all fat cattle of 5*s* a hundredweight because the farmers couldn't make beef pay. Until then there were no weighing machines and so every animal my father and

Mr H.H. Pickering's shop in the Old Bank House, High Street, Market Harborough butchers like him bought had to be assessed by eye to see if it was suitable and whether it was going to kill out properly. Although he'd left school at twelve he was an amazing man: he could look at a beast and tell you how much a pound deadweight it was going to be. He was very seldom without a halfpenny out. He knew exactly the type of beast he was used to and wanted. You see we're talking about a time when Harborough market was booming. I suppose there were 600 or 700 beasts there every week from June until Christmas. They were selling cattle from half-past ten until half-past three in the afternoon. You've got to remember we're talking about a time before there was any local transport. Everything came in on foot. If he bought two beast from a farm at, say, Marston Trussell, it was a question of walking them in. I started walking cattle I suppose when I was about six. My earliest memories are of driving stock off the railway station in Harborough, straight through the middle of Harborough and up Coventry Road. We had two fields [off Welland Park Road], there'd be about 12 or 14 acres I suppose and they'd be used exclusively for lairage.[12]

Driving cattle through a built-up area was not without its dangers. In April 1896, the *Market Harborough Advertiser* reported that a bullock had found its way into West's confectionery shop. Being driven through the High Street it made a rush down a passage and into West's side door. Mrs West who was behind the counter was so alarmed that she jumped over the counter and fainted![13]

From the time that the grass beef stopped in Harborough, which would be virtually Fatstock Show at Christmas . . . from then until May or June he went every week to North Walsham in Norfolk, drove there and back in a day, and brought a load of stall-fed cattle which was one of the great by-products of the cereal-producing counties in those days. They were cattle that were bought from round here in the autumn and fattened on the by-products from the cereal farms. He used to go down and buy a load of cattle every Thursday. They'd come on the train, arrive Harborough sometime on the Friday and be fed with hay and stuff and then he'd pitch them on the cobbles privately at Harborough market on the Tuesday and all the local butchers took advantage of it and he supplied them virtually with their meat all winter, people like Gregory's and Warners . . . a minimum of eight and a maximum of twelve in a railway wagon. He was [the only one doing it] in Harborough, although this was the regular thing that somebody did it.

I understand that my father . . . killed in Miller's Yard, some arrangement with Jackson Loomes [in addition to the council-run slaughterhouse opened in about 1906]. Mr Loomes in those days killed in Miller's Yard, right up to the war. There were three slaughterhouses [in Springfield Street]; my father rented one and the others [butchers] rented the other two between them. Monday was a killing day because the shop didn't get going on a Monday: people had a joint on Sunday and had it cold on a Monday. You sold very little meat on a Monday and in effect the whole shop was cleaned on the Monday morning, from top to bottom, everything was scrubbed and polished, the windows and the doorsteps were whitewashed and everything. That was Monday morning while the two slaughtermen were killing. The shop would close at dinner time on a Monday but the killing would go on, they'd work in the afternoon as well, the whole staff and then it would be a question of demand after that. If they were beginning to eat into next week's stock by Wednesday then they'd spend Wednesday afternoon killing as well.

He always bought top quality animals and he always presented them in a top way. He always insisted on this hanging period. Even before refrigeration, and except in the middle of summer when it was impossible, you always had one week's meat in stock. You had the meat for next week hanging up in the shop and you weren't selling that, you were selling last week's. And it was hung for a week before it was thought fit to eat. It's about three or four days now, but being much younger stock that goes to make the meat, it doesn't matter so much today. There was more flavour in the mature stock that was killed in those days, I'm certain of that. I mean a piece of mutton was really something . . . mutton was mutton [i.e. lamb was lamb]. Often the sheep had been shorn twice which you never see today. . . . But everything had a season, which is difficult to understand now. You would never sell lamb at any time except between May and July; it was mutton after that. Spring lamb was spring lamb, it was suckling lamb. Soon as the lambs were weaned it wasn't lamb any longer. . . . Everybody else sold New Zealand lamb but my father wouldn't touch anything that was frozen, it was all high-quality home-killed meat.

Very little pork was sold between May and August because nobody had fridges, not even the butchers. I can remember my father's first refrigeration room when I was eight or ten [about 1927] and that was the first butcher to have a refrigerator in the town. It wasn't automatic; every time the temperature rose you had to start it up. In Harborough there'd be several hundred pigs kept in back yards and there was a whole list of people who expected my father to buy them, not always because he wanted to because not all of them were top quality, but they had to be bought and keep people happy. They'd be sold by the deadweight. We had a steelyard in the shop and they'd come in and have a conference [on] how much they weighed, how much they were going to get paid.

The days started on Tuesdays, Fridays and Saturdays at half-past five. The full staff except for the errand boys arrived at half-past five because all the preparation for the shop that day was done that morning because there was no way of keeping the joints presentable. This [refrigerated] room was all right for sides of beef and whole sheep but it wasn't much good once you'd cut it up. So the meat for sale that day was cut up on the morning and all the orders that had been taken the previous day were cut up before breakfast that morning for that day's delivery. It closed for lunchtime from one, opened at two and closed half-past six on Wednesdays, one o'clock on Thursdays and half-past seven Tuesdays, Fridays and Saturdays.

There'd always be a couple of lads who were apprentices in a way. They weren't old enough to do the regular killing but they were old enough to do these odd jobs and sweep out the shop. I mean, labour was cheap, I suppose but there'd be a total staff often of six; four adults and perhaps one full-time boy and one who came in after school. It had a double window with a door in the middle and each window had a sloping marble slab on which the meat was presented. The floor was wooden and it was sawdusted at least twice a day. There was a very large solid-topped wooden block for cutting up carcasses on the right-hand side of the shop and on the left-hand side was a smaller similar block which was the retail counter and the meat was cut up before the customer's eyes; they wouldn't buy it if it wasn't. Very few joints as such were presented in the window; a few on a Saturday morning and perhaps a few on a Friday morning.

It was a silvered rail, hanging from the ceiling by iron rods, that took the carcasses you see and if you wanted to, you could swing these carcasses right round the shop. It was a continuous rail. If he hadn't got it cut off already, the hind quarter of beef would be put down on the big block and it would be cut up then and there. [In the window] there were large pieces mainly, pieces which were cut into the various joints like a whole sirloin or a whole rib of beef or a whole steak and people would come in and say I want a bit of that. But people were much more definite, they knew a lot more about what they were buying than today, so there were lots of joints of meat you never hear of today which people asked for by name; aitch-bone of beef or tail-end of beef and they knew what they wanted, you couldn't fool these ladies, they knew exactly what they were buying. If you hadn't got it they wouldn't have anything else. It was an old, traditional, way [of cutting up] these joints. It isn't done today. You go to a supermarket and you buy a piece of lean beef. It could come from anywhere. It's none the worse for that because it's a young animal. In the days that I'm talking about, the hind-quarter of meat was roasting, virtually, and the fore-quarter was stewing. If you wanted stewing meat it was near the horn, if you wanted roasting meat it was near the tail. But people always came and asked for joints of meat by name. They didn't want a 'bit of beef' . . . If you'd got a loin chop and they wanted a best neck chop they wouldn't have it.

Now today you go and ask for a chop and you get whatever the butcher's got in front of him. You can buy steak today but a lot of it is from joints that in my father's day were roasting meat. 'T-Bone' steak is sirloin; that would never be anything but roasted in my father's day. Instead of, say, 10 per cent [being] grillable or fryable in my father's day, now 40 per cent is fryable. . . . The farmer has to tailor an animal to the customer, that's what's happened so now we're killing cattle 18 months younger and also of course a lot of peculiar things go into meat to make it tender today. When he [father] was there, . . . the shopman was his assistant. He was the top man, he could do everything, he'd serve the customers, do everything.

[The lady in the cash office] was a permanent fixture, all my childhood, the same lady. There was big business with all this booking and accounts, and weekly slate. My mother and father spent all Saturday afternoon finishing it off, because there wasn't much to do in the shop from Saturday dinner time until you closed at 7.30 p.m., so that was the time. [Credit] was very important: a lot of big customers paid once a year. This was one of the problems that had to be solved. The only reason we let customers go was because they weren't credit-worthy. You're better without them than with them. Bad debts were a constant headache. Of course it was the bigger customers who were longest to pay, the ordinary shilling steak people had to pay every week or else there would be questions asked. A certain class of customer had bills every month, that's the people who came in and ordered meat and had it delivered. The ordinary cash customer had credit for a week. They used to come in and pay on a Friday or a Saturday.

Until the late 1920s they were still running a high butcher's cart. You could get a carcass of beef under the seat so that was used not only to deliver joints but also to bring stock from the slaughterhouse to the shop. But very quickly we had vans, at one time we had two or three vans, unheard of now. . . . We supplied a lot of big houses in those days. You've got to remember we're going back to the time when hunting lodges were fashionable, especially in the winter-time; Sulby Hall, Hothorpe Hall, West Langton Hall. I've been fetched out to go there on my bike regularly, somebody'd rung up; they'd never refuse an order, somebody'd take it somehow. They were days when nothing was lost, no business was lost. The orders that were taken out to these places were ridiculous. I've been to Sulby with two lamb's kidneys times!

There was a customer for every cut in those days, because people were on the whole much poorer. Course meat was very cheap; I can remember they sold brisket of beef, which is the cheapest cut, for *4d* a pound, plate of beef was *6d* a pound. Steak, people would come every day for 1*s* worth of steak for their husband's dinner, it was a regular thing. The only thing that was a speciality in the shop was sausage and these were prepared from a recipe he had bought from the Miss Holts. Pork sausage was *6d* a pound and beef sausage was *4d* a pound. Just before the war they went up to about 1*s* and 1*s* *2d*. . . . We had a tremendous trade for sausage. I'm sure that at Christmas time we were selling thousands of pounds of pork sausage and they were going all over the country. They used to go through the post to London, people who had them in the hunting places would send in an order for so many pounds of sausages. We're talking about the time before there were any multiple[s'] sausages. These were pure meat and rusk with this special seasoning.[14]

Most of the town's butchers carried on their trade between the wars along similar lines to that of Pickering's, although few had the size of business undertaken at the Old Bank House. As well as the dozen or so butchers' shops in Harborough, many butchers were to be found in the country villages beyond the town; in 1912 there were twenty-eight butcher's shops in the fifty-four villages around Market Harborough. Most middle-sized villages had a butcher's shop, while the larger villages boasted several. In 1912, for example, there were two butchers each in Hallaton, Medbourne, Cottingham, Great Bowden and Welford, three at Clipston and four in Kibworth Beauchamp.[15]

John Jesson's butcher's shop and slaughterhouse at Gumley, *c.* 1905. Note the characteristic butcher's high cart used for deliveries, and the sides of beef hung outside the shop

In 1987 a typical country butcher's premises could still be seen at Gumley. A purpose-built slaughterhouse and shop had been opened as a private museum by Mr and Mrs Davis. This showed, among other things, the tools of the trade, account books and a high cart for deliveries made by Johnsons on St Mary's Road, Market Harborough. The former proprietor of the shop, John Jesson, was born in 1865 and had followed his father Thomas Jesson as a small grazier, raising cattle, pigs and sheep. In 1894 he had the shop and slaughterhouse built for him by Edward Martin of Great Bowden for £22 19*s* 4*d* and, branching out, he began to kill and sell meat. The shop enterprise seems to have been relatively short-lived; it was apparently disused from around 1910. Unfortunately the museum closed following the death of Mr Davis, and the collection was finally dispersed by auction in January 1994.[16]

Villages without the benefit of a shop were supplied by the butcher's round. A country butcher's trade was dependent to a far greater extent than the townsman's on the delivery round. It was also more likely to be combined with raising livestock, running a smallholding or other employment. Mr Charles Kirby worked for Vendy's at Cranoe just after the First World War: 'I went there and he still done it [slaughtering] with a pole-axe. . . . Country butchering ain't like town butchering. . . . You still had to go round from village to village, and all those outlying farmhouses, well off the road. Cold old job I'll tell you in the winter. . . . Another thing, there wasn't enough in the country to keep you going every day, not all butchering you see. He'd [Mr Vendy] got a bit of land and he used to mix the land with the butchering'.[17]

John Jesson used a blue-painted trap or high cart for his regular round in Foxton, Laughton and Mowsley. A similar vehicle was used by Welch and Son, butchers in Wilbarston from 1918 until 1975:

> We used to have a carrier bike then, and I used to bike all around the villages to various places: Ashley, Weston, Carlton, Carlton Park and round the village. This village, Stoke Albany, used to deliver quite a considerable amount of orders. We started with a horse and cart . . . the traps, just the two wheels and the box at the back . . . We used to pack

Mr O.M. Lillyman's butcher's shop at Wilbarston, *c.* 1910. This business was later taken over by Welch & Son. The thatched building on the left was the slaughterhouse

the meat inside the cart and we had a small block on four legs that used to clip underneath the trap between the two wheels. The back used to let down and in those days we had what they called spring balances to weigh on, you know, the old hand used to swing round on the spring, and we used to clip the scales on an arm on the side of the cart. Of course she used to come out no matter what the weather were like and she'd bring a plate with her and she'd have a look, see what sort of stuff we'd got, various cuts, joints, she'd perhaps choose a bit; 'Cut me a piece off that, I like that, it's got a nice bit of fat on it'. Out it used to come, plonked on the old block and father used to cut it off while I used to have to stand there and hand him the various things that he wanted. Then of course he used to load the customer's plate up with as much as he could, as cheap as possible and another satisfied customer departed.[18]

Until recently, butchers sold meat and very little else. Meat preparations such as pork pies and faggots were rarely seen in a typical town butcher's shop, being found with bacon and cooked meats in a pork butcher's shop (such as Garner's in Adam & Eve Street) or on the provisions counter in a grocer's shop. Sausages were the only exception to this as most butchers made their own. A village butcher commonly had a more broadly based trade. Welch & Son at Wilbarston, for example, fed twenty or more Middle White pigs themselves and made their own sausage, pork pies, hams, potted meat and faggots:

. . . pork pies and faggots, that's another thing we used to do on a Thursday. We had great long tins . . . we used to make our own faggot mix, pack it in these tins, put it in the van and we used to take them up to the local bakehouse. We'd take them up, say, just after dinner and we'd leave them in the bakehouse till the children came out of school, and then their mothers used to send them down with basins and jugs or anything, for sixpenn'orth of hot faggot. They used to know that we used to fetch them from the bakehouse just after they came out of school and they used to come tearing down with the jugs and the basins! We hadn't got ovens then. If we wanted hams boiling, we used to send them up to the bakehouse, you see it was only a stone's throw up the village. We always used to nip up with the van and fetch them or if they wasn't too big we used to put them in the carrier bike, bring them down on that.[19]

As with sausages, the meat used in pies was often of high quality by today's standards and minced more coarsely:

Pork pie seasoning was pepper, salt, pinch of nutmeg, something like that just to flavour it up. The same with the sausage, that was more or less the same, we used to make our own seasoning, pepper and salt, a little bit of nutmeg, a pinch of sage, anything to put a nice little bit of flavouring in it. There used to be plenty of meat in it too. The sausage in those days wasn't made like it is today, it was put through a mincer and when it was filled

J. Welch & Son's butcher's shop at Wilbarston, *c.* 1930. Mr Welch and his son (to the right) stand with their delivery van

into the skins you could see the meat, in the skins, but today it's just whipped up into a paste. 'Course we 'adn't used to put any preservatives in, it was just a matter of making the sausage and selling it while it was fresh. We never used to have any sausage left because it was only ½*d* a pound. We used to take the best middle cuts out the legs of pork, the remainder of the leg, with the exception of the hock, used to be boned out and put into the sausage. People wouldn't believe you put leg of pork into the sausage, but we used to.

The advent of the motor van in the 1920s provided the country butcher's round with serious competition:

There were two butchers in this place when we came here. There was one higher up the street, in a small way, but he was a man getting on in years and the competition got keener and eventually the old fellow got a bit too old for the job, it got too much for him and the trade began to drop off, so he closed down, just left us in the village. But then, vans became quite common then; the baker had a van, the butcher had a van, the coalman had a lorry and then they started to get in to the villages you see and that's when things really did get keen, the advent of the motor. You see they couldn't get in before, only by horse and cart and there wasn't many that would do that.

As I say, when they got the vans in, then it started: they came in from Kettering, they came in from Desborough, they came in from Harborough. The Desborough Co-operative Society, they started to deliver round here, bread, everything the Co-op delivered, coal, every mortal thing you could think of, and, I say, we had to really keep on our toes and then, of course, that went on until the last war broke out, that started to cut them down. That left us more or less the only butcher in the village, with the exception of a butcher named Kilborn from Desborough; he stuck it for a time then he gave up. Well the whole lot came in to us because all customers had to register with a local tradesman because of the ration book you see.[20]

In small towns such as Market Harborough, multiple butchers' shops do not appear to have drastically affected the trade of the independent butcher. There were three chain shops in the town by 1932: Eastmans, the Empire Meat Co. and the London Central Meat Co., all occupying small cramped shops; the London Central Meat Co. had its cutting room on the first floor at 66ax High Street. These shops were all, however, in prime positions in the middle part of the High Street. Despite this competition, eight independent butchers remained in business in the town. Since the 1960s, they have faced another major threat to their trade, the movement into fresh and frozen meat by the giant supermarket chains. Over the following twenty years, the butcher's trade saw a second high street revolution. In 1987 it was possible to shop under one roof for all basic foods, including meat, at Tesco, the Co-operative, Kwik Save and Gateway, and in superstores made accessible by wide car ownership at Corby, Kettering, Wigston, Oadby, Leicester and Northampton.

Nevertheless, undoubtedly aided by steadily rising standards of living, the independent butcher has proved remarkably resilient. There were still six independent butchers in Market Harborough in 1987 (Bates, Hobbs, Gregory's, Morris, Freeland, and Chambers). They differed from their pre-war predecessors largely in their concentration on retailing and in the broader range of meat, poultry and meat products which they stocked: flavoured sausage, pates, cooked pies, burgers, kebabs, barbecue-ready cuts, chicken, turkey and duck. On the other hand, traditional sidelines and by-products such as pork scratchings, black pudding and tripe were less frequently found. Butchers could buy the specific parts of the animal they required from wholesalers and meat preparers, such as Swifts and Weddels, and not having the whole carcass to deal with, they no longer had these by-products to clear. No Market Harborough butcher was killing his own meat by the time of our study, although Morris's at Kilworth were still doing so, and Mr Wise at Medbourne had only finished killing lambs in late 1986.

Gregory's have been established in Granville Street for over ninety years. The proprietor is Alan Bott, who learnt the trade as errand boy and assistant to Mr Frank Gregory in the 1950s before taking on the business himself. Alan Bott's methods are broadly traditional. He is the last butcher in the town to regularly buy locally finished stock, he hangs meat for ten days before selling it and he still does a weekly delivery round. He has also made a reputation for innovation in the meat products he sells – sausage, pies, oven-ready dishes – and in the publicity he gains from winning a national sausage competition and in stunts such as champagne and strawberries for his customers. Speaking to him in 1987, his business came across as a good example of the flexibility and entrepreneurial zeal of the independent shopkeeper which in this trade is successfully resisting the onslaught of the supermarket giants:

> I started as an errand boy in the first place. When we were lads we all wanted pocket money to go to the pictures and wherever. . . . It just happened to be that was the job I got. I'd done paper rounds and all sorts of things but that was the early morning job, delivering orders on the bike, and tea-time job. . . . When I was errand boy I used to go in at night to do the washing-up and then deliver the orders, then that finished when I went full-time. Then there was only the two of us, me and the boss. . . . Four of us now, plus a part-timer. My boss asked me when I took over the shop, 'The only thing I ask you would you leave it as Gregory's?' It's a town name, it would be silly to change it I think. It's an established name. You change the name, you change something else, you know. The name is linked with quality, whatever. This is why and I'd got no intentions of changing it anyway.
>
> I buy a percentage on the farm and the rest from an abattoir, from a wholesaler. I have the help of the local farmers, you know, I'll go to one and he'll say, 'I've got these which I think might be all right for you', so then I'll go and see what he's sorted out and they help me. They're customer farmers, people that come in the shop and I go to them to buy the meat. Possibly 50 per cent [is locally raised]. Because we buy a lot of meat in for pies and sausage, well it's not convenient to buy carcass meat for that from off of the farms. We want special bits for that so we buy tremendous amounts of parts of animals. I can go down to Swifts and buy 200 fore-ends of pork, because I want that, but I don't want to buy 50 pigs, because I'm going to have an awful lot left and I don't want to put legs of pork in sausages and this kind of thing. We buy a normal week's stock and top up with all these bits and bobs that we want.

Gregory's still occupy a small shop, tucked away just off the main Northampton Road in Granville Street. Although storage space is limited, the ready availability of meat from local wholesalers means quite a low level of stock is all that is necessary for the shop. Mr Bott described the situation in 1987 as follows:

> Two pretty good cold rooms. One is 4 ft by 8 and another big one is about 8 by 10. This is one thing we don't need a lot of, you see, 'cause we can top up with Swift's. We leave our meat down Swift's, the lambs and the pig carcasses until we need them. If they were

twenty miles away we would fetch it all up and store it in the shop but I can go down this morning and fetch some of it up, use it, go down this afternoon and fetch some more of it up you see, so we haven't got a terrific amount in the shop at one time.

We deliver; we've now got it down because of the cost of it to three mornings a week. We deliver a small round Tuesday morning, ten orders is small, and Friday afternoon and evening we do a big round round the villages, we took over Mr Wise's round [former Medbourne butcher, retired 1986]. He asked us if we would like to do his round. One thing I do like to think, right or wrong, is that he picked us because we probably butcher the same way as he does. We'd got the same ideas as what he had, you know, customer relations, quality. It's an order round. We're delivering all Saturday mornings too, locally. Fridays is round the villages from Harborough, Great Bowden that way to Ashley, Langtons and back again, and Saturday mornings round town. 85 per cent of them are elderly people and I don't know whether anyone else delivers in town. Possibly they're wise, it costs money, but then again, if you make your round worthwhile it gets money in too. [We have] one van.

Alan Bott by the refrigerated display counter in his shop in Granville Street, Market Harborough, June 1992 (Photograph by Andrew Carpenter)

I stay in the shop all the while. Monday mornings, we get in, make a stock of sausage for Tuesday morning, get the fridges all shone up, the windows, cabinets all shone up and sorted out and have a look at what meat we want for the rest of the week. We pack up about midday Monday. It's quite a short morning, or, like today, a farmer sends a beast in to be cut up for freezing, shall we say, and so we get that done Monday morning, it's quieter so it's convenient to do that Monday morning. It's a lot of work. It's a fair old load out of a day, it took six hours. We boned it all out, we minced it and we bagged it, chopped it all up, done as we would in the shop. It wasn't like a lot of freezer places, chop it in half and throw it in a bag quick! It was all processed as we would have it in the shop.

Tuesdays we prepare meat for pies, steak and kidney, we get that cut up and we sort all that out. We get a lot of pork cut up, this is what we buy in, extra meat for sausages, we get a lot of that cut up and minced and seasoned, which takes two of them three-quarters of a day to do. There's a lot of sausage we do, plus the fact that they're all small batches of different kinds. Every time we finish one lot we've got to wash the bowls out and start on another one because we use garlic and tomato and herbs which will go into another sausage if you don't wash everything up, you know, so you've got to do every one separate.

Wednesday is deep freeze day. We do deep freezes and big contract orders. We serve several restaurants around town and that, Wednesday is a day we like to do that. We make more sausage Wednesday too, because Wednesday was half-day closing in town, [early] closing some years ago, and it's a little bit quieter, Wednesdays are, all over town, even the traffic wardens say there's not a lot of trade on Wednesdays. So generally a bit quieter so we do freezer orders, shop freezer orders, and more sausage. Thursday we get the bulk of our weekend meat in and we cut that up and break that down, bone it and we roll it and do all the stuffings, and we get our supplies of chickens in, that's how we do a lot of boning-out of chickens and turkeys and that, making Chicken Kievs and all this sort of stuff, takes a lot of time, and we make the weekend sausages.

Then Friday it's full tilt in the shop and we cut – Thursday night, I go in after hours on Thursday and cut the Friday night orders for the round, no time in the day to do that – the Saturday morning orders. Two of them get on with that as best they can, in between the shop but it's full tilt. We've got a YTS lad who feeds the shop, he's the one out the back, refilling the trays and hanging the sausages up and boning-out quick, and stuff such as this you see, and getting the meat ready for mincing and the trays of stew and this that and the other. And in the meantime we have all the people in. I like to be there, yes, I like talking to folks and having my finger on it all obviously, knowing what's going on. The majority of people come from ten miles around, we have folks in regular from Lutterworth and from [Great] Glen and Oadby, and Uppingham, Sutton [Bassett], Ashley, Weston [by Welland], round there. Since our sausage job, there's a lot of people we still don't know the names of, come in regular and we still don't know where they come from or who they are.

I do like to call my customers by name. It's nice if you can say 'Hello Mrs Smith', it's nice, I like that. It's more personal; we call everybody 'Sir' or 'Madam', it's nicer if you know a name: 'Did you enjoy that? Would you like one booking for next week?', 'And what name is it?' Then we've got the name then. It's nice if you can call a lady by a name. Where we're situated we don't have any passing trade, 'cause nobody passes my shop to go anywhere unless they do happen to go to visit people up the road, they don't go past our shop. So that anybody that does come into the shop, we've got to be very nice to them and we've got to make sure they come again. We can't rely on anybody just walking by and seeing something in the window, 'Oh, we'll just pop in there'. So we do need to be nice to people. So customer relations, yes, very important.

I mean, like, supermarkets, they need customers but if somebody don't go in they don't miss them, 'cause they don't see them. You never see butchers in them places do you. There's no butchers in them anyway! What I do worry about is when somebody advertises something at less than I can buy it at. That worries me, the fact that they have got this buying power, but other than that I don't worry about it. . . . Yes, I try and do all sorts of things for advertising. It's got your name whether you do anything or not. Whether you've got special offers or not, you put your name forward all the while. People have seen your name, they don't forget your name. Plus the fact we're doing these sausage things and our strawberry and cream job and the haggis job, I mean we're getting photographs in, and the kids' painting thing, we're getting our name put forward all the while, not necessarily advertising lamb chops at tuppence a pound or anything like that, but we get the name, that's Alan Bott the butcher.

The freezer trade in general has slowed right down. Two or three years ago everybody had got the colour television so they all bought a freezer, basically, and there's a terrific amount of people have sold them as well now, yes, really in the last two years freezers have gone down. We used to have rows and rows of orders, probably ten or fifteen, of freezer orders, probably if we get three or four a week now; I think everybody is quite similar. Most butchers, most butchers I talk to anyway, the freezer side is quite quiet. I would sooner have my customer come in twice a week than once a month. We can keep contact with them, they can see what we're selling in the shop, you know, what good things we're selling in the shop, plus the fact that they keep up with prices as well. You know, you get somebody coming in every six months and prices alter, it looks a terrific difference then, they're out of touch. Plus the fact if they come in the shop you can sell them more can't you! Looking at your cabinet, 'Oh yes, we'll have some of that while we're here'. It's contact and getting your people in your shop. People say freezer work's easy, you got one customer with £50 worth instead of ten customers at £5, but I'd sooner have ten in, you're filling a day up and you're, you know, more people coming in your shop.

All Alan Bott's meat was hung for up to ten days before being sold:

This is how all the butchers used to do it. This makes a level quality all the way along.

Yes, it matures it better, I'm sure it does, but we don't know any other way, it's all done like that, it's all matured. It cuts better as well, the meat sets and it cuts nicer. When we're cutting up it cuts nicer, it's got a feel about it. If it don't look nice people don't look at it do they. I know everything of mine is in there on a Tuesday and we fetch it up, we shall fetch some up tomorrow, Wednesday, Thursday get it all ready for the weekend so in actual fact it's probably ten days killing. And I know that stuff I buy from them, they turn their meat round quicker 'cause they don't want meat hanging around of their own for ten days obviously because a beast hanging up is six hundred quid's worth, they don't want 150 of them hanging around for a week, they want to get it out, so if I buy any of theirs I bring it up and put it in my fridge and we know when it's come up there, so this is part of stock control isn't it, part of the business.

My boss told me, 'Go the other side of the shop once or twice a day and have a look or go outside and have a look what your customers are looking at and see what your customers are seeing'; hooks are hanging in the window without anything on them or meat that's not hanging symmetrical you know, dirty trays and this sort of thing or anything pushed under your counter, bits and bobs of paper pushed under your counter, paper bags and this that and the other, and yes I do, I go round and have a look, and look at the cabinet where my customers look. I mean from my side it looks all right but you go round the other side it might look not right.

I know in myself you can set a tray out, make it look beautiful then you get another one up there that's not, that you haven't got to yet, the nice tray will go first. This is why we've set it all out, make it look nice, and the things that are difficult to go, such as breast of lamb, that need titivating up, things like that, I mean, chump chops we can sell them in bed. My boss's old saying, you can sell fillet steak and chump lamb chops in bed, you don't even have to get up in the morning to sell those. But it's the other bits that you've got to sell. So you've got to make them look nice on your trays, the awkward bits. No, this is part of the trade, making sure that you don't get left. At the end of the day, you want topsides and steaks and legs of lamb left, you want to get rid of all the shoulders of lamb and the breasts of lamb and the stew. Any pork that's left we've got this nice fridge plus the fact that we can fridge it now for four or five days quite easily. Years ago when you hadn't got fridges or such efficient fridges, you'd got to get rid of everything, which did cut your buying down probably a little bit. Now if there's any pork left, we can make it into sausages, or brawn, or if there's any beef left we can mince it and make it into pies again, or sausages, potted meats.

Everything can be used up for something, burgers and sausages are a great way of using your bits and bobs up. They're all different animals and we rely on the quality of each animal being consistent, but meat content and seasoning is exactly the same. We were making sausages when we won the competition, we made a batch of sausages to a recipe and we're still making the exact same ones, this morning we made exactly the same recipe sausage. Everything else, the burgers are all the same recipe, the sausages are and the pies are; they've got to be. If the lady comes and has some nice ones, she wants to come back and have some more, doesn't she, you don't want to change the recipe, or else she's going to say, 'They weren't very nice, I shan't have any more'.

Fortunately I had the prices when I went there. But this Meat and Livestock Commission do a very, very good thing. All my prices are on computer, all my meat prices, not poultry or pies or sausages, they're worked out as we go along, but my meat prices, we've got them on computer. I do what's termed as a block test. I cut meat up and I prepare it for sale, exactly as my customers want to come in and buy it. All the fat's taken off, all unnecessary fat, all the bone's taken out so it's right on point of sale, and then I know how much it's cost me, how much profit I want to make and how much I've got to sell it for. Obviously a leg of lamb you want more money than you do a shoulder of lamb, which you want more than a breast of lamb and then again more then a neck of lamb. So you work it all out.

I admit that I look in shop windows to see what everybody else is selling the bits and bobs at and I'm sure all the other butchers do too. So you do know that a leg of lamb's £1.50 and a shoulder's only £1. Over the years you work it out, that you need your leg of lamb to be £1.50 if your shoulder's only going to be a quid you see. But I've done block tests over a period of six months and then these are all computed and averaged out and I can ring the Meat and Livestock Commission up tomorrow morning and say, 'I've got a lamb in my shop, cost me 80p a pound, how much do I sell it at?' and they can flick it over on the old computer and I've got a code, my code number, put it in the old computer and within a couple of minutes they've got prices of what I should be charging, for my own personal cutting list.

A lot of them don't cut the way I do, from Suffolk, to Birmingham to Scotland, I've got my own personal cutting list and personal names, what I call each bit as well you see. The facility's so I can tell them I want an extra 5 per cent profit on it. They will recompute the prices adding 5 per cent on everything and then if I happen to do a special, like legs of lamb, I can ring them up, say I've got these lambs here cost me 80p per pound, I want to do a special on legs, I want to sell legs of lamb at 50p a pound, compute the rest to get me the same profit at the end of the day and they press a button and they can throw that out in two minutes. Very handy . . . I've only been doing it for about three years. . . . To do this I cut ten beasts up, and ten lambs and ten pigs and got an average of what meat I get out of a leg. I have a thing come when, they will tell me on the phone how much I should charge and then they will print this out and it will be in the post the same day, arrive the following day. It's 1987, we've got to keep up with the times . . .

Like the sausage we tried leek sausage out years ago. English people wouldn't use garlic and peppers years ago. But you've got to do it, you've got to keep up, young people are reading the papers about these sort of things. They come to you and you've got to have them or else they'll go down the road and get them.[21]

*Chapter Nine*

# The Clothing Trades

*Everybody wants clothes, don't they? Dresses, stockings, hosiery, knitwear, haberdashery.*
(Employee at Wood's the drapers, 1930s[1])

Changes in the way clothes have been produced and sold over the last two centuries have been almost as dramatic as the rise and fall of different fashions. Up to the middle of the nineteenth century, the retail clothing trades were split between craftspeople who sold garments they made themselves and merchants who dealt in clothes made by others. In the first category were the bespoke tailors and dressmakers who sewed as their customers ordered, and the clothiers, hosiers, corsetmakers and milliners who commonly sold ready-made clothes produced in their own workshops or by outworkers. The other side of the trade was handled by general and specialist retailers – the linen and wool drapers and haberdashers, who between them sold cloth and trimmings to their customers to make and repair clothes at home – and second-hand-clothes dealers.[2]

The introduction of new technology in the mid-nineteenth century altered the relationship between production and retail in the clothing trades in two ways. First the invention and perfection of the sewing machine, in the 1850s, eased the making of clothes at home, and therefore boosted the sale of cloth-lengths and other piece goods by drapers and haberdashers. This resulted in greater numbers of general drapery stores, a notable feature of the trade in the late nineteenth and early twentieth centuries. Drapers were mostly to disappear from the clothing trades in the latter part of this century.

Secondly, although the sewing machine initially strengthened the position of outworkers, further technological developments soon undermined their ability to compete in the market for heavy clothing (men's suits and women's coats, for example). At first British capitalists were slow in bringing their workers together in tailoring and clothing factories; there were only fifty-eight factories listed for the trade in 1871. However the invention of the oscillating shuttle in 1879 enabled sewing machines to be powered by steam and gas engines, instead of the machinist working the treadle, and thus increased the advantages of factory production. The development of the band-knife (which could cut through many thicknesses of cloth at once) and blind-stitching, button-holeing, buttoning and pressing machines all added to the speed and economy of factory production.

The new factories produced ready-made, serviceable and cheap clothing in set sizes.

This encouraged the growth of the outfitting trade, particularly those sectors catering for the working-class and lower-middle-class markets, and reduced the importance of the second-hand clothes trade which previously had been the staple source of working-class men's outerwear. A new group of shops came into being, the multiple men's outfitters and tailors, operating on the same low-cost high-turnover philosophy as multiple organizations in the grocery trade. Mass-produced footwear was also suited to the multiple style of selling. Indeed, one of the first multiple stores of any kind in Market Harborough was a branch of Freeman, Hardy & Willis, which occupied 1 High Street for nigh on a century (British Heart Foundation charity shop in 1994).

In the hosiery and knitwear trades, the transition from production by hand outworkers to the employment of factory machinists started sooner and took place quicker than in the heavy clothing trade: in 1871 there were already 129 hosiery

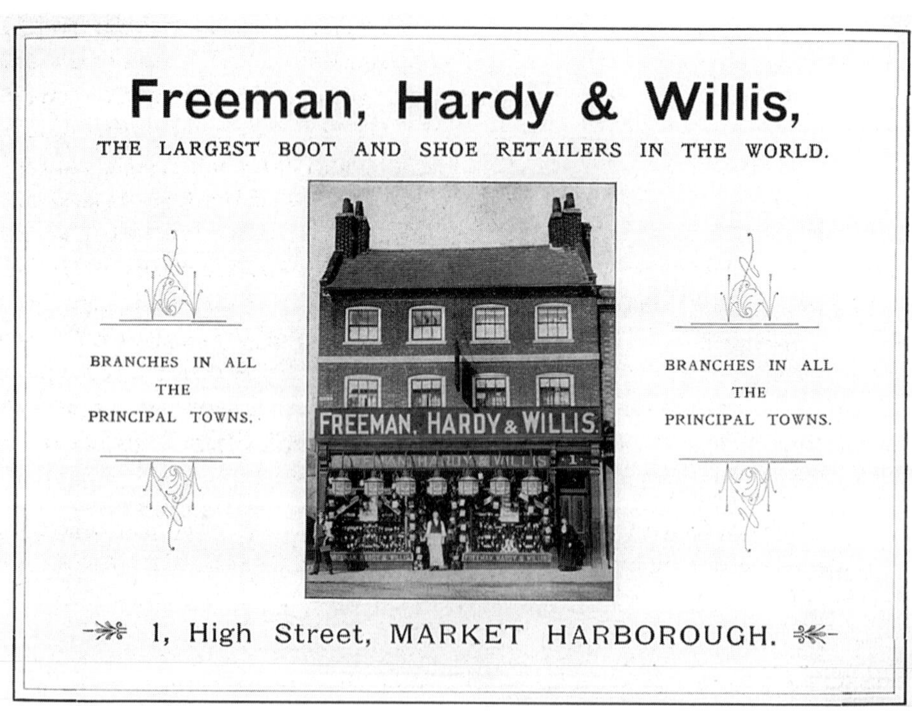


Freeman, Hardy & Willis' advert in the Market Harborough souvenir for the coronation of Edward VII, 1902. In the centre is a photograph of the shop at 1 High Street, Market Harborough, decked out for the occasion. The retail shoe trade led the way in the development of multiple stores

and knitwear factories in Britain. By contrast again the change to factory production for light clothing (underwear, hats, aprons and dresses for instance) was even slower; in 1914 most women's clothing was still made by hand and to order. In the long term though the combination of factory production and multiple outfitting was to triumph here as well.[3]

How did these developments affect Market Harborough? Since at least the sixteenth century, general 'mercers' could be found in the town who stocked goods from a range of woollen, silk and fine linen materials, as well as clothes, drugs and medicines, soap and candles, spices, dyestuffs, sugar, haberdashery, hosiery, stationery and books. The 'mercer' in a small town was the general store. When for example the goods in the shop of Frances Hunt of Harborough were appraised in a probate inventory of 1620, a list was made which recorded many bolts of both coarse cloths and fine linens, clothes and underclothes, haberdashery, soap and raw fleeces.

The terms 'mercer', 'woollen draper' and 'haberdasher' were applied loosely to clothing retailers in seventeenth and eighteenth-century Harborough, with five mercers listed in 1647, and four mercers, a woollen draper and a haberdasher in 1655. The description 'mercer' went out of use in the course of the eighteenth century, and, by 1801, the term 'draper' was used exclusively when recording ready-made clothes dealers. The mercer's trade had in fact become fragmented among a number of more specialist retailers. In 1796 Market Harborough boasted nine drapers, eight grocers, a hosier, a hatter and a tailor, three staymakers, two mantua makers (dressmakers), four breeches makers, and a glover. Throughout this period as well as the owners of fixed shops there were also travelling pedlars and market dealers, who might pitch their wares in the 'Cloath Market' on Church Square, or at one of the annual fairs. These itinerant traders hawked their cloths and other goods round the market circuit. This mixture of craftspeople and specialist retailers persisted in Market Harborough for much of the nineteenth century. An example of the made-to-measure side of the trade was the firm of Healey's. When the Healey brothers opened shop at 5 High Street, in October 1864, they put an advertisement in the local paper:

> To the Nobility, Clergy, Gentry and Inhabitants Generally . . . We beg most respectfully to inform you that we have commenced business as TAILORS, HABIT MAKERS and HATTERS at the above address, and also to solicit your kind patronage and support.[4]

The transition from small-scale hand production to large-scale factory-based automation also had a particular relevance for Market Harborough. R. & W.H. Symington's works , which opened in 1861, pioneered the factory-made corset, using the new Singer sewing machine. Within twenty years the firm owned four factories – the other three were in Desborough, Rothwell and Rugby – and was producing corsets for the national and international markets.

Messrs Healey and Barnsley stand outside their high-class tailor's and outfitter's shop at 19 High Street, Market Harborough, *c.* 1897. By 1899 James Barnsley was the sole proprietor of the business

The story started with James Symington (younger brother of William Symington, the grocer and tea dealer), who set up business as a tailor, hatter and woollen draper in Church Street in the 1830s. James soon made a canny marriage to Sarah Gold, a staymaker who had moved to Harborough with her mother from Warwick, and the shop added stays (corsets) to the lines it sold. The Symingtons employed three women staymakers in the yard behind the shop. The couple soon moved to a shop in the High Street.

The Symingtons' business was revolutionized by the introduction of the new Singer sewing machines from America. The second generation of the family partnership, the brothers Robert and William Henry Symington, established a 'stay manufactory' in a disused factory in Adam & Eve Street in the 1860s. By the 1880s the stitching and strengthening of the corsets by the cording process was all done on machines working off steam-powered line shafting; the firm then employed 1,600 people, some of them outworkers. The economies of factory production meant corsets were then available for as little as 1*s* 11*d* a pair.[5]

Another local example of factory production (although one which was not on the scale of R. & W.H. Symington), was C.T. Freestone, 'Boot, Shoe and Upper Manufacturer'. Unlike Symington's, Freestone also kept his own retail outlet in Market Harborough, as the 1892 guide to the town describes:

> Occupying a fine position in the centre of the town at 13 The Square, [YMCA charity shop in 1994] with a handsome plate-glass front, and a most attractive show of goods, Mr Freestone certainly holds good vantage ground in the boot and shoe trade of the locality. His business is of a wholesale as well as a retail character. In the vicinity of Church Street he possesses a factory, in which, by the help of machinery, and a number of experienced workmen, he produces good work in the shape of boots and shoes, and particularly in the manufacture of uppers, which is a speciality. The general stock is extensive, consisting of all varieties of ladies' and gentlemen's and children's boots, shoes and slippers – which are also made to order when required. The business has been established about forty years.

Boot and shoe manufacture was a 'sunrise' industry in Leicestershire in the 1850s and 1860s, where there had been no opposition to use of the Singer sewing machines as there had been in the traditional boot and shoemaking areas of Northamptonshire and Staffordshire. From the 1870s outworkers were brought into large factories, so that by 1900 there were over 200 footwear factories in the county.

Mass production of footwear enabled multiple retailers to distribute boots and shoes cheaply. Two early multiples, Hilton's and Freeman, Hardy & Willis, started from a Leicester base. Both these firms opened Harborough branches in the 1890s, two of a handful of multiple retail organizations which arrived in the town at that time.[6]

The rise of the general draper, which was linked both to factory production and rising incomes among the lower-middle and upper-working classes, brought changes to the trade. In the larger towns at the end of the nineteenth century there were specialized outlets for ready-made clothes – hosiers, milliners, corsetières, and mantle and gown shops; in the smaller towns like Market Harborough this demand was served instead by general drapers and outfitters. The general draper sold a very wide range of goods, including ready-made clothes, though the sale of piece-goods was a major part of business. Some of these features can be seen by looking at one well-known general draper's shop in Harborough, John Wood & Son.[7]

John Wood first came to Market Harborough in 1894 or 1895. He was the son of a Midlands businessman (also called John Wood) who had originally hailed from Cumberland:

> [John Wood senior] came from Carlisle, and made money, I don't know quite how. Retired very young, then he went to America twice. He produced too many children, I think – the money wasn't sufficient that he retired on – and started up businesses, one in Leamington and one in Leicester. He opened this business in Market Harborough, and my poor father, at the age of eighteen, was pushed into it.

The senior John Wood had bought for his son the Harborough business of G. Emery, a linen draper, at 8 The Square, two doors up from another draper's. One of the junior John Wood's daughters, Joyce Dexter, recalls what her parents had told her about the venture's early years:

> He was very green, he'd only just left school. My father wanted to do law, he didn't want to go into this at all. But being the eldest of the family – in those days you were told what to do. So that's how he became a draper.
>
> It was in the days when the assistants used to live in. And in the yard at the back there was a cottage and that's where the men used to sleep. And the women used to live over the shop [on the first floor, which much later was turned into a stockroom], and there was a kitchen downstairs. They worked very hard because they were open – I think it was until eight o'clock most nights and on Saturday they were open till ten o'clock at night.
>
> Tuesday of course was a very busy day, being market day in Harborough. All the women used to come in with their menfolk who were coming to market . . . and the most embarrassing thing – I think my father used to hate walking through – was when the women used to bring their babies and start feeding them as they were buying stuff. And he was rather a shy man. [It] used to embarrass him very much I gather.[8]

In 1897 John Wood was advertising as a 'family draper and gent's outfitter', who also sold dresses, mantles (women's coats and cloaks), millinery, and mourning clothes and accessories. He also sold 'Manchester goods' – household linen, and other cotton materials used for making light clothes, curtains and furnishings – so called because the Lancashire textile firms specialized in such piece goods. Likewise a 'Bradford' warehouse stocked woollen cloths, whereas a 'London' house reputedly sold the latest fashions and fancy goods.

The 1890s were boom years for general drapers and outfitters in Market Harborough. Smart new businesses sprang up and competition was intense. Some of these aspiring shopkeepers had already run local drapery businesses, or had at least served their time in one, but others were newcomers to the town. Two clothing multiples opened branches in Harborough: Webb Bros in 1892 and Herrington Ltd in 1901. The local Co-operative Society also started a Drapery and Boot & Shoe Department. In 1900, out of twenty-three clothes shops in Market Harborough, sixteen dealt in general drapery or outfitting.

Perhaps inevitably there was some shake-out from such intense competition. A few firms lasted only a matter of months. One tradesman, Charles Richard Lloyd, survived two bankruptcies before failing. In 1912 there were the same number of clothes shops overall as in 1900, but only ten of the general drapers and outfitters from twelve years previous were still in business. For those who survived there were rewards as the town's population continued to grow and demand increased. The Co-operative Society rebuilt its premises at 3 High Street between 1915 and 1917 to house its expanded Drapery Department.[9]

The rising star among Harborough's constellation of drapers at this time was Frederick George Shindler, 'draper, milliner and ladies' outfitter'. In 1896 he opened a new 'well lighted and roomy' sales area, selling heavy drapery goods, in the basement of his shop at 6 The Square, which he had opened ten years earlier. In about 1900 he took over 7 The Square, a former cabinet-maker's and boot and shoe retailer's, building outwards and upwards to match the height of his own London House shop. The expanded premises now boasted eleven display windows and three showrooms on the first floor, and was the biggest draper's in the town. An advertising feature described the business in December 1905:

> Mr F.G. Shindler, dressmaker, milliner and general draper. – Taking each window of this enterprising tradesman's shop, one sees a very large variety of goods suitable for Christmas presents. Blouses in silk, delaine, voile and flannel; under-skirts, children's dresses for outdoor and indoor wear, dressing gowns, and jackets, furs in great variety, pinafores, lace-collars, collarettes, and fichus, table linen and a host of other things. Mr Shindler is always thoroughly up to date . . .

Shindler made his name as the premier general drapery and women's clothes establishment in Market Harborough, selling everything from stockings to sewing machines. The shop's local reputation was such that the draper's on The Square was warmly referred to as Shindler's long after the business was no longer his.

> Whatever the Period of the Year we are always ready with Seasonable Goods. Our guide words are Value, Variety – Always. Careful and Quick Service.[10]

Winnifred Hardwick got her first job at Shindler & Douglas' in 1918:

> I suppose when it came to the time that I was about twelve or thirteen, he, Mr Shindler, asked Dad if I could go to work for them at Shindler & Douglas. He said if he didn't get them early (and I was very young, I could hardly see over the counter) he didn't get them at all, they went into the corset factory.
>
> And I only got 5*s* a week. It was an apprenticeship, three years – got 5*s* the first year, 7*s* 6*d* the second year, and 10*s* the third year.
>
> I'd only been working there about a week when the Armistice was signed, and of course everybody went mad. We sold every blessed bit of red, white, and blue ribbon, red, white, and blue buttons, flags. And of course, we apprentices were not allowed to serve customers, we only did all the odd jobs and tidying up; but they were so busy that week that I had to serve a few customers.
>
> When I first went to Shindler's I was put into the glove department as an apprentice. We used to have to stroke the gloves each day. They were mostly kid gloves, you see . . . And we used to have a strip of blue flannel, and had to stroke the bits off – pull them back to shape if anyone had stood and tried to put them on.

Advertising for Shindler & Douglas

> And we used to have to dust, we had to put chairs up every night; chairs down again, dusted, and counters dusted in the morning. If we sold out, boxes had to be turned upside down so that people knew they were empty.

Mr Shindler, the owner and manager, 'was always round about, always shop-walking and making sure you were doing your job properly, things like that'.

> We never closed for lunch. We used to have 'parties', first party and second party. First party went from 12 to 1 p.m., second party went from 1 to 2 p.m. And in my very early days, when it was Shindler's, on Tuesdays we were not allowed to go home at all: we had our lunch upstairs in one of the stockrooms. The housekeeper from Bridge House [in Northampton Road] – it's pulled down now, but it used to be the lodging house for the assistants – she used to come over and prepare the lunch for us on Tuesdays. We only had three-quarters of an hour because it was market-day.[11]

Like the other drapers in the town, Shindler's could not afford to be exclusive. It catered for all classes of customer. Furs and kid gloves were obviously aimed at the wealthy, but the shop also ran clothing clubs to boost its working-class trade. By making a regular contribution to a club the customer could spread the cost of buying clothes and often receive a discount as well.[12]

Shindler's had previously offered a dressmaking service too, but when Winnifred Hardwick worked there the shop only arranged alterations, which they farmed out to a tailor in Northampton Road. Shortly after Miss Hardwick started as an apprentice, Mr Shindler retired. He then leased the shop to an incomer from London, William Smith, who carried on the trade in drapery, ladies' clothes and millinery, adding a dry-cleaning service. He kept on most of the staff, and brought in 'one or two assistants from London' who lived in the lodgings at Bridge House.[13]

William Smith was not able to run his business on the scale Shindler had done, and Shindler commissioned architects to divide half of his premises into two new shops, 6 and 6a The Square, in 1924. The shop at the end of the block, No. 6, was taken by Melia's, a grocery multiple. The middle unit, No. 6a, was leased to John Wood, the draper, who turned it into a millinery department. It was John Wood rather than William Smith who was destined to inherit Shindler's position as the leading draper in the town.[14]

John Wood's drapery business on The Square had been in direct competition with the neighbouring Shindler's shop for over twenty years. Only the gents' outfitting part of Wood's trade had not had its counterpart in the older firm. Yet John Wood had done well out of his business, living in a big house in Northampton Road. He had become a respected person in the community and he served on the Market Harborough Urban District Council. When John Wood's youngest brother returned from the First World War, he was taken into the business. The two brothers had quite different personalities: John Wood was a strict manager who keenly supervised the running of the shop and the staff, Stanley was 'a charmer, not a businessman'. He was in charge of the gents' outfitting side, helped with the shop's management and looked after the order rounds in the villages: 'He used to go about twice a week, I think. One week one district, another week another. He had his districts, and I think he used to enjoy going out and having a gossip to the ladies and taking their orders'.[15]

William Smith's shop, now sandwiched between Wood's main shop on one side and Wood's millinery department on the other, did not last long. By 1927 he had ceased trading and left No. 7, which was quickly snapped up by John Wood.

> Mr Smith went bankrupt. He had a shop in Plumstead as well, you see, he was running two. And his wife came down, and then she opened a shop at Rugby for herself, so I suppose they overdid it . . . Then I think they went back to London.[16]

William Smith's drapery premises on The Square, Market Harborough, 1921. Note the large first-floor window on the left and the densely packed displays, so characteristic of retail window-dressing until recently

John Wood celebrated his expansion by modernizing Smith's old shop-front. He narrowed and deepened the two windows, and installed an island display case between them. The whole effect was completed with a terrazzo entrance and art deco tracery in the windows:

> The fitters of shop-fronts was a firm in Northampton, and I can remember going with my father in the car. . . . That was quite . . . modern in those days, you see, where you walked in. And I think we had millinery in [one] side, and dresses and things shown [in the other window]. Then the door, you went in, and then there was the stocking counter and the glove counter, and the handkerchiefs and scarves. Then there was the cash [desk] where Miss Miller and Miss Hardwick worked. Then it had quite a nice curving staircase which went up to the top. [Upstairs] there was the millinery in the front and the mantles [and the] dresses behind.[17]

The late 1920s and '30s were the heyday of Wood's the drapers. By 1930 the shop had eleven departments and employed about fifteen staff. Soon afterwards Melia's withdrew from the end unit, and John Wood bought it, putting a baby clothes department into this extra sales area. At the same time he also purchased No. 6a and No. 7, which up till then he had been leasing from the Shindler family. John Wood now owned the whole block on the north-east corner of The Square, fronting Symington's corset factory.

Joan Freestone started as an apprentice at Wood's in 1931, and worked in most of the departments during her eleven years there:

> We sold everything from haberdashery right up to coats, dresses, millinery and all the lot . . . It was the largest shop in the town [for drapery and women's wear], if you couldn't get it at Wood's you couldn't get it anywhere. They used to come in from the country, you know, the old dears out in the villages used to come in, and Mr Stanley Wood used to go travelling as well, out to the villages.
>
> [I] started in the haberdashery, and then you work your way through . . . Oh, we sold knitting needles, pins, needles, buttons, press-studs, all different types of braid, mending wools and all this sort of business, reels of cotton – 'Silko', 'cause people used to do a lot of dressmaking in those days – it was a busy department. Then, of course a lot of, tremendous lot of dress materials were sold. And the Manchester department where you sold bed-linen. Then hosiery, knitwear, oh dear, everything really. Yes, it was a busy shop.
>
> A person used to do alterations upstairs but there wasn't actual dressmaking done, no. They used to do a lot of alterations: buy clothes, want dresses altering or coats altering. They used to have someone in to do all that. She used to come in so many hours, she used to work upstairs in the dress department. There was two floors. We used to have stairs going up in the middle, and it was the tremendous big showroom – he used to sell millinery, coats and dresses [up there].
>
> Tremendous lot of gloves we sold. Ribbons and all this business, you know, fancy goods. But we didn't touch upholstery because that was done through a furniture shop.
>
> I think I liked [working on] the knitwear and underwear, jumpers and cardigans . . . Well mostly jumpers, 'cos knitted dresses were upstairs. We sold a tremendous lot of dressing-gowns, underwear, bras, corsetry. And we were lucky we could go into Symington's and get anything we wanted. Well it was Alcock & Priestly's, then . . . it was the back of Wood's. So if we hadn't got anything in the corsetry line, we used to just nip in there, you see and get the things they wanted. . . . Oh, children's wear, we sold a lot of children's wear, coats and all the baby equipment and everything. It used to be a busy department, there used to be a lot of us in there.

The shop also sold men's shirts, ties, socks and underwear, and 'fancy goods' – laces, buttons, collars, ribbons and headscarves.[18] Because his was a large shop selling a wide variety of goods, John Wood depended on the skill and knowledge of the buyers:

> He didn't do all the buying because he had a buyer for each department. And then he'd go up to London, buying occasionally. When you served your apprenticeship you went as

> second sales, and then first sales. I never got to be a buyer, which I would have liked, you know, to travel to different parts buying. . . . But they used to have a tremendous lot of travellers round, and the buying was done from them [as well].

> The travellers used to come on the train, and Mr Wallis used to get his brougham out [and brought] the skips, all the hampers. They used to come and plant them outside here, outside the shop, and kept bringing the stuff in to show.

> They used to sell dress materials, you know, summer-weight, winter-weight . . . The travellers would say 'Now this is a leading colour for the winter, or autumn', you see, and you'd stock that material which was the leading colour.[19]

A draper had to buy carefully to be successful. Not enough variety of stock would mean customers going elsewhere, but it was dangerous to buy items, especially ready-made clothes, that might remain unsold and go out of fashion: 'We didn't buy stuff – not hats and things like that – to store . . . they were present-day fashion. If they had something good, and it sold out, or sold rather well, they'd buy some more of the same thing. The boss used to write orders every night'.

The sales were the only opportunity to sell stock that was out of season or shop-soiled:

> We used to cater for the spring, the summer and the autumn, well autumn and winter fashions. . . . We used to have January sales and July sales. Ever so busy they were. Some of them nearly go mad – oh dear, I always remember they had a eiderdown reduced and there were two women fighting nearly over this eiderdown to get it first.
>
> And they didn't buy it – 'cause some of the shops buy sales stuff – but Wood's didn't, it was genuine reductions. Perhaps one or two items shop-soiled or that, but they were all genuine bargains. Oh, it was hectic at times – we earnt our money, we really did.

> All the oddments had to be done up into remnants, and stitch the tickets on them. Things like [ribbons and laces] were reduced and put in baskets, and people would go for the reduced things first, like they do now. . . . We used to have remnants of coat materials, dress materials, and they used to be put on remnant boards outside the shop. Soiled blankets and sheets, or anything like that, were all put together and marked 'Sale Price', 'Special Sale Price'.[20]

'Genuine reductions' gave some return on problem stock, even if sometimes it barely covered the buying price. 'Generally the good stock was kept separate and anything else that went into the sale went in at cost price.' Items that still 'stuck' in the sale were then reduced to 'throw-out price'. Staff also got bonuses on the sale of certain items:

> During the sale things had got a mark – after the boss had been round and marked them

The staff of John Wood's drapery shop in their 'uniforms' outside the newly refurbished entrance, *c.* 1927: 'We all had to wear brown uniform – dingy colour, everybody dressed in dark brown'

> up [with a letter code] and put a premium on them, to encourage you to sell them because they were oddments. And we used to have a little box each and put all our premium slips in there. And then they were added up at the end of the month, and then we were given money that we made. Perhaps it'd only be 3*s* 6*d*. [Weekly wages at Wood's in the 1930s ranged from 7*s* 6*d* for a first-year apprentice to £2 or more for a departmental buyer.] Some of them in the gown department, or heavy overcoats department, had bigger premiums on, so they would get more money.[21]

The sales marked the end of the autumn/winter season and the spring/summer season. The buying of the new season's stock would have started well in advance. Spring clothes, for example, were bought in September and October time. 'We didn't usually put out the new stock until about the last week of the sale, till there were only the bits and bobs that were left.'[22]

Wood's required two cashiers to look after the books. The junior cashier was Winnifred Hardwick, who had been taken on at Wood's when Smith's closed. She remembers the system of allowing clothes out on approval:

> We used to send things out on 'appro' . . . If somebody said they wanted a hat, any special hat,

or 'Would we please send a few corsets up' for somebody to try on – a great big pile of them! Send this, send that! And if the boss was around, and he suggested it, well we sent it. 'Oh yes, you can have them up, we'll send them within so long, you can have them today', whether it mattered or not . . . Used to give them two or three days 'appro' with the goods, and then we used to have to send the errand boy back to the house for the things back again. And the lady would have kept whatever she wanted, and come in and pay for it when she was ready.[23]

The shop staff were given a 10 per cent discount if they bought clothes from Wood's.

Well when I first went it was Shindler's – we wore black: black stockings, black shoes, black everything. And two assistants in the old department had black ribbon bows – I think they used to see which one could have the biggest one, great big butterflies sticking up! – stiff black taffeta ribbon . . . But then [under Smith's] we had navy . . . Then after that [at Wood's], of course we got a bit fed up with black and navy, so we asked if we could change to brown. Boss was quite agreeable, so we all had new dresses on the same day. We had to buy our own of course.[24]

At the beginning of the Second World War, John Wood died suddenly. Stanley Wood and his wife took over the business, but after the war the shop went into a slow decline. The premises were eventually sold in 1961 and were demolished.

During John Wood's lifetime the shape of women's clothes retailing continued to change. Nationally, the years of Wood's greatest success – the 1920s and '30s – were the time when womenswear multiples started to make major advances in the trade. However, at this time in Market Harborough there were no multiples selling only womenswear.

This did not mean that Harborough women lacked a choice of places to buy clothes. In the inter-war years a new type of shop appeared – the small outlet for fashionable clothes, usually owned and run by women, and nicknamed 'Madame shops' in the trade – which may reveal something about its attitude to the aspirations of the women proprietors. Market Harborough had several of these small costumiers. The shops had names like 'Maison Eve', 'Violette' and 'Madame Gertrude's, which was opposite Boots . . . she had very high-class stuff'. Madame Gertrude's stayed in business until the 1970s. Similarly, Grace Duckmanton opened her own shop at 2a, Church Square, in 1925, and then moved to the top of Northampton Road; she had previously run the ladies' department of Webbs the outfitter's in Church Street.[25]

The viability of such shops was helped by the spread of branded goods, greater mass-production of women's clothing and an increase in consumer demand. This allowed at one end of the market the growth of this type of high-fashion shop, and at the other end a diversification into selected lines of clothing by the variety chain stores, like Woolworths and Marks and Spencer. The coming of Woolworths to

Market Harborough in 1927 was quite a big event: 'To think Harborough was going to have a Woolworths. . . . It was thruppence and sixpence then – anything – nothing above sixpence. It was an absolute child's dream'. 'It was somewhere you could go in and walk all around, and see and not buy.'[26]

The new 'Woolies' had a haberdashery counter, selling trimmings, cotton, buttons and the like. From there it was not a big step to start selling limited ranges of children's clothes. In the 1950s Woolworths no longer priced goods solely at 3*d* and 6*d*, but it was still a cheap and cheerful store which attracted a lot of custom.

> It was a 'cheapie' shop; for all that, everyone loved it. All the little bits and pieces – bootlaces, combs – you'd just go into Woolies and they'd have it . . . Dinner time you get all the factories [workers] just walk round – something to do really.

Margaret Cork was sales assistant on the drapery counter at Woolies in the mid-1950s. She sold 'underwear, all the kiddies' stuff . . . socks and vests, things like that', 'tea cosies and tablecloths' and she also measured out oilcloth (linoleum) from a fixture in the corner of the shop. Unlike Kettering or Leicester, Harborough had no Marks and Spencer. The only other big store which dealt in clothes and drapery was the local Co-op.[27]

In 1941, as well as Woolworths and the local Co-op, Market Harborough had thirteen shops selling mainly women's clothes or associated goods, three of which provided tailoring or alterations. Six of these were general drapers and outfitters, demonstrating this type of establishment's hold on the trade. There were also two 'Madame shops', three wool shops, one 'art needlework repository', and one haberdasher's.

By the late 1950s a local directory listed three shops advertising themselves as drapers; the Co-op's new ladies' and children's wear department on Coventry Road also stocked drapery lines. By 1970 there was only one self-styled draper's left in the town – Phillips of Church Street.

Why did the success of the general drapery shops come to an end? What caused establishments like Wood's and all the 'odd little shops selling skirts and things' to go out of fashion? As we have seen, general drapers sprang up at the end of the nineteenth century to serve an increased demand for clothing, especially in piece-goods for making up at home, but also to some extent for ready-made items. In the first half of the twentieth century the balance of this demand continued to shift towards ready-to-wear clothes and away from piece-goods. The general drapers had to change their stock accordingly, but this made them vulnerable to competition from the multiples and chain stores who had more buying power and could sell ready-made clothes cheaper. From the 1930s these large organizations were able to dictate styles and sizes to the manufacturers that supplied them. Nor could the

Arthur Elliott's tailor's shop at 2 Church Street, Market Harborough, 1913

general drapers match the choice offered by small private shops which specialized in one area such as coats and dresses, or underwear, or knitting wools.[28]

In Market Harborough the trade that once belonged to drapers like John Wood, Muriel Hodgson and Thomas Scarborough had fragmented. Haberdashery could be bought off the counter at Woolies and the market stall. Market traders also sold children's wear, as did specialist children's and babies' clothes shops and Tesco for a time in the early 1970s. Vivien Panter, a teenager working part-time in the 1950s, was able to get clothes for herself from Market Harborough and Kettering markets. She remembered from her childhood one alternative for poor families:

> There was a shop called 'Uncle' Charlie's . . . That was a Harborough man – I think he got seconds and things, and it was a family joke that everything I wore came from 'Uncle' Charlie's. It was a back street shop . . . used by people who didn't have any money, of which we were very much a part.[29]

Until very recently (with the arrival of Dorothy Perkins) Harborough had no womenswear multiples, so it was the fashion specialists who stood to gain from the decline of the drapery stores. The types of these shops has varied over the years, as have their fortunes, but collectively they represent an important sector. Costumiers, boutiques, and today's private fashion retailers pursuing the latest trend are all part of the story. One particularly noticeable change has been the growth in numbers of shops catering for young people as the disposable income of this group has increased since the 1950s.

Vivien Window and her husband recently had a shop in Desborough selling clothes which they made at home. Their main problem was the location:

> People are not used to shopping in Desborough, and if they want say, a skirt or a dress for their little girl, they'll go to Kettering, they'll go to Harborough, they might go to Northampton or Leicester. . . . And one or two people said, 'We didn't realize how cheap you were.' People equate small shops with expense. And actually we were as cheap as MacKays here in town, or any of the cheap shops. . . . In the end it didn't pay enough – we were paying out in the end, so [my husband] just makes his jog-suits at home now.[30]

In the 1980s, despite competition from the Leicester clothes shops, both large and small, Market Harborough supported a sizeable private sector. Most of the shops were small and highly specialized in what they sold. Second-hand clothes were sought after for fashion as much as out of necessity, and the town had a successful second-hand womenswear shop, Dress Circle, in St Mary's Road.

The history of menswear shops in Market Harborough has followed a similar pattern to that of womenswear shops. Tailors, hatters, shirtmakers and drapers were the first shopkeepers to serve the needs of those who wore new rather than second-hand clothes. Later on, factory production of ready-made clothes provided the stock for the men's outfitter as well as the general draper who sold mens' and boyswear.

Geoff Johnson went into the Co-op's drapery department at 3 High Street straight from school in 1926 and worked there until 1940. The department was quite large, employing ten people. They sold women's, men's and children's clothes, hats, boots and shoes, household linen and heavy textiles. Like other general drapers, the department's sales were very mixed:

> We used to sell a lot of matting strips, the old coconut matting strips. [In] everybody's kitchen, as they climbed up the social scale, they graduated from the red tiles to a strip of coconut matting.
>
> The trade was so different: I can remember a typical couple coming in from Welford, and make a special journey in somewhere round about Easter time. . . . She bought shirting by the yard to make him shirts, and lining, 'cause the old boys in those days, a lot of them liked lined shirts. And she'd either be buying Oxford shirting, which is a hard-wearing shirting, or flannelette shirting, which is a warmer shirting. And then she would buy all the buttons and bits and pieces to make shirts.
>
> Then she would buy underwear, trousers, jacket, waistcoat, usually in what was then the old Derby tweed, which was a heavy tweed. In those early days you were still selling breeches

> and leggings. You got him with . . . John White's impregnable boots, and leggings and breeches, which meant stockings as well, which meant long pants [too]. And of course a cap, or a couple of caps if they were in the money. . . . Generally they had a good do early in the spring. And then they would come in again late autumn and renew all the parts.[31]

This couple could have bought cheap factory-made shirts at any draper's or outfitter's in the town. Customer conservatism was to remain a powerful influence on men's clothes shops.

The rise of menswear multiples shaped that side of the retail clothes trade sooner than it did in womenswear. Factory mass production was applied earlier and more extensively to men's clothes than it was to women's, and the first multiple shops appeared in the 1870s. Indeed throughout the first half of the twentieth century menswear multiples were more widespread than womenswear multiples. Hence Market Harborough has had a number of branches of menswear chains but never any of the women's clothes chains before 1989.[32]

Webb Bros Ltd was a very small multiple, a private chain of seven or so shops in the south-east of the Midlands, including shops in Kettering and Luton. Their Market Harborough branch was opened in 1892 in Church Street. It finally closed in 1986. Charles Wimlett was an apprentice at Webb's in the 1920s. Most of their trade was in menswear though the shop also sold some ladieswear:

> Webb Bros Outfitters Ltd, that was their name. . . . There were three people [on the menswear side]. There was the manager, Mr Samuel Ward, the first sales came next, then there was myself, a very important one. After a customer had been served, I had to clean up all the pickle; in other words, socks were not in cases, they were all tied together in cardboard plaques, and they would serve a customer and leave the lot there, and the apprentice would learn to tie up his string and his knots and get ready for the next customer to come along.
>
> There was another piece on [the shop], that was our tailoring department. It all came from Kettering. Webb's did as many still do, send all their goods to a factory, Wallace & Linnell.
>
> If I met you at the door, and I didn't know who you were, I should pass the time of day to you and 'What can I do to help you?' If you said a suit you wanted, I should immediately call Mr Ward the manager. He would come along with his tape round his shoulders and he would then take you into the tailoring room, into this other department, and show you all his patterns and quote his prices and measure you. If he were not there, the assistant, what we called the first sales – there was only one there but he was the first – he would do that.
>
> He would have his order book there and write all your widths for the trousers and stuff. Then that would go to Kettering and they would decide whether it should be made bespoke, because they had a tailor on the premises, or whether it should go to one of the tailoring firms. It would all depend on the price. If you chose a low-price cloth, then it

would go to the manufacturers. If you were choosing a high-grade cloth, a wedding order, or someone you recognized as someone of standing, you wouldn't try and push anything off with him, you'd sell him the best you'd got, and it would be made by hand at Kettering.[33]

The household names in menswear arrived in Market Harborough in the 1920s, a period of national expansion for the multiple clothes shops. The Leeds firm Hepworth's and the Birmingham-based Foster Brothers (founded 1876) came to the town in 1923. Whereas Foster's only sold ready-made clothes, Hepworth's offered a bespoke tailoring service by sending orders away to their own factories in Leeds, in the same way as Webb's had some orders specially made up at Wallace & Linnell's. Both Foster's and Hepworth's, like most of the large multiples, were self-sufficient in as much as the factories and the retail outlets were part of the same company.[34]

Wholesale bespoke tailoring chains had taken off at the beginning of the twentieth century. Their attraction was that they could offer a cheap suit, fitted and styled to the individual customer. The crucial factors in running this type of operation were an administrative system that could transmit the customer's order to the factory and deliver a satisfactory product back, and the ability to match retail demand with output. When demand was slack, the factories were put over, where possible, to the production of off-the-peg clothing instead. Capacity could also be, and was, reduced by laying workers off. To raise money for their hectic expansion of retail branches many of the larger menswear multiples became public limited companies in the inter-war years. Nevertheless the multiples that solved these organizational problems prospered. Both the wholesale bespoke tailoring firms and the multiple outfitters took greater shares of the menswear trade between 1914 and 1939, but by no means at an equal rate. According to one estimate the wholesale bespoke tailors were expanding four times as fast as the multiple outfitters, and therefore picking up more of the business, during this period.[35]

The national menswear chains set their stalls by the price of their main lines, as they competed for custom in the high streets of small towns and city suburbs. In Market Harborough Foster's and Hepworth's faced each other across The Square, advertising ready-made suits for 35*s*, 45*s* and 55*s* at Foster's, and a made-to-measure garment from Hepworth's for 45*s*. Webb's offered made-to-measure suits from 50*s* upwards. In marked contrast the independent High Street tailor, G.E. Remington, started his prices at 55*s*, and went up to 7 guineas (147*s*).[36]

The Hepworth's shop in Market Harborough was quite small, employing only two members of staff in the early 1930s. Made-to-measure suit orders were a major part of the business, as was typical for the wholesale bespoke tailoring multiples, but the shop also stocked the standard range of men's clothing as well as working men's bib-and-brace overalls. All trade was for cash only.[37]

Charles Wimlett, after he had left Webb Bros in the early 1920s, got a job at

Smith's Clothing Stores, a large independent shop in Leicester's High Street:

> I was there for eleven years. I went through all the departments, became a departmental buyer and also a hatter; and I was the only hatter in the city of Leicester. If you came in, if you'd got bumps on your head like bunions, I could fit you on the spot. . . . Say you wanted a bowler hat or a set style – that's a soft felt hat, generally either fur felt or wool, and it would be rigid, so I had to melt that hat down. First of all I'd take the shape of your head on a conformeter. That was like a typewriter, inverted, which I put on your head, and little segments all round recorded the shape of your head [on a piece of paper]. . . . Then you took that piece of paper out, cut it round the dots, place that on this segmented block and you adjusted the block all round to fit the shape of your head.
>
> [At] Dunn's [a menswear multiple which had a branch in the centre of Leicester], if a customer went in – I did this myself to find out what they did do – they would put the conformeter on your head, press the doings, show you the paper that had been marked out, and say 'That's your head, sir'. They never did heat the hat up – they would warm it, and put it on their knee like this, and pull it like the devil. That was their idea of being a hatter![38]

Multiple firms, as in other trades, depended for their success on a high volume of

The imposing premises of Richards & Son, in the 'Manor House', the west side of the High Street, Market Harborough, *c.* 1952. Richards were the leading independant bespoke tailors in the town during the period between the wars

sales. The Leicester branch of the London menswear multiple, Horne Bros, had a system of heavy sales pressure. Any member of staff working there, once he had finished serving a customer in his own particular department, was required to take him over to another department. 'Would you like a shirt, Sir?' If the customer made a further purchase, the first assistant would receive an introductory commission.[39]

The pattern of clothes shops in Market Harborough in 1941 reflected the local demand for menswear. Out of twenty-seven retailers, twelve dealt to differing degrees in men's clothes. Six of these shops offered a tailoring service, ranging from Hepworth's 45*s* suit to the riding wear made for the hunting set by Richards & Son and F. Hall.[40]

After the Second World War the tendency of the wholesale bespoke tailoring firms nationally was to increase their production of ready-made clothing, which made more efficient use of their manufacturing capacity. At the same time the greater popularity of casual clothes for men, particularly sports jackets and knitwear, gave a boost to this part of the trade. Burton's, one of the best-known chains of wholesale bespoke tailors, came to Harborough in the early 1950s. They opened shop on a prime High Street site next to Woolworths (Gateway and Thrifty respectively in 1994), and closed down again a few years later to be replaced by MacFisheries Supermarket.[41]

The wholesale tailoring firms had to adapt to national fashions if they were to survive. Although the independent men's outfitters had to keep pace with fashion as well, they could do so more locally as long as they could find the right suppliers.

Geoff Johnson, who had worked for the Co-op before the Second World War, came back to Market Harborough after serving in the RAF and set up in business for himself. Samuel Ward, the former manager of Webb's in Harborough, was selling his gentleman's outfitter's in Adam & Eve Street, and Geoff seized the opportunity. He stayed in the trade, and the same shop, for forty years before retiring in 1987. When he started in the late 1940s, rationing of clothes manufacture and retailing was still in force:

> All the firms were rigid. They came to an agreement that a shopkeeper would get a percentage, according to his turnover. According to his trade with them, they would guarantee him a percentage so that he'd always got some goods to come in. . . . I think I had about four dozen socks a month from Wolsey, two or three dozen ties from Tootal. . . . The underwear came in with Wolsey as well, and Tootal's included the shirts. . . . So you were getting basically over your main suppliers, you were getting your bread-and-butter'.

Geoff struck a deal with a High Street retailer to get round one of these restrictions:

> There again why I always liked old man Burn – he had always been uppercrust, and he had the two bob and half-crown [ties], but he'd been in business longer than I had – his turnover was bigger, from the past. So he was entitled to shilling and 1*s* 6*d* ties, so old

> Burn used to buy them and flog them to me – that enabled me to put ties in my window.

He saw a great deal of change over the years, both in men's fashions and in the economics of the trade:

> The dinner-suits we used to sell, they were quite heavy. You can't imagine anybody going to a hop now in a great thick suit, can you? They used to sweat like the blazes, didn't they?
>
> The days have gone when I used to sit down on a Saturday evening with my order book and write away. Post them on a Sunday morning, and the stuff would arrive on Thursday. The customer would be satisfied and the money in the till by Saturday. You'd done your business in a week without holding stock. You can't do it now.
>
> This sort of self-service has always gone against my grain. If a customer comes in with the intention of buying a shirt, you ask him what size he takes and he says fifteen, you're getting somewhere aren't you? Now, they wander in, half of them don't tell you what they want, and eventually you screw it out of them that he's looking for a shirt – inevitably he's looking at the [size] seventeens or the thirteens. By the time you get him on . . . you could have had the ruddy thing in the bag and the money in the till and the bloke on his way quite happy.

Today, most of the manufacturers that supplied Johnson's for years have disappeared; those that have survived are now distributing clothes made abroad. In the town two of the shop's main competitors, Webb's and Hepworth's, both closed in 1986. The latter outlet was not retained by its new owners, Next, who were then restyling former Hepworth's branches to serve younger, fashion-conscious customers, who had more money to spend on clothes. The converted shops were concentrated in the cities and larger towns, and smaller branches such as Market Harborough were sold.

By 1989 men's clothes shops in Harborough varied widely in the clothes they sold and the market they served. These differences were most marked among the small specialist private shops. The hunting set could still have their riding gear made at the firm of F. Hall's. Henry's in the High Street offered suits, shirts and Barbour jackets, and also hired formal wear. At Geoff Johnson's old shop there was still a gent's outfitter run on similarly conservative lines to its predecessor. In the same street however, shoppers with an eye for smart style could buy upmarket Italian clothes at Martel's, or go to Apollo for a cheaper, more casual range.

Perhaps the most interesting recent development is the return of Burton's to the town. Burton and Dorothy Perkin's have a joint outlet (they are both part of the Burton group) at 3 High Street. Certainly the Burton venture has increased competition in Market Harborough. At the same time the town's clothes shops remain in the shadow of nearby cities with large markets and a wide range of independent and chain stores. In Geoff Johnson's words: 'It doesn't make that much difference, because there's just as many people go into Leicester and Kettering and Northampton'.[42]

## *Chapter Ten*

# Bakers and Confectioners

The baker's trade was the last of the food trades to experience an industrial revolution. It was only from the 1880s that technical advances began to be made in bakeries with the introduction of mixing machines and ovens more capable of close control. This was both a result of legislation compelling standards of cleanliness and of capital investment stemming from the introduction of limited liability. By the turn of the century all but the smallest bakeries had a dough-kneader and in larger establishments machinery was employed for sifting flour, mixing, moulding and rolling dough. While mechanization led to the plant bakery and the mass production of sliced bread, ultimately it has enabled the small producer-retailer to compete successfully on the basis of a locally produced fresh product.[1]

For much of this century, the baker's trade in Market Harborough was dominated by small bakers, producing a range of breads and confectionery for sale in their own shops and bread rounds. Large scale centralized baking passed this small town by, at least until the arrival of the supermarkets in the 1960s. It would be wrong however to think of all the bakers with archaic ovens, baking in the traditional way. Steam ovens and other technical innovations were to be found in the more progressive bakeries before the last war. The small baker was not obliged to do everything by hand. The mixing of bread baking with catering, confectionery and the sale of biscuits and other groceries has also helped small bakers to stave off large-scale competition. They also had the advantage of offering a fresh product (factory-made bread is usually at least twelve hours old), the loyalty of their customers and the lure of credit.

In 1900 there were eight bakers in the town. They could be divided into two broad types: those who baked a limited range of bread for shop sale and a delivery round, such as Francis Pepperday in Gladstone Street and Mrs Bird in Rectory Lane, Little Bowden, and those who baked bread and confectionery for the supply of a shop and refreshment rooms, such as Herbert West at 54 High Street and J.A. Emerson at 11 The Square. Herbert West also baked for outside catering. In addition to the independent bakers, the Market Harborough Co-op had built a bakery behind their premises at 4 High Street in 1892. Garner's in Adam & Eve Street, and their successors Stokeley's, also baked pork pies and other meat products on the premises:

Jinks, he had a horse and cart and Muggridges in the back [Church Street] but they didn't used to deliver a lot as I remember it. Then there was Harrison's of Bath Street, they did an awful lot, they came second to Emerson's in actual fact but they did bread only . . . Stokeley's in Adam & Eve Street, they used to bake pies and sausage rolls, and a thriving business too, but they only baked meat products, nothing else . . . Miss Muggridge didn't make her own bread, it was bought in from Frear's and Black's in Leicester.[2]

On a national scale, bread consumption has declined since the 1880s. An affluent society eats less bread and as purchasing power has increased, people have turned

The Buswell family bakery in Clipston, 1952. Ralph Buswell is holding a 10 ft 'peel' to slide the loaf tins into the oven

away from cheap, filling foods, based on bread, towards more palatable foods. In 1841 bread took one third of total expenditure on food, in 1881 one sixth and by 1960 only one sixteenth.[3] In Market Harborough, however, as the population of the town grew steadily up to the First World War, the number of bakers also grew to meet the demand for bread. Thereafter bakers combated the decline in bread consumption by diversifying into catering and confectionery. By the period covered in this book, most Harborough bakers had begun this process. It was usual, for instance, to sell a range of confectionery and cakes, particularly at Christmas time:

> Mrs West, the confectioner, who has a larger establishment across the way [67 and 54 High Street]. At either of these premises the Christmas shopper will find, not only iced cakes and high-class confectionery, but crackers from *6d* per box upwards, and chocolates of all descriptions. Mr Emerson [11 The Square] is noted for cakes, specially iced and trimmed for Christmas, whilst their veal and ham pies are certainly of the best, and cannot be beat. Here will also be found a speciality in chocolates and sweets assorted in fancy boxes, in addition to a very large and extensive collection of crackers. (*Market Harborough Advertiser*, 20 December 1904)

West's was the longest established of the bakers' businesses in the town, still owned and run in 1987 as Emerson and West's by the fourth generation of the family, Mr Michael West. Mr West's great grandfather, Herbert West, opened at 54 High Street in 1897, continuing the tea and coffee rooms formerly run by Mrs Annie Lakin from whom it would appear the celebrated Harborough cheesecake recipe was obtained.[4] 'The cup that cheers but not inebriates', ran an advert in 1898, 'If you want a genuine and refreshing CUP of TEA, go to West's (late Lakin's) Tea and Coffee Rooms. The original shop for Cheesecakes, Celebrated Pork Pies and Fancy Confectionery. Ices in Season. The best of everything at moderate charges. Wash and Brush-Up, *2d*.'[5] Another newspaper advert placed by Herbert West in 1899 lists a broad range of:

> Sponge, Pauna, Madeira, Birthday, Bride, Christening, Genoa and Tea Cakes . . . Pastry Cook and Confectioner, Genuine Home-Made Pork Pies, Veal and Ham Pies, Vienna and Tritcumina Bread. Sole agent in Market Harborough for the London Broken Tea at *6d* and *1s 8d* per lb, and the London *1s 10d*, *2s* and *2s 4d*. Dinners and Teas Catered for at Reasonable Prices.[6]

In December 1901 West's moved to 11 High Street and in the following February opened new Dining Rooms there. Hot joints were available every day from 12 to 2 o'clock.[7] Herbert West died in 1932, leaving the business to his son Arthur. Another son, H.G. West, set up in business at 55 Northampton Road, which was later to become Wesses (the current bakery of that name no longer has any family connection with West's). Arthur West's son Donald became the third generation of the family to bake when he started full-time in 1933, learning the trade from the Swiss chef employed by his father. He had started as early as 1926 by helping as a boy to put the crosses on hot-cross buns at Easter. He was to follow in Herbert West's footsteps with a particular interest in the catering side of the enterprise:

> My grandfather did quite a lot of catering and did it in a simple sort of way; a horse and cart used to transport the staff and equipment about. I'm going back to 1930 now. He used to do the polo teas at Thorpe Lubenham and Arthingworth in particular, and . . . the cricket lunches and teas as well, going down to Symington's ground and doing the catering there for all kinds of sporting events. . . . His wife was very keen on the shop trade and she did that part. She was always at 11 [High Street] We used to have the bank managers, bank clerks [and] company directors, who didn't have canteens of their own in those days. They didn't eat rolls at lunchtime then, they came for a three-course lunch – soup, meat and sweet – and paid 1*s* 9*d* for it. We used to get quite a lot of passing custom because we were in the middle of the High Street which was a very prominent position. Every day of the week for years and years we sent filled rolls and sausage rolls and pork pies to R. & W.H. Symington's between

The bakery delivery van of Weston & Sons, Gumley, 1920s. Note the bread piled up on the shelf inside and the ledger for recording sales under the woman's arm

ten and eleven o'clock and it used to be an awful fight to get them over there. We used to hand-carry the lot over there. The girl used to come back worn out because she'd probably served 300 or 400 customers in that time, but that was for mid-morning, not for lunch. They used to start work at half-past six or seven in those days in the factory.[8]

Mr Jack Faulkner retired in 1983 after a long career as a baker, most of which was spent in Market Harborough. He had worked for several of the town's bakers – Emerson's, Todd's, Eades and the Co-op – after being apprenticed to the prestigious Simpkin and James in Leicester and following a short period baking in Nottingham. He was brought up in Leicester during the First World War and initially learnt the trade from his father, Ernest Faulkner of Marston Street, Leicester. His childhood memories of Leicester give an insight into the work of the small baker:

When I was with my Dad, it was all bread, we didn't do any confectionery. . . . They were long days too; six o'clock in the morning, I had a carrier bike [to do deliveries], then when I'd done that I had to go in the bakehouse and weigh up bags of flour and grease the tins ready for the next day. There were scores of 'pony bakers' in Leicester in those days . . . I could name you sixty bakers in Leicester, family bakers that employed two or three people.

In those days dough was made overnight and allowed to prove in a big long trough. Then in the morning it was risen to the top and you knocked it down, cut it out and made it up into bread. In those days you blended the flour yourself. We'd have what we'd call a local mill – that was perhaps Wellingborough or Northampton – then a port flour which mostly consisted of Canadian winter wheat, which was strong; that gave you the strength, the local mills, the sweeter flavour. Most bakers had two or three mills and they blended them. In those days it was ten-stone hessian sacks.

It was a side-flue, coal-fired oven; the fire actually went in the oven. Of course there were no thermometers in those days. You tested the temperature by the degree of whiteness round the wall. Then the fire was raked out and we had what were called a 'devil', that was a pole with a sack and we used to dip that in a bucket of water and sling it around the oven and clean all the muck off the bottom. That was heavy work. Then after the bread was made and moulded and put into tins or whatever, that was put into the oven. You had to be quick about that because the first bread to be put in was the last to come out. If you'd got a hot oven, twelve foot square, you'd got to nip about a bit. [It took] about forty-five minutes. The baking temperature in those days was usually 500 degrees.

People used to come to us to bake their Sunday dinners in our big oven. Of course we had to fire it on a Sunday too, so it didn't get too cold for Monday. I had that money, penny a time. You'd get all sorts of dinners: Dad used to say, 'Has the twenty-to-one been yet?' I used to think, 'What was twenty-to-one?' 'Twenty potatoes to one bit of meat!' Some would come respectable with a nice white cloth over it, others with a bit of newspaper. Still, I didn't care, I was getting the pennies. And we used to bake Christmas cakes for them, people had made their own Christmas cake [mixture]. There were some rare specimens, some like Yorkshire batter!

You'd always got company while you'd got a horse. His ears would be going and you could talk to him. [The horse] always got first treatment. Go and feed the horse and water it before you loaded up. Then on a nice wet day you've got to wisp him down. . . . Then if heavy snow came, you'd have to take him down and have him what they called 'frost-nailed'. They put nails in that stick out like cricket studs [from the horse's hoof]. They knew when they were going home as well, when they'd served the last customer. If they'd been half dead during the day, when they'd got their heads towards home, it was a wonderful feeling. They were living things. You could talk to them, you could see their ears going backwards and forwards. If you moved to get the whip, they'd [move sharply].[9]

Mrs Dorothy Springer's father, Frederick Murkitt, ran a small bakery and general store from about 1918 at 18 Church Street (Squibbs in 1994). Mr Murkitt's methods were typical of the smaller baker, with his bakehouse situated behind the shop. As with many family businesses, his young daughter often helped:

[He started baking] about six o'clock. . . . At the far side of the shop was a whole set of wooden shelves where my father would stack the bread when he brought it from the bakehouse. . . . He didn't do any fancy confectionery. He did his bread of course, lots of pastries, meat pies – he'd got quite a name for his meat pies – mince pies, cakes, plain cakes really, fruit slab – his fruit slab again was something that he had quite a reputation for – jam tarts, cheese cakes, 'Nelsons'. No fresh cream or decorated cakes or anything. He really was a baker and confectioner, but not fancy bakery.

He would mix his bread mix in a great big wooden 'trough', he used to call it. He would mix the dough in that and leave it to rise and then he would knock it back and lift it out. It was a great big armful of dough which he would just put his hands under and carry it from that side of the bakehouse to the other, he called it the 'board', but it was a wooden table against the wall. Now I would help him then, I would weigh off the dough while he moulded up . . . If he was doing jam tarts or cheese cakes, he would roll out and put the pastry in the tins and then I would add the filling. I'd probably keep an eye on things if he'd put it in the oven and he probably wanted to go and have a rest for quarter-of-an-hour. . . . There were four ovens set one above the other with a firebox at the bottom which was fired with coke . . . it had – he used to call it a barometer but obviously he meant a thermometer – at the side of the oven which told him the temperature it was roughly at. His only way of regulating it was the amount of coke that he put on the fire. The oven at the top was always the hot one and by the side of the oven was a big steel cupboard which he called the 'prover', where he proved the bread.

He wouldn't be finished before five o'clock. The afternoons would be when he did his pastry and cakes. It used to take him most of the morning to do bread. He didn't deliver bread at all. Everybody came to the shop and collected it. . . . White bread and wholemeal, rolls, all sizes, 1 lb, 2 lb and then a big 4 lb sandwich loaf, cottage loaves and he used to bake a round loaf . . . in 7 lb jam tins. Everybody liked these round loaves for some reason or other.

On a Good Friday morning he would always be up really early that morning, three or four o'clock, and make hot-cross buns. My brother and I used to have to take those out on our bikes to as many of the regular customers as we could supply so that they got hot-cross buns hot for Good Friday morning breakfast. That was something I remember we did year after year.[10]

By 1932 there were a dozen bakers working in Market Harborough. There were several family concerns, such as Murkitt's, Harrison's in Bath Street who had a considerable delivery trade second only to Emerson's, and J. Bird in Little Bowden. Joe Jinks at 99 St Mary's Road (Todd's bakery in 1994) also kept a small refreshment room, the Station Refreshment Room. On a much larger scale, the Co-op bakery, with separate bread and confectionery bakehouses behind 2–4 High Street, supplied all but four of the society's branch shops and employed seven men. Another type of baker, such as West's or Emerson's did much more on the confectionery and catering side. Rowland Gardiner, brother-in-law to H.H. Pickering the butcher, bought J.A. Emerson's bakery business at 11 The Square, retained the name, and moved to new purpose-built premises at 7 Northampton Road in 1923. Between the wars, R.K. Gardiner's 'Emerson's' was the largest baker in the town, catering for hunt balls and functions in many of the country houses of the district. He later required a second bakehouse for his trade at 95 St Mary's Road. His bakers worked around the clock: 'They used to have the bread bakers in at night and the confectionery bakers in the daytime so it was used all the while'.[11]

In 1946, Joe Jinks sold his St Mary's Road bakery and the new owner, Mr Eades, employed Jack Faulkner, then with the Co-op in Market Harborough, as his baker. The bakery was rather run-down and required considerable modernization as Jack Faulkner recalled:

I thought I'd get back into private trade. Well I went to see this place. The old chap, Mr Jinks, I woke him from his afternoon nap and he came in his carpet slippers and we went into the bakehouse and he lit a gas jet. I thought, 'Crikey, just a gas jet in the bakehouse', that was the light. . . . He says, 'The oven's a bit bad'. I looked in and there was a bloomin' great hole in the middle. I said, 'How do you manage?' and he says, 'You have to be a bit careful'. The top oven was all right but you couldn't get it hot. There was no machinery, none at all, everything was hand. There were chickens running about in the bakehouse and there were pigs in the yard . . . I thought, 'Good Lord, you've done something here'. However, we survived. I had a fortnight with Mr Jinks to get used to the place and Mr Eades took over and we did all right. When he retired he sold it to Todd's.[12]

The old coal-fired oven was pulled out and a new gas-fired one was installed by Hunt's of Leicester. The work took three months and in the meantime, Hunt's provided an Army-type field service oven, which was installed temporarily in the yard. With the work completed, the bread round was built up and the dining-room improved:

> First thing we'd make the dough. We'd always put the flour in the day before, ready you see . . . then got the dough machine going and then went and got the other things ready for the pastry out of the fridge and got the oven lit. By that time the dough was mixed and we'd get that out and then start on the bread.
>
> We used to start with the hottest things first, build the oven up to the required heat for bread. You didn't want it too hot for cakes and pastry, so you organize your work so it's done on a cooling oven. There was enough heat in the afternoons for meringues. You didn't want it hot, you only wanted to dry them you see.
>
> Our bread was really what we built the business up on from taking over from Mr Jinks . . . [The bread round covered] pretty well all over the town but mostly around Welland Park Road, Highfield Street and round there, and Clarence Street. He bought a

Mr Eades standing by a field oven at the rear of his St Mary's Road shop, Market Harborough, 1946. This was his temporary measure while a new oven was being installed shortly after taking over Joe Jinks' bakery

little bakery business at Welford . . . eventually he shut the bakery down and supplied the Welford shop from here. [Eades sold to one or two other shops] and Symington's corset factory. We supplied their canteen with bread and rolls. That was a good thing. We used to make big long sandwich loaves, put six or eight of them in one basket, load the other basket up with rolls and send Florrie off. As things got on, Symington's used to send a man with a sack barrow, little Joey Taylor.

There wasn't so much [baked] but there were more varieties of brown. There was Hovis, Turog, Vitbe, Burmaline, no end of brown breads but you had to make a bit of each. You had to make Hovis according to their recipe. They always used to send you a card and you had the tins from Hovis. Hovis always had to be 120; you sieve the flour, so that you got the grains out of it and you didn't add salt to Hovis because salt was already in and then you make a thin slurry of a dough, then add the wheatgerm back again and give it another mixing. But to me Hovis was the best, when it was made right, it was the best of the wholemeals. Then there was Allinson which was as dry as dust. That was the idea, you had to chew it, that's where it aided your digestion. Jink's made a lot of Allinson, Eades did. I should think we made more Allinson than any other baker in the town. But then patterns changed. At that time millers were all competing to get their product on the market. You could get all sorts of things from Hovis. With a small place, whatever you make has got your name on, whether good or bad. People know, 'Jack Faulkner made that'.[13]

Multiple grocery and provisions stores diversified through the 1950s and 1960s and impinged on the markets of many independent retailers: outfitters, greengrocers, hardware dealers and bakers. The mass produced products of the plant bakeries, the wrapped and sliced steam-baked loaf, squeezed out the small independent retail baker who produced his own bread. The Co-op bakery closed in the face of this competition. By 1970, a pattern similar to today's had become established, with mass-produced bread a popular line in the multiples, and also sold, helped by its long shelf life and delivery network, in many village stores and suburban corner shops. The fresh bread, speciality and confectionery market was the province of three independents, Emerson & West, Wesses and Todd's. As we have seen, each of these concerns could trace their origins in bakery businesses founded earlier in the century. In the 1980s Peter Todd was baking bread and cakes in the premises formerly occupied by Eades and before him Jinks on St Mary's Road. Wesses continued the business founded by H.G. West in the 1930s on Northampton Road. They also baked for the associated 'Champers' café on The Square, as well as a busy filled-roll and lunchtime takeaway business on the corner of Coventry Road and The Square, formerly the premises of Clark's the saddlers. Emerson and West, run by Michael West in 1987, built its success on the twin advantages of West's baking pedigree and Emerson's large premises at 7 Northampton Road.

These three enterprising and modern businesses, each occupying its own niche in the bakery and catering market, left the factory loaf to the multiples. They traded

Donald and Michael West behind the counter in their Northampton Road shop, 1973

successfully upmarket, with fresh granary and crusty bread baked on the premises, value-added lines such as filled rolls and takeaway pizzas, and confectionery baking from wedding cakes and gateaux to doughnuts and fresh-cream buns. There would seem to be little scope in Market Harborough for the 'Oven Door' or other 'baked-on-the-premises' style of chain bakers, seen in many other high streets and shopping centres. The bakery trade is one of the larger retail sectors where the long-established producer-retailer has resisted the advance of the multiples. The product is invariably fresher, more closely tailored to the local market and something for which many customers are prepared to pay more.

In 1987 Mr Michael West gave us an account of Emerson & West's diversified retail and catering business which illustrates the blend of innovation, flexibility and the accumulated experience of a family business which contributed to his own success and that of other independent bakers in the town:

We're trading on 7 Northampton Road in a multitude of guises really, we're bakers and confectioners, we do a little bit of outside catering, we do some associated equipment hire, we retail wines and spirits and we also stock a large range of delicatessen items, both fresh and preserved.

On a full-time basis we've got six [staff] and then we've got a floating pool of part-timers of approximately twenty-five, some of whom obviously only do one or two days a week. Most of the full-time staff are associated with the bakery. We've got four full-time in the bakery and two full-time working on the retail side, and then we've got a couple more part-time in the bakery and then the rest of the part-timers are split between the shop and on the restaurant and restaurant kitchen side. . . . Because of the nature and the volume of the work we do, we don't need a permanent staff just for the catering.[14]

Donald West, Michael's father, had made catering his speciality and from 1946 to 1970 was reckoned one of the best caterers in the Midlands, servicing functions all over the county and beyond and for as many as forty hunt balls in a season. 'There aren't the hunt balls there used to be', Michael West told us, 'it's a dying art'.[15] His catering business was of a different type and geographical range to years gone by:

We can do a small buffet lunch for a local company's board meeting for perhaps two or three people, or we can do a wedding or a private party for a couple of hundred, and everything in between really. We do a lot of company business locally where the numbers tend to be quite small but their demands and expectations are quite high. We don't go much outside a twenty-mile radius.

My week tends to vary, very much depending on whether we've got any outside catering business and what that entails. Obviously if you've got an outside catering function ten miles away for 200 people that's going to absorb a certain amount of my time and other members of the staff's time, actually being there and preparing for it. As far as the actual day-to-day running of the business is concerned, certainly on the bakery side, it's very much a routine, with certain functions being done on certain set days. That's the only way we can organize the production and it gradually runs as a continual process, and then special orders and one-off things are fitted in as and when they're needed.

Well at the beginning of the week, on a Monday, Tuesday, Wednesday, we tend to make the things that are going into the shop and can stay in the shop with the shelf life of approximately a week. Towards the weekend, obviously we concentrate where the greater volume of trade is, we concentrate on the things that are going to go out with one day shelf life only, things that involve fresh cream, meat products. Obviously the day is split up. The first part of the day, whichever day of the week it is, is involved in producing daily requirements of bread and rolls, buns and confectionery required for that day and can only be sold for that day, and then the rest of the day revolves around preparing confectionery bases for finishing off later in the week.

Different times of the year there's obviously going to be different routines. The build-up to Christmas, as far as Christmas cakes, Christmas puddings, those sort of things, that starts from the early part of October and goes all the way through October and November and then once we're into December we start thinking about gateaux for Christmas, yule logs, mince pies, those sort of things, and the thing gradually snowballs over the three weeks up to Christmas.

We supply three private grocery shops between here and Oadby, one in each village actually, we go to Foxton, to Kibworth and to Great Glen and then of course we've got our own business in Oadby [since 1975], that we supply on a daily basis with our own home-made bread and rolls and confectionery. . . . We sell a combination of our own bread and bread that we buy from Geary's at Ratby. They are an established bakers in Leicester with established lines particularly of health breads. They make two loaves in particular, 'Warden' and 'Rearsby'. They have a very strong following so we stock them for that reason and from a practical point of view; making our things fresh daily, it's not that easy getting our bread to the shop for an 8.30 a.m. opening without completely disrupting our routine at Market Harborough. The bread we deliver doesn't arrive there until perhaps 10.30 a.m. which is quite late.

The dining-room is an integral part of the business. We started originally without it but because we'd got so much space upstairs on the first floor and because carrying on from when my father was in business, we'd got people who'd been very regular customers then, perhaps not necessarily coming weekly, but we still now get people who come once a year whenever they're in Market Harborough and we were getting a demand, we'd got the room so we felt we should do it. It's very much the people who come into the shop, they're looking round and they see they can have a cup of coffee, they can pop upstairs for afternoon tea. People travelling through the town stop for lunch, and having stopped for lunch they come back in the shop and they wander around and see things we offer in the shop.

The style of the operation is very similar to what we did at both 11 and 13 High Street. It's all table service, waitress service, we offer the same sort of set lunches. It's always roast, either a two or three course, moderately priced. We're serving other meals throughout the day, whatever people want and they can have their morning coffee in the afternoon and they can have their afternoon tea in the morning. Whatever's there is immediately available.

I think we're fortunate in Market Harborough that at the moment the demand is there but I think if you were in other situations you might be swimming very much against the tide. Because of the locality, it is still, very rural, people still expect to find an operation like ours and will still patronize it, whereas if you go in the centre of Leicester for example, I wouldn't think there'd be any chance of running on that format.

I'm involved with the actual organization of the staff, running who does what and how, where and why. Hopefully normally that runs without too much trouble because again we've got some staff who've been with us for quite some time, so we're fortunate in that respect.

The buying obviously is my principal concern and that involves quite a lot of time because it's such a wide spectrum of products that we're dealing with. We're buying for the restaurant and catering, we're buying bakery ingredients in all sorts of different guises, whether it's bags of flour or tins of fruit, dried fruit. Unfortunately it all tends to come from different suppliers. You can't really go through a particular wholesaler and still get what you want at the right terms. Then there's the buying associated with all the delicatessen items, whether it's fresh pâtés, continental sausages, hams, cooked meats some of which we do ourselves; we make our own salads, we cook our own hams, quite a lot of the cold meats we cook ourselves, and then all the items whether they're tins or packets or jars . . . you tend to be dealing with perhaps twelve to twenty [suppliers] on a monthly basis. Obviously stock control is very important on them, as you are well aware, most foods now come with labelling regulations and particularly sell-by dates and codes which take an awful lot of time.

The delicatessen side of the business has really developed since 1973. The restaurant that we are operating now started in '75, on the first floor. The delicatessen has really expanded more in the last six to eight years. We've really now got quite a large range.

It's certainly rising standards of living, it's also associated with people generally now take a lot more holidays abroad so they come into contact with different varieties of food and when they come back from holiday they then begin to think, let's try what we had on holiday and where can we get it, so a lot of the demand stems from that. There's also in Market Harborough quite a lot of people of foreign origin, associated with the Second World War, there's quite a large Italian community and Polish community and they're obviously very keen on buying certain things of their particular origin.

The current trend is certainly towards healthier eating, which we're all aware of; a greater perception of labelling, E-numbers and exactly what is in, particularly, manufactured foods. There is a tendency for us to use less salt in recipes, sugar, than there was previously, a greater use of wholemeal pastry and greater use of vegetable fats in the bakery whereas perhaps in the past we might have used butter or margarine, we now use more vegetable margarine and the same with oils that we use, we now use a vegetable oil which we wouldn't necessarily have done in the past.

I would imagine if we could turn the clock back thirty years, we would be using the same style of equipment and working in the same way really. I think the only material change that we have made in recent years is the type of mixer that we use to principally mix the dough and make the pastry whereas in the past we've always had what would be known as an upright mixer, like the Kenwood mixer you might have at home . . . today we're using a spiral mixer which is exactly the same style of machine except it has a twisted arm and it mixes the dough or the pastry in a spiral action and supposedly it does the job better. The rest of the equipment that we use is very much based on traditional lines. We still divide and weigh the dough manually and mould all the dough manually because most of our bread production is for fancy loaves and for bread rolls that actually involve doing it by hand. On our scale you can't fully mechanize. If you're running a plant bakery, it can be fully mechanized. That's obviously not our wish.

We're unfortunately blessed with electric ovens, that's something we inherited which are very expensive to operate although they do retain the heat very well, so we're very anxious that we should get our ovens switched off as early as we can and then use the latent heat on a reducing basis and end up at the end of the day using them for drying bread so that we can make our own breadcrumbs and for drying meringues which stay in the oven overnight.

The [bakery side] isn't very different compared to thirty or forty years ago. We're still making many of the lines that have been made for so many years, [such as] these oval Market Harborough cheesecakes that we're obviously well-known for. The recipes we use for our Christmas cakes, our Christmas puddings, our wedding cakes, many of the recipes that are involved in producing part of the elements of the confectionery are the same recipes that say Billy Cotton, who was working for us for fifty years would have known the second day he started. They just haven't changed, the books are so well-thumbed . . . occasionally we have to have a rewrite because they are so well-thumbed, because they're used consistently.

We're making a large variety of different items, particularly on bread. We now sell a lot more brown bread than we ever did in father's time. There are certain days when we sell more brown to white. The ratio used to be something like 20 per cent brown, 80 per cent white and we do all sorts of different varieties of brown now. We obviously do the stone-ground wholemeal, we do a rye and a granary all in various different sizes and guises.

Well I think Market Harborough is pretty unique in the fact that for such a small town there is three independent bakers. I was talking to an equipment supplier who obviously knows us, he couldn't believe there were also two other independent bakers . . . there still must be a very good demand for the products. Having said that, obviously our bakery is only part of our business. It's not the main part . . . and people come in our shop for several different reasons apart from buying bakery products.

At the moment we haven't got a supermarket in Market Harborough which has got its own in-store bakery which supposedly is the most direct form of competition. Most of the bread that is sold through the supermarkets is still in sliced form and the sort of volume that they're working in, we're just not in that league. You see them trolleying in perhaps a thousand sliced loaves. It's not our wish to be involved in that sort of business.

You could split up the catering side of it, including the restaurant upstairs and you could say that that would account for about 30 to 35 per cent, something like that. The other 65 per cent would be split fairly evenly in the shop between business that's associated with the bakery and that associated with the delicatessen counter.

Tuesday is still the second busiest day of the week, with Saturday the first and then, usually, Friday third, not necessarily always these days. . . . I think apart from the actual farmers and their wives and people like that who are involved directly in the [livestock] market when it's a market day, yes that generates a certain amount of business but I think where the real increase in business comes, is people tend to visit the town on the market day and that is really where the extra trade comes from, certainly for us . . . More [from people using] the retail market these days.

It would be unusual for people to come and have lunch with us as part of their working day, whereas in the shop, we're involved in selling, particularly over lunchtime, large quantities of things like filled rolls, pork pies, canned drinks, which all the staff from the various shops, building societies, banks nip out for. . . . As a general rule I start normally somewhere between seven and eight [a.m.]; I'malways there by eight, this morning I was there at six, and I usually like to think I'll be away by half-past five, six o'clock in the evening, six days a week. We reckon to do about an hour on a Sunday morning, which is purely administrative for our own purposes, rather than doing an extra hour on a Saturday night . . . Lunchtime is our busiest time, both in the shop and in the restaurant. As far as the bakery staff are concerned, we've now stopped the very early start because we think that was one of the problems we find with recruiting staff and as a rule of thumb we now start in the bakery about six a.m. and the bakery staff only work a 40–42 hour week which is considerably less than they were working ten years ago. It's still unfortunately split over the six days but they do have most of their afternoons free, they basically finish work at lunchtime.[16]

Mr Jim Knight at work in Wesses' bakery, Market Harborough, September 1988
(Photograph by Doug Millhouse)

# Postscript

During the eight years that have elapsed since the research for this book was undertaken shops and shopping in Market Harborough have dominated local opinion, news and gossip. At the heart of this lay two issues: the continued advance of multiple (especially grocery) shops and the problem of heavy through-traffic, together with the state of road communication in general. As this book goes to press both of these issues seem to be reaching some sort of conclusion and the retail life of Market Harborough is now set to adjust to many exciting new opportunities.

Ironically, the latest advance of the multiple shops has been made because of the changing fortunes of the town's livestock market. Since the Second World War, there has been a fundamental shift in Welland Valley farming away from stock fattening to a mix of pasture and varied arable agriculture. This change steadily reduced the operations of the weekly Tuesday livestock market, to a point where Harborough District Council decided to move it to an out-of-town site to the south of Foxton village and redevelop the area between Springfield Street and the River Welland as a retail centre, with a large Sainsbury's supermarket as the flagship of the enterprise. The livestock market duly moved from its 1903 site on 24 November 1992 and the new retail centre, named 'St Mary's Place', opened between 19 October and 4 December 1993.

Reactions to St Mary's Place, with its mix of supermarket, small retail units and impressive stall-market hall have been predictably mixed. Few deny the high quality of the build and the important retail opportunities which it has created, but many people worry that in the sluggish consumer economy of the early 1990s, the rest of the town's shops will find it hard to compete. The relocation of a number of retailers from the High Street to St Mary's Place, along with the main post office from St Mary's Road, seems to confirm that the commercial centre of gravity is shifting south of the historic town centre.

These changes have been aggravated by a series of changes to the road transport network. The 'bypass ethos' of post-war Britain finally affected Market Harborough with the opening of a north-eastern bypass for A6 traffic on 26 June 1992, and the completion of the long-awaited A14 road, linking the M1 and A1, on 15 July 1994. Although the environmental benefit of these new roads is considerable – radically reducing the amount of heavy through-traffic – some retailers are worried that passing trade will be equally diminished. Of more general concern has been the considerable disruption to local traffic by extensive roadworks which began in 1992 with replacements of storm water mains and has then developed with traffic calming measures associated with the Department of Transport's 'Bypass Demonstration Project'.

Depite many doom-laden predictions, born mostly out of an inherent dislike of change, it is certain that these difficulties are only a temporary problem and are in fact a rather unpalatable tonic to Market Harborough's retail capabilities. The facilities on offer today mean that the town can now compete effectively for the long-distance, car-based shoppers who, since the mid-1980s, have sustained the retail success of neighbouring towns such as Corby. It is perhaps a symbolic irony that the St Mary's Place car park occupies the site of the pens formerly used for selling cattle and sheep from the surrounding Welland Valley. Market Harborough has indeed become 'Supermarket Harborough'.

Steph Mastoris
The Harborough Museum, 1994

The logo for St Mary's Place, Market Harborough, 1993

# References

(see also the Sources and Bibliography)


## Chapter One

1. Mrs Joan Catling (née Freestone), MH.OR 104.4.
2. Johnson (1983), p. 35.
3. M. Randall, 'Supermac of the Supermarkets', *The Sunday Times*, 26.04.1987 p. 69.
4. Mr Bill Wood, MH.OR 73.7–8.
5. Whyte-Melville (1862).
6. Mr Hubert Reeve, MH.OR 101(A).7.
7. Mrs Joyce Dexter (née Wood), MH.OR 106.5–6.
8. MH.OR 101(A).5.
9. MH.OR 106.6.
10. Mr A.C. Wimlett, MH.OR 85.2.
11. Mr F.W. Lee, MH.OR 71.2.
12. MH.OR 85.6.
13. Mr Cecil Copson, MH.OR 78/1.2–3.
14. MH.OR 104.10.
15. MH OR 78/1.5.
16. MH.OR 73.7–8.
17. Winstanley (1983), pp. 220–1; Yamey (1954 & 1966), *passim*.
18. Mr Ronald Hodby, MH.OR 99.11.
19. Mr Arthur Wilford, MH.OR 05. Mr Wilford's father was the Naseby carrier; MH.OR 104.7, re Wood's.
20. Mrs Dorothy Springer (née Murkitt), MH.OR 89.12.
21. Holcombe (1973), pp. 131–2.
22. MH.OR 89.8.
23. Mr W. Ingram, MH.OR 113.2.
24. MH.OR 71.5 & 7.
25. Mrs Elizabeth Bristow, MH.OR 54.3.
26. Mr L. Buswell, MH.OR 70.2.
27. Mr Jack Whitbread, MH.OR 14.2–3.
28. MH.OR 85.8.
29. Calder (1969), *passim*, esp. pp. 318–19, 439–40; Bonner (1970), pp. 209–11.
30. Mr George Scrimshire, MH.OR 115.11–12.
31. Mr Michael Kelly, MH.OR 81.8, 10.
32. Mr Geoff Johnson, MH.OR 12/3.9.
33. Winstanley (1983), pp. 220–1; Yamey (1966), p. 277.
34. Bonner (1970), p. 248; 'Cohen, Sir "Jack"', *Dictionary of National Biography*.
35. Jefferys (1954), p. 330.
36. Mrs Vivien Window (née Panter), MH.OR 109.5.
37. MH.OR 71.8.
38. MH.OR 71.8, 14.
39. Mrs Josie Walker, MH.OR 74.4.
40. MH.OR 78/1.23–24.
41. Mr Ken Wylie, MH.OR 105.3.
42. Mr Ted Ashby, MH.OR 102.14–15.
43. MH.OR 71.11.
44. MH.OR 74.5–6, 8.
45. MH.OR 74.11.
46. Mrs Carol French (née Dainty), MH.OR 112.2.
47. MH.OR 74.3.

## Chapter Two

1. Fraser (1981), p. 92.
2. Mr Cecil Copson, MH.OR 78/1.4.
3. Mr Fred Tuffs, MH.OR 27 (side 10).10.
4. MH.OR 78/3.10.
5. Mr W. Ingram, MH.OR 113.11–12.
6. MH.OR 78/1.6; Mr F.W. Lee, MH.OR 71.3; Mrs Winnifred Monroe, MH.OR 124.4–5.

7. MH.OR 124.4–5.
8. MH.OR 78/3.16 & 78/1.6.
9. Mr Ronald Hodby, MH.OR 99.4; Mrs Joyce Dexter, MH.OR 106.6, referring to barter at Wood's the draper's.
10. Mr Norman Marlow, MH.OR 75.2–3; Mrs Dorothy Springer, MH.OR 89.9.
11. MH.OR 75.2–3; MH.OR 78/1.4; *Market Harborough Industrial Co-operative Society quarterly report*, June 1899.
12. Mr A.C. Wimlett, MH.OR 85.8.
13. MH.OR 99.12.
14. MH.OR 71.7.
15. Mrs Carol French, MH.OR 112.13.
16. MH.OR 85.8; MH.OR 99.11.
17. MH.OR 124.9–10.
18. MH.OR 75.3; Mr George Scrimshire, MH.OR 115.10–11.
19. Mr Charles Kirby, MH.OR 72.6; MH.OR 89.9.
20. Mr Michael Kelly, MH.OR 81.10–11; MH.OR 99.12; MH.OR 124.10.
21. Fraser (1981), p. 86; Golby & Purdue (1986), p. 57.
22. *Market Harborough Industrial Co-operative Society half-year report*, January 1931; MH.OR 124.17–18; C.R. Lloyd's draper's advertisement, *Market Harborough Advertiser*, 27.02.1900, p. 1.
23. Fraser (1981), p. 92; Stevenson (1984), p. 113.
24. Mrs Josie Walker, MH.OR 74/2.4.
25. MH.OR 74/2.13.
26. Mr Ted Ashby, MH.OR 102.13–14.
27. Kay (1989), *passim*.

## CHAPTER THREE

1. Mr Cecil Copson, MH.OR 78/3.9.
2. MH.OR 78/3.3–5. & MH.OR 78/1.2; Mr Norman Marlow, MH.OR 75.1,5.
3. Mr Hubert Reeve, MH.OR 101(A).17–23.
4. MH.OR 78/2.7–8.
5. Johnson (1983), p. 42; MH.OR 78/1.12; Mr Raymond Tack, MH.OR 15/2.8, 11.
6. MH.OR 15/2.6, 9.
7. Mr Geoff Johnson, MH.OR 12/3.2, also Johnson (1983), *passim*.
8. See Notts Archives Office DDRN for Raleigh bicycle catalogues.
9. MH.OR 15/2.4–6.
10. Mr W. Ingram, MH.OR 113.4–5.
11. Mr Arthur Wilford, MH.OR 5, *passim*.
12. Mrs Prince, MH.OR 122/1.10–11.

## CHAPTER FOUR

1. Mrs Gladys Wimlett, MH.OR 84.8.
2. Mrs Joan Catling (née Freestone), MH.OR 104.2.
3. Mrs Joyce Rhodes, MH.OR 107 (side 1); Mr Charles Kirby, MH.OR 72.2; Holcombe (1973), p. 112.
4. MH.OR 104.1, 3 [cf. Mr Geoff Johnson, MH.OR 12/3.2, for the identical duties of a Co-op drapery junior].
5. Mr & Mrs Lines, MH.OR 86.6; Mr Peter Todd, MH.OR 77; Mr Bernard Kemp, MH.OR 79.1.
6. Mr Michael Kelly, MH.OR 81.2; Mr W. Ingram, MH.OR 113.3 & 4; Mr William Gardner, MH.OR 108; Mr A.C. Wimlett, MH.OR 85.2.
7. MH.OR 79.1; Mr Ronald Hodby, MH.OR 99.8, 16; Mr Cecil Copson, MH.OR 78/1.1&2.
8. Mr S.G. Stanger, MH.OR 114.2; Carol French, MH.OR 112.2; Mrs Josie Walker, MH.OR 74/2.2.
9. Routh (1965), p. 36; Holcombe (1973), pp. 104–7.
10. Cronin (1984), pp. 51–5.
11. MH.OR 12/3.3 & 4.; MH.OR 78/3.15; for Wood's, see below Chapter Nine.
12. MH.OR 84.2&3, 5, 8&9; Mr Hubert Reeve, MH.OR 101(A).22; Cronin (1984), p. 54.
13. Mrs Olive Reeve, MH.OR 101(B), 8–11, 22–4, 27.
14. Routh (1965), pp. 92–6, 108; Cronin (1984), pp. 149–50.
15. Mr F.W. Lee, MH.OR 71.9, 12; Mr Bill Wood, MH.OR 73.13.

16. Mrs Vivien Window, MH.OR 109.1–8, 11–13; Margaret Lawrence, MH.OR 111, *passim*.
17. Cronin (1984), p. 195; Ted Ashby, MH.OR 102.2, 4.
18. Winstanley (1983), pp. 72–3.
19. Interview with USDAW official, Leicester area office, 17.07.1986.
20. *Market Harborough Advertiser*, 29.11.1904, p. 5, col. 2; Mr L. Buswell, MH.OR 70.5; Mrs Winnifred Monroe, MH.OR 124.15; MH.OR 71.10; MH.OR 101(A).24; Gwendoline Parke, MH.OR 98.11–12.
21. MH.OR 12/3.1; Webb (1921), pp. 193–4 ; Norman Marlow, MH.OR 75.6–7; MH.OR 78/2, side 8.
22. MH.OR 12/3.1–2; MH.OR 75.6–7; MH.OR 78/1.10 & 78/2.12.
23. MH.OR 78/1.10 & 78/2.12; Mr Raymond Tack, MH.OR 15/2.9.
24. Holcombe (1973), p. 121; MH.OR 78/2.12 & 78/1.12; MH.OR 75.16; *Leicestershire Co-operative Society, yearly report*, January 1971.
25. Holcombe (1973), pp. 122–40; Winstanley (1983), pp. 96–9.
26. Mr Ken Wylie, MH.OR 105.6–7, 14; MH.OR 102.5–6.
27. USDAW Leicester area office, as above (19.); MH.OR 109.15.
28. MH.OR 78/1.15; Routh (1965), pp. 74–5, 92–3, 95: source for 1924/5 is Board of Trade enquiries into the grocery, drapery, outfitting, fancy goods and butchery trades, quoted in Routh (1965); source for 1960 is information from retail businesses and employment exchanges, also in Routh (1965).
29. MH.OR 85.7–8; MH.OR 105.14–15.
30. Winstanley (1983), p. 38; for Allied Suppliers see Mathias (1967) and Levy (1948), pp. 69, 146.
31. MH.OR 113.1–4, 6–13.
32. MH.OR 112.6–7, 11.
33. MH.OR 85.8; MH.OR 71.6–11.
34. MH.OR 78/1.18–19, 24.
35. MH.OR 105.2–4, 6, 18–19; MH.OR 102.9.
36. MH.OR 104.9–10.
37. Mrs Joyce Dexter (née Wood), MH.OR 106.3, 7–8.
38. MH.OR 99.10, 18.
39. MH.OR 84.7.
40. MH.OR 106.3, 12; MH.OR 104.4, 9–10.
41. MH.OR 98.12.
42. MH.OR 112.2; MH.OR 74/2.1.
43. MH.OR 105.6; MH.OR 102.15.


## CHAPTER FIVE


1. Mr Charles Kirby, MH.OR 72.7.
2. V.A. Hatley (ed.), *Northamptonshire Militia Lists, 1777*, Northants. Record Society vol. xxv (1973).
3. *Whelan's History and Gazetteer of Northamptonshire* (1849); *Hagar & Co.'s Directory of Leicestershire* (1849).
4. Mr George Scrimshire, MH.OR 115. 3–7, 9–11.
5. *Kelly's Post Office Directory of Leicestershire* (1888); *Kelly's . . . Northamptonshire* (1885).
6. *Kelly's . . . Leicestershire* (1936); *Green's Directory of Mkt. Harborough & District* (1937).
7. 1981 Census; Harborough Museum, village shops survey file.
8. MH.OR 72.7.
9. Mr William Gardner, MH.OR 108.
10. *Market Harborough Illustrated* (1902); HMSO, Census of England & Wales, 1871 & 1911; Mullins & Glasson (1985).
11. Mrs Pickering, Harborough Museum written reminiscence file.
12. Mr Ronald Hodby, MH.OR 99.
13. Anon., MH.OR 96.4.
14. Mrs Dorothy Springer (née Murkitt), MH.OR 89. 1–11, 13–15.
15. Mr Michael Kelly, MH.OR 81.
16. MH.OR 81.
17. MH.OR 81.9–13, 20.
18. Mr Geoff Bonnet, MH.OR 91/1.10–12.
19. Mr Alan Clayton, MH.OR 69/1.17–18 & 69/2.1–3.
20. Mr Ramesh Radia, MH.OR 95/1.6–7.
21. MH.OR 95/2.5, 12–13.

22. MH.OR 69/2.9–12.
23. MH.OR 91/1.18–19.
24. MH OR 91/1.7.
25. MH.OR 91/1.5.
26. MH.OR 91/1.
27. MH.OR 69/1.2, 5, 8.

## CHAPTER SIX

Abbreviations:

MHICS: Market Harborough Industrial Co-operative Society

MHICS Rpt.: *MHICS quarterly reports*, 1887–1902; *half-yearly reports*, 1904–69

LrCS Rpt.: *Leicester Co-operative Society half-yearly reports*, 1955–69

LCS Rpt.: *Leicestershire Co-operative Society half-yearly reports*, 1969–73

CWMCS: Coalville Working Men's Co-operative Society

DIPCS: Desborough Industrial & Provident Co-operative Society

KCS: Kettering Co-operative Society

HDC: Harborough District Council

*MH Advertiser*: *Market Harborough Advertiser and Midland Mail*

1. MHICS Rpt., April, June 1899; *The Co-op Directory* (1951), p. 242.
2. *Midland Free Press*, 01.02.1862, p. 3; *Peterborough Co-op. Congress 1898*, pp. 247–8; MHICS Rpt. June 1892; *Kelly's Leicestershire Directory* (1888), p. 684.
3. *Kelly's Leicestershire Directory* (1900); *MH Advertiser*, 17.12.1901, p. 6; MHICS Rpt. June 1899, Nov. 1905, May 1907; MHICS Jubilee Calendar, 1912; building stone date (1913), Co-op premises, Bitteswell Rd, Lutterworth; *Leicester Co-op Congress Souvenir, 1915*, pp. 176–7; Mr Norman Marlow, MH.OR 75. 3–4.
4. MH.OR 75.4–5.
5. Mr Cecil Copson, MH.OR 78/1.6 & 78/3.9.
6. MH.OR 75.3–5.
7. For MHICS and CWMCS see *Leicester Co-op. Congress Souvenir, 1915*, pp. 171–3, 176–7; for DIPCS see Webb (1921), p. 20; *MH Advertiser*, 19.05.1896, p. 6; *The Co-op Directory* (1951).
8. MHICS Rpt., Jan. 1920=Jan. 1939; MH.OR 78/2.6, 78/3.3.
9. MHICS Rpt., Jan. 1933.
10. Mr Geoff Johnson, MH.OR 12/3.5 (1920s and '30s).
11. MHICS Jubilee Calendar, 1912; MHICS Rpt., April 1894, May 1907, July 1920.
12. MH.OR 78/1.5 & 78/2.7.
13. MH.OR 78/1.5; MH.OR 75.6.
14. MH.OR 78/2.7.
15. MH.OR 75.6.
16. MHICS Rpt., 1920–8, 1931–42.
17. *Ibid.*, 1945–69.
18. *Ibid.*, Jan. 1936–Jan. 1960; MH.OR 75.9–10.
19. Bonner (1970), pp. 249, 260–1; LrCS Rpt., March 1961; MHICS Rpt., July 1967.
20. LCS Rpt. Jan. 1971; MH.OR 75.10; 1986 'Passport to Value' promotion.
21. MH.OR 12/3.1; MH.OR 78/2.5–6; MHICS Rpt. Dec. 1899, Jan. 1920; *MH Advertiser* 19.05.1896, p. 6.
22. Mr Raymond Tack, MH.OR 15/2.10; MH.OR 78/2.7; MHICS Rpt. May 1907; MHICS Jubilee Calendar 1912.
23. MH.OR 78/2.11 & 78/1.15; MHICS Rpt. 1896=1969.
24. *MH Advertiser*, 25.03.1902, p. 2; MH.OR 78/1.15 & conversation.
25. *MH Advertiser* 23.01.1900, p. 6.
26. *Ibid.*, 25.03.1902, p. 2; MH.OR 78/2.6 & 78/1.19; MH.OR 15/2.10.
27. MH.OR 78/2.7.
28. Enfield (1927), p. 15; MH.OR 78/2.5–6.
29. MHICS Rpt. Jan. 1969; LrCS Rpt. Nov. 1968; LCS Rpt. May 1969, Jan. 1970, July 1971; MH.OR 75.14; MH.OR 78/3.8; LCS Membership Control Form 11.12.1986.
30. Conversation with MH.OR 78.
31. LCS Rpt. Jan. 1970, Jan. 1973.
32. Based on a comparison of accounts from four Co-op staff with those from private shopworkers; MH.OR 15/2.14; MH.OR 75.5; conversation with Mr P.G. Preston,

LCS Personnel Manager, 22.12.1986; Mr Ted Ashby, MH.OR 102.2.

33. MH.OR 78/1.15 & 78/3.11; MHICS Rpt. Jan. 1931.
34. MH.OR 78/1.14; MH.OR 15/2.9.
35. MH.OR 78/1.13 & 78/3.2; MH.OR 15/2.6; MHICS Rpt. July 1920.
36. MH.OR 78/1.14; MHICS Rpt. Jan. 1923, July 1925; conversation with MH.OR 75.
37. MHICS Rpt. Jan. 1940, July 1951, Jan. 1969.
38. *Ibid.*, Jan. 1969.
39. MHICS Jubilee Calendar 1912; Winstanley (1983), pp. 36–7; Pollard (1960), pp. 100–12; *MH Advertiser*, 19.05.1896, p. 6, 17.11.1896, p. 5, 16.02.1897, p. 5 and 30.01.1900, p. 5.
40. *Ibid.*, 19.05.1896, p. 6, 17.08.1897, p. 3, 07.06.1889, p. 8; MHICS Rpt. June 1901, Nov. 1904, Nov. 1905.
41. *Ibid.*, July 1926; MH.OR 78/2.9.
42. MH.OR 78/1.11, 21 & 78/3.10.
43. *MH Advertiser*, 30.01.1900, p. 5, MHICS Rpt. Jan. 1902, Nov. 1905; MH.OR 78/2.11, 15, & 78/3.18; LCS Rpt. Jan. 1970.
44. MH.OR 78/2.10.
45. Pollard (1971), pp. 185–207; *The Midland Free Press*, 12.07.1862, p. 1, 'Papers on Co-operation No.VI – Co-operation in Northamptonshire'.
46. *MH Advertiser*, 15.03.1898, p. 3, 29.08.1899, p. 6 (pro-labour, Mr Richards, Mr Griffiths and Mrs Hodgett; pro-brotherhood, Mr Panter KCS President, Mr J. Stevens MHICS President).
47. *Ibid.*, 21.01.1896, p. 5, 19.05.1896, p. 6; MHICS Rpt. Jan. 1895, March, June, Oct. 1892, Oct. 1893.
48. MHICS Rpt. July 1917, July 1933; Bonner (1970) p. 194.; MH.OR 78/3.5–6; MH.OR 15/2.1.
49. MH.OR 78/1.27–28 & 78/3.1.
50. Mrs Joyce Dexter (née Wood), MH.OR 106.7; Mr Ronald Hodby, MH.OR 99.7, 9.
51. MH.OR 15/2.13–14; MH.OR 75.7.
52. Davies & Brown (1981) p. 3; *MH Advertiser*, 19.05.1896, p. 6, 17.08.1897, p. 3; MHICS Rpt. 1895–1907, 1917–27.
53. MH.OR 78/2.13; S. Pollard (1971), pp. 185–207.
54. Pollard (1960), p. 205; Webb (1921), pp. 267–71; MHICS Rpt. Jan. 1922, Jan. 1923, July 1925, July 1926, Jan. 1931, Jan. 1935, Jan. 1936, Jan. 1939, 1943=1954; Gaffin & Toms (1983), pp. 109–11; Branson (1975), pp. 82–7; MH.OR 78/2.13–14.
55. MH.OR 78/2.13.
56. MH.OR 78/2.13–14.
57. MH.OR 75.7.
58. LrCS Rpt., 1955–69, e.g. March 1959, p. 10; MH.OR 78/2.15; LCS Rpt. July 1973.
59. MH.OR 78/2.1–3,11.
60. LCS Rpt. July 1972, Jan. 1973; conversation with Mr R.C. Knight, Oct. 1986.
61. MH.OR 78/3.9.
62. MH.OR 78/3.7.
63. *Idem*; HDC Planning Applications 76/1001/3P (built in 1979).
64. Mr John Collins, MH.OR 110, side 1; MHICS Rpt. June 1892; HDC Planning Applications (Co-op Superstore, Coventry Road, 1986).

## Chapter Seven

1. Mr Bill Wood, MH.OR 73; Mr F.W. Lee, MH.OR 71.
2. *Market Harborough Illustrated* (1892); L.R.O: 1871 Census, Market Harborough.
3. Mr Fred Tuffs, MH.OR 27. 5 & 11.
4. *Market Harborough Illustrated* (1892).
5. HDC Planning Dept.: Building control plan no. 441.
6. Mr Hubert Reeve, MH.OR 101(A).15, 16–20.
7. Mrs Gladys Wimlett, MH.OR 84.1–2, 4–6.
8. Mrs Olive Reeve, MH.OR 101(B).
9. Mr Les Buswell, MH.OR 70.1–5.
10. O. de Rousset-Hall, MS History of W. Symingtons, kindly loaned by the firm; *Pigot & Co.'s Directory of Leicestershire* (1835);

*Cook's Directory of Leicestershire* (1842); *White's History and Gazetteer . . . of Leicestershire* (1846); Harborough Museum: W. Symington & Co., printed price list, July 1904.

11. Jefferys (1954), p. 148.
12. *Market Harborough Industrial Co-operative Society Quarterly Report,* June 1901 (Committee Report); *Market Harborough Advertiser*, 18.10.1904; *ibid.*, 14.12.1915.
13. MH.OR 101(A).7.
14. *Ibid.*
15. Mr Norman Marlow, MH.OR 75.17; Mr W. Ingram, MH.OR 113.1–5, 7–12, 15–18.
16. Jefferys (1954), p. 174.
17. Mr Ronald Hodby, MH.OR 99.25.
18. Jefferys (1954), p. 174.
19. MH.OR 73.1–3, 7–8, 13.
20. *Keesings contemporary archives*, 1954, p.13688; MH.OR73.13; MH.OR71.12.
21. MH.OR 71.12.
22. Mrs Margaret Prince, MH.OR 122.24.
23. Corina (1971), quoted in *Dictionary of National Biography, 1971–80* (OUP, 1986).
24. Mr Ken Wylie, MH.OR 105.2, 3, 5–7, 11.
25. Corina (1971), *Supra* (23.).
26. MH.OR 105.9–10.
27. Mr Ted Ashby, MH.OR 102.1–3, 6, 11–15. With particular thanks to Tesco plc and the staff of the Market Harborough store for their ready assistance in our recording of their operation and interview of the manager, Mr Ashby.
28. *Harborough Mail*, 16.04.1987.

## Chapter Eight

1. Stocks & Bragg (1890), p. 166. The term *shambles* is derived from the Old English *sc(e)amul*, a stool or table (*Oxford English Dictionary*).
2. Stocks (1926), p. 275; *ibid.*, pp. 169, 170, 173.
3. L.R.O.DE 4354: Rowland Rouse, MS History of Market Harborough (started *c.* 1764), p. 22.
4. *Barfoot & Wilkes' Universal British Directory* (*c.* 1796), pp. 890–1.
5. *Market Harborough Advertiser*, 22.12.1896.
6. *Green & Co's Directory and Guide to Market Harborough and District*, 17th edition (1912); *Kelly's Directory of Leicestershire* (1922).
7. Mr Charles Kirby, MH.OR 72.
8. Duncan (1957).
9. Critchel & Raymond (1912).
10. *Market Harborough Industrial Co-operative Society quarterly report,* April 1899.
11. Mr A.C. Wimlett, MH.OR 85/2.1, 8 & 9.
12. Mr G.H. Pickering, MH.OR 68.1–3.
13. *Market Harborough Avertiser*, 28.04.1896.
14. MH.OR 68, *passim.*
15. *Green's Directory* . . . (1912).
16. Mr and Mrs Davis (granddaughter of John Jesson) gave ready assistance in the recording and research of the butcher's shop at Gumley in 1986. See also Gilding's sale catalogue, 25 January, 1994; a few items were purchased by the Harborough Museum (LEIMH 17.1994).
17. MH.OR 72, *passim.*
18. Mr Arthur Welch, MH.OR 119.
19. *Ibid.*
20. *Ibid.*
21. Mr Alan Bott, MH.OR 121.

## Chapter Nine

1. Mrs Joan Catling (née Freestone) MH.OR 104.5–6.
2. Jefferys (1954), pp. 292–352.
3. *Ibid.*, pp. 292–5; Fraser (1981), pp. 58–65, 175–92.
4. Trinder & Cox (1980), pp. 26–7; Stocks (1926), pp. 202–3, 233; *Barfoot & Wilkes' Universal British Directory* (1793–6); *Midland Free Press*, 28.01.1865, p. 4.
5. Page (1981): the account of Symington's early history recounted by Page may well contain apocryphal elements.
6. *Market Harborough Illustrated* (1892), p. 19; Fraser (1981), pp. 180–4; Welding (1985);

*Kelly's Directory of Leicestershire* (1888), (1895) & (1900).

7. Jefferys (1954), pp. 322–3.
8. Mrs Joyce Dexter (née Wood), MH.OR 106.1–2, 15.
9. Fraser (1981), p. 187; *Market Harborough Advertiser*, 1896–1905 *passim*; *Green's Directory of Market Harborough* (1900) & (1912); *Market Harborough Industrial Co-operative Society quarterly/half-yearly reports*, June 1899 & July 1917.
10. Shindler & Douglas advertisement, 1912; *Market Harborough Advertiser*, 16.03.1897, 12.10.1897, 17.03.1896, 23.12.1902, 23.12.1905, 15.07.1913; Harborough District Council, Planning Department, Building control plans no. 717; *Green's Directory* (1909), p. 10, *idem* (1912), p. 10; Anon., MH.OR 103.8.
11. Winnifred Hardwick, MH.OR 124.1–3, 5–6, 16.
12. *Market Harborough Advertiser*, 29.09.1903, also 22.09.1896, 05.10.1897, 01.11.1898, 27.2.1900 (see above Chapter Two).
13. *Green's Directory* (1912), p. 10; MH.OR 124.4, 8.
14. Harborough District Council, Planning Department, Building control plans no. 1388; MH.OR 103.6; MH.OR 106.2.
15. MH.OR 106.2–4, 10, 11; MH.OR 124.17.
16. MH.OR 124.11, 17; MH.OR 106.2; L.R.O.DE 3581: Documents relating to John Wood & Son.
17. MH.OR 106.5, 14–15; Harborough District Council, Planning Department, Building control plans no. 1927.
18. MH.OR 104.2–5; MH.OR 103.2; MH.OR 124.7.
19. MH.OR 106.1–2, 8, 13; MH.OR 104.1–2, 6, 8.
20. MH.OR 104.6; MH.OR 124.8, 12
21. MH.OR 103.6; MH.OR 124.5.
22. MH.OR 104.6; MH.OR 124.12.
23. MH.OR 124.4, 9–10.
24. MH.OR 104.6; MH.OR 124.14.
25. Jefferys (1954), p. 334; MH.OR 106.7; Joyce Rhodes (née Gardiner), MH.OR 107, side 2; *Market Harborough Advertiser*, 13.02.1925, p. 4 & 01.01.1926, p. 4.
26. MH.OR 107, side 2.
27. Vivien Window, MH.OR 109.11–12; Margaret Lawrence, MH.OR 111.2–3, 4.
28. Jefferys (1954), pp. 342–52; MH.OR 104.9.
29. MH.OR 109.9.
30. MH.OR 109.14.
31. Mr Geoff Johnson MH.OR 12/3.3, 6–7.
32. Jefferys (1954), pp. 292–7, 315, 349.
33. L.R.OPE box: agreement for letting a shop and premises lately occupied by Mr W. Eland to Mr Webb of Kettering; Mr A.C. Wimlett, MH.OR 85.2–3.
34. Harborough District Council, Planning Department, Building control plans nos 1302, 1323.
35. Jefferys (1954), pp. 302, 308–11.
36. *Green's Directory* (1937) (Foster's advert); Mr S.G. Stanger, MH.OR 114.2; *Gartree Parish Magazine*, June 1935 (Webb's); *Market Harborough Advertiser*, 21.06.1935 (Remington's).
37. MH.OR 114.1–2; Jefferys (1954), p. 307.
38. MH.OR 85.4.
39. Mr & Mrs W.E. Lines, MH.OR 86.7.
40. *Green's Directory* (1941); MH.OR 12/3.5.
41. Jefferys (1954), p. 310; Harborough District Council, Planning Department, Building control plans no. 2907.
42. MH.OR 12/3.9–13; Jefferys (1954), pp. 302, 308–11.

## CHAPTER TEN

1. Burnett (1966).
2. Mr Donald West, MH.OR 120, side 3.6.
3. Burnett (1966).
4. *Market Harborough Advertiser*, 06.07.1897.
5. *Ibid.*, 04.01.1898.
6. *Ibid.*, 03.01.1899.
7. *Ibid.*, 17.12 1901, & 25.02.1902.
8. MH.OR 120, side 3, pp. 3–6 (Donald West).
9. Mr Jack Faulkner, MH.OR 82.15–16.

10. Mrs Dorothy Springer (née Murkitt), MH.OR 89.4–8.
11. *Kelly's Directory of Leicestershire* (1932), *Green's Directory of Market Harborough and District* (1932); MH.OR 82.
12. MH.OR 82.4–5.
13. MH.OR 82.7–8, 11–13.
14. MH.OR 120 (Michael West).
15. MH.OR 120 (Donald West).
16. MH.OR 120 (Michael West).

# Sources

## WRITTEN SOURCES

In addition to local commercial directories, census returns and parish magazines, the following proved useful:


Blakeman, P.J. (1982): *The rise and fall of the Harborough Bus.*

Cole, G.D.H. (1946): *A century of Co-operation*, Co-operative Union, Manchester.

Co-operative Union (1898): *Peterborough Co-operative Congress* 1898.

Co-operative Union (1915): *Leicester Co-operative Congress* 1915.

Co-operative Union (1951): *The Co-operative Directory, 1951.*

Davies J.C. & Brown, M.C. (1981): *Yesterday's town: Victorian Harborough*, Barracuda Books, Buckingham.

Davies, J.C. (1969): *Georgian Harborough*, Market Harborough.

Davies, J.C. (1974): *Town affairs*, Market Harborough.

de Rousset-Hall, O.: unpublished MS History of W. Symington & Co.

Harborough District Council, Planning Department: Building control plans, 1890s to date.

Harborough Mail offices: *Market Harborough Advertiser* (1854–1923); *Market Harborough Mail* (1890–1897); *Midland Mail* (1897–1923); *Market Harborough Advertiser & Midland Mail* (1923–1968); *Harborough Mail* (1968– ).

Johnson, G. (1983): *The Stream of Days, Market Harborough.*

Leicester Co-operative Society: *Half-Yearly Reports of the Leicester Co-operative Society*, 1955–1969.

Leicestershire Co-operative Society: *Half-Yearly Reports of the Leicestershire Co-operative Society*, 1969–1973.

Market Harborough Guide (1892 & 1902): *Market Harborough Illustrated*, Robinson & Pike.

MHICS: *Quarterly Reports* (1887–1902), *Half-Yearly Reports* (1904–1969), *of the Market Harborough Industrial Co-operative Society.*

MHICS (1912): *Market Harborough Industrial Co-operative Society Jubilee Calendar 1912.* Midland Free Press.

*The Midland Free Press*, microfilm. Pen Lloyd Library, Market Harborough.

Mullins, S.P. & Glasson, M. (1985): *Hidden Harborough: the making of the townscape of Market Harborough*, Leicestershire Museums, Leicester.

Page, C. (1981): *Foundations of fashion*, Leicestershire Museums, Leicester.

Rouse, Rowland: Unpublished MS history of Market Harborough, circa 1764, Leicestershire Record Office [L.R.O.]: DE 4354.

R. & W.H. Symington Ltd (1956): *In our own fashion*, Market Harborough.

Stocks, J.E. & Bragg, W. (1890): *Market Harborough Parish Records to AD 1530.*

Stocks, J.E. (1926): *Market Harborough Parish Records, 1531–1837.*

Welding J.D. (1985): *The Leicestershire Boot and Shoe Industry*, Leicestershire Libraries and Information Service.

Whyte-Melville, G.J. (1862): *Market Harborough.*

## Oral Sources

The following recordings and interview summaries form part of the sound collection of the Harborough Museum, Market Harborough. Most were recorded specifically for this project. Those marked with an asterisk are written summaries of unrecorded interviews.

MH.OR 05: Arthur Wilford (9 March 1984: Naseby carrier's son).
MH.OR 10: Reg and Maisie Wright (22 June 1985, 23 June 1986: Shops and shopping in Great Bowden and Market Harborough [MH]).
MH.OR 12: Geoff Johnson (10 July 1986: MH Co-op employee and proprietor of gents' outfitter's).
MH.OR 14: Jack Whitbread (30 August 1984: Childhood in King's Head Place).
MH.OR 15: Raymond Tack (12 August 1986: MH Co-op roundsman).
MH.OR 27: Fred Tuffs (3 January 1985: Shopboy before First World War).
MH.OR 54: Elizabeth Bristow (26 September 1985: Cook/housekeeper).
MH.OR 68: George Pickering (24 June 1986: Pickering's the butcher's).
MH.OR 69: Alan Clayton (28 July 1986: Hallaton post office and stores).
MH.OR 70: Les Buswell (29 July 1986: Symington & Thwaites, grocer's).
MH.OR 71: Frederick Lee (30 July 1986: C.F. Lea's, Symington & Thwaites, Burton's, Fine Fare, grocers' shops).
MH.OR 72: Charles Kirby (1 August 1986: Butchers' shops and Slawston post office).
MH.OR 73: Bill Wood (4 August 1986: C.F. Lea's, grocer's).
MH.OR 74: Frank & Josie Walker (6 August 1986 & 3 September 1986: Little Bowden store and multiple stores).
MH.OR 75: Norman Marlow (6 August 1986: MH Co-op shopman & manager).
MH.OR 76: Frank Taylor (11 August 1986: Fish & chip shop proprietor).
MH.OR 77: Peter Todd (11 August 1986: Bakery proprietor).
MH.OR 78: Cecil Copson (12 August, 24 & 27 October 1986:
MH Co-op shopman and manager).
MH.OR 79: Bernard Kemp (13 August 1986: Pharmaceutical assistant).
MH.OR 80: Kevin Quinn (14 August 1986: Bookshop proprietor).
MH.OR 81: Michael Kelly (15 August 1986: Greengrocery proprietor).
MH.OR 82: Jack Faulkner (18 August 1986: Baker).
MH.OR 83: Bill Falkner (19 August 1986: Shoemaker and shop proprietor).
MH.OR 84: Gladys Wimlett (20 August 1986: Symington & Thwaites assistant).
MH.OR 85: Charles Wimlett (20 August 1986: Butcher's son, Webb's – gents' outfitters, Brooke Bond representative).
MH.OR 86*: Mr and Mrs Lines (20 August 1986: Tailoring and shoe trades).
MH.OR 87: John Tate (27 August 1986: Tate's the chemist's proprietor).
MH.OR 88*: The Misses Brown (14 August 1986: Foxton post office and shop).
MH.OR 89: Dorothy Springer (29 August 1986: Murkitt's, Church Street).
MH.OR 90: M.W. Clarke (1 September 1986: Greengrocery trade in MH).
MH.OR 91: Geoff Bonnett (4 September 1986: Great Easton post office and store proprietor).
MH.OR 92: John Pugh (5 September 1986: Pugh's the saddlers).
MH.OR 93: Maurice Saunders (9 September 1986: Mawer & Saunders proprietor).
MH.OR 94: Audrey Pearson (10 September 1986: Chemist's shop assistant).
MH.OR 95: Ramesh Radia (12 September 1986: Northampton Rd post office proprietor).
MH.OR 96: Anon. (September 1986: Post office and small shop proprietor).

MH.OR 97: Mrs Elliot (15 September 1986: Miss Fox's shop, Leicester Rd).
MH.OR 98: Gwendoline Parke (19 September 1986: Shop assistant, W.H. Smith, and Elliott's clothes shop).
MH.OR 99: Ronald Hodby (22 September 1986: Post office and grocery, Nelson Street, proprietor).
MH.OR100: Sidney Payne (23 September 1986: Burditt's cycle shop).
MH.OR101A: Hubert Reeve (24 September 1986: Grocers, Smith's, Star Supply Stores, Symington & Thwaites).
MH.OR101B: Olive Reeve (24 September 1986: Symington & Thwaites).
MH.OR102: Ted Ashby (1 October 1986: Tesco supermarket manager).
MH.OR103*: Anon. (3 October 1986: Draper's trade in MH).
MH.OR104: Joan Catling (7 October 1986: Wood's drapery sales assistant).
MH.OR105: Ken Wylie (8 October 1986: Tesco superstore manager).
MH.OR106: Joyce Dexter (15 October 1986: Daughter of John Wood, draper).
MH.OR107: Joyce Rhodes (21 October 1986: Daughter of G.B. Gardiner, Gardiner family shops, draper's trade, and wool shop proprietor).
MH.OR108: William Gardner (22 October 1986: Family village store, Welford).
MH.OR109: Vivien Window (23 October 1986: Woolworths assistant).
MH.OR110: John Crawford (28 October 1986: Manager, Great Glen Co-op store).
MH.OR111: Margaret Lawrence (4 November 1986: Sales assistant, Woolworths and shop manager in North Kilworth – Rugby Co-op).
MH.OR112: Carol French (4 November 1986: Chemist's sales assistant).
MH.OR113: Bill Ingram (5 November 1986: Maypole Dairy, Kettering).
MH.OR114*: S.G. Stanger (11 November 1986: Hepworth's assistant).
MH.OR115: George Scrimshire (17 December 1986: Family village shop, Husbands Bosworth).
MH.OR117: Mr H.W. Webb (4 February 1987: Webb & Goward/R.J. Webb photographic business).
MH.OR118: Mr R. Rhodes (13 February 1987: Grazier of Manor Farm, Welford).
MH.OR119: Mr A.J. Welch (19 February 1987: Butcher, Wilbarston).
MH.OR120: Donald and Michael West (5 May 1987: West's the bakers, Emerson & West's bakers, delicatessen and restaurant).
MH.OR121: Alan Bott (9 March 1987: Gregory's of Market Harborough, proprietor).
MH.OR122: Margaret Prince (10 March 1987: Lipton's sales assistant).
MH.OR123: Mr Len Robinson (27 March 1987: Projectionist, Oriental Cinema).
MH.OR124: Winnifred Monroe (1 April 1987: Drapery trade, including Wood's).

## Pictorial Sources

All photographs and illustrations reproduced here are, unless otherwise credited, part of the collections of Leicestershire Museums, Arts and Records Service.

# Bibliography

(All titles published in London except where stated)


## KEY WORKS

Bonner, A. (1970): *British Co-operation*, Co-operative Union Ltd, Manchester.
Davis, D. (1966): *A history of shopping*, Routledge.
Fraser, W. Hamish (1981): *The coming of the mass market*, Macmillan Press.
Jefferys, J.B. (1954): *Retail trading in Britain 1850–1950*, Cambridge University Press, Cambridge.
Levy, H. (1948): *The shops of Britain*, Kegan Paul.
Mathias, P. (1967): *Retailing revolution* [Allied Suppliers], Longman.
Ward, S. (1990): *The village shop*, David & Charles.
Winstanley, M.J. (1983): *The shopkeeper's world, 1830–1914*, Manchester University Press, Manchester.

## RECENTLY PUBLISHED LOCAL AND REGIONAL STUDIES

Hartwich, V. (1981): *Ale 'n' a'thing*, Dundee Art Galleries & Museums, Dundee.
McCullough Thew, L. (1985): *The pit village and the store*, Pluto Press.
Millet, F. (1988): *Going up town: shopping in Oldham*, Oldham Leisure Services, Oldham.
Williams, N. (1986): *Shop in the Black Country*, Uralia Press, Wolverhampton.

In addition to these works, the books and articles listed below were used more selectively:

**Chapters One to Three**
Calder, A. (1969): *The people's war, Britain 1939–1945*, Granada ed., 1982.
Golby, J.M. & Purdue, A.W. (1986): *The making of the modern Christmas*, Batsford.
Kay, W. (1989): *The battle for the high street*, Piatkus.
Stevenson, J. (1984): *British Society 1914–45*, Pelican.
Yamey, B.S. (1955): 'Competition in the retail grocery trade, 1850–1939', *Economica*, xxii.
Yamey, B.S. (1966): *Resale price maintenance studies*, Weidenfeld & Nicolson.

**Chapters Four and Five**
Cronin, J.E. (1984): *Labour & society in Britain 1918–1979*, Batsford.
Holcombe, L. (1973): *Victorian ladies at work*, David & Charles, Newton Abbot.
Routh, G. (1965): *Occupation and pay in Great Britain, 1906–60*, 1980 ed., Cambridge University Press, Cambridge.
Webb, S. & B. (1921): *The consumers' Co-operative movement.*

**Chapter Six**
Branson, N. (1975): *Britain in the 1920s*, Weidenfeld & Nicolson.
Enfield, A. H. (1927): *Co-operation*, Longman.
Gaffin, J. & Toms, D. (1981): *Caring & sharing: a centenary history of the Co-operative Women's Guild.*

Pollard, S. (1960): 'Nineteenth Century Co-operation – from community building to shopkeeping', in A. Briggs & J. Saville (eds), *Essays in labour history, 1*, Macmillan.
Pollard, S. (1971): 'Formation of the Co-operative Party' in A. Briggs & J. Saville (eds), *Essays in labour history, 2*, Macmillan.
Webb, S. & B. (1921): *The consumers' Co-operative movement.*

**Chapter Seven**
Corina, M. (1971): *Pile it high, sell it cheap* [Tesco].

**Chapter Eight**
Critchel, J.T. & Raymond, J. (1912): *A history of the frozen meat trade.*
Duncan, R. (1957): 'The Demand for Frozen Beef in the U.K., 1880–1914', *Journal of Agricultural Economics*, xii.

**Chapter Nine**
Trinder, B. & Cox, J. (1980): *Yeomen and colliers in Telford*, Phillimore, Chichester.

**Chapter Ten**
Burnett, J. (1966): 'Changes in bread consumption' in T.C. Barker, J.C. MacKenzie & J. Yudkin (eds), *Our changing fare: 200 years of British food.*